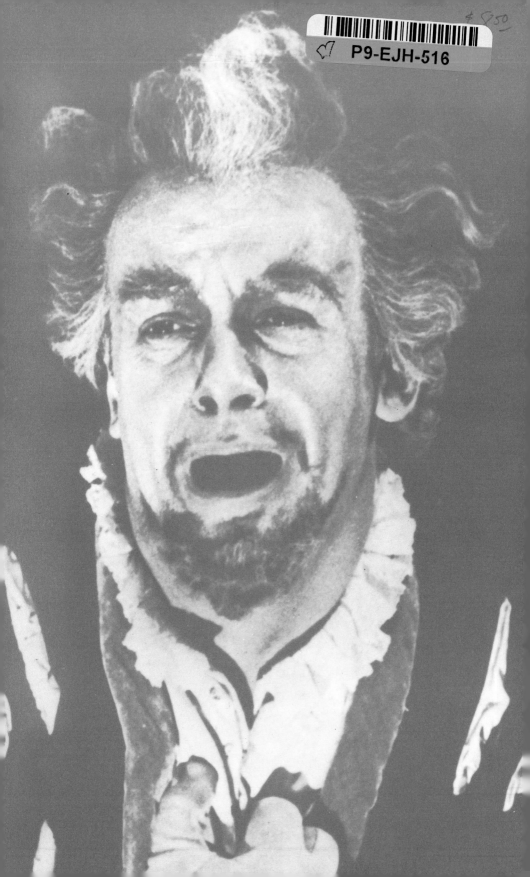

TITO GOBBI

My Life

TITO GOBBI

My Life

Doubleday & Company, Inc., Garden City, New York
1980

ISBN: 0-385-15627-8
Library of Congress Catalog Card Number 79–7784

Copyright © 1979 by Tito Gobbi and Ida Cook
PRINTED IN THE UNITED STATES OF AMERICA
FIRST EDITION IN THE UNITED STATES OF AMERICA
BOOK DESIGN BY BEVERLEY GALLEGOS

Illustrations

As Count Almaviva in *The Marriage of Figaro* (*Houston Rogers, London*).

With Amy Shuard in *Macbeth* (*Dominic*).

Rigoletto—in close-up.

With Boris Christoff in *Don Carlo* (*Houston Rogers, London*).

As Gianni Schicchi (*Foto Marchiori, Florence*).

With Maria Callas in *Tosca* (*Photo Pic*).

As Baron Scarpia in *Tosca* (*Fayer-Wien*).

Leonard Boden's studio in London (*Leonard Boden, R.P., F.R.S.A.*).

Following page 160

With Maestro Serafin.

With Carol Fox.

With Ida and Louise Cook at a Verdi Society of Liverpool party (*Paul Wilson*).

Four studies in make-up for Falstaff (*The Age, Melbourne*).

Falstaff delivering the Honor Monologue (*Michel Petit, Paris*).

Falstaff after his ducking in the river (*Fayer-Wien*).

Falstaff in the guise of Herne the Hunter (*Agence de Presse Bernard*).

Backstage with ex-King Umberto.

With Del Monaco and the Queen Mother (*Press Association*).

As King Moomba in Melbourne.

Tilde and my parents on their Golden Wedding.

Papa Giovanni and Papa Raffaello.

Cecilia as a little girl.

Cecilia today (*Erika Davidson*).

With Isabella (*Erika Davidson*).

Teaching at the Villa Schifanoia.

Front endpapers:

Iago; Rigoletto.

Rear endpapers:

Simone Boccanegra (*Foto A. Villani, Bologna*); Rodrigo, Marquis of Posa, in *Don Carlo* (wearing the famous Stracciari costume) (*Paul Hansen, Chicago*).

TITO GOBBI

My Life

1.

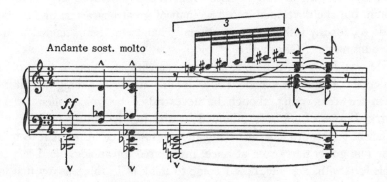

Andante sost. molto

THOSE ARE THE CHORDS which herald the appearance of Scarpia in the first act of *Tosca*, and although I must have repeated that spine-chilling entrance nearly nine hundred times, the spell which Puccini casts never fails to inspire me. He hands to the artist playing Scarpia one of the finest moments in all opera, and if that artist cannot administer to the audience an immediate sense of shock and revulsion, then in my view he must leave the role alone.

Ruthless, elegant, and terrifying, Scarpia should instantly register a force for evil which spreads through the house from the orchestra pit to the last row of the gallery. Not only does all Rome tremble before him; every member of the audience must be made to do so too.

But for once I, who have so often impersonated him, propose to defy the overwhelming authority of Baron Scarpia. Even though he has cleverly appropriated the opening paragraphs of this book—and will no doubt make a more lengthy appearance later—I insist that this is the story of *my* life, which began in the Church of Sant' Andrea in Rome, many years before I met the baron. In fact it began not in Rome but in the country town of Bassano del Grappa in the Veneto, where I was born on October 24, 1913, the third son in a family of three boys and two girls.

Our family came originally from Mantua in 1272 and though we never climbed aristocratic heights neither did we plumb poverty-stricken depths. The Gobbis lived on the whole a good, solid, comfortable life, producing lawyers, goldsmiths, literary men, doctors, merchants, and so on. My mother, born Enrica Weiss, was Austrian and came from Bolzano, which was then part of the Austrian Tyrol. She was a pretty, feminine type of girl, as can be seen from the photographs in the family album, but she developed into a woman of great character. She needed to do so, for my father, an exceptionally handsome man, tended to live up to his name of Giovanni.

He was, however, a parent I remember with affection in spite of his undeniable faults. He exercised considerable authority among us children when we were young, though he never raised his voice when he was angry. If one of us boys offended at the family dinner table it was sufficient for him to look at us and thoughtfully pass his napkin over his lips. The guilty party rose at once, murmured an apology, and left the table forthwith. Possibly, now I come to think of it, this was my first lesson in what can be accomplished with a glance rather than a great show of action.

I remember both my grandfathers with affection and also a great respect for their position in the family circle. Grandfather Weiss was a handsome old man with a white beard and a rather gruff manner. He carved beautiful wooden toys and told wonderful stories, some of them rather frightening—cautionary tales about the devil, which made us put our heads under the bedclothes at night. But the delicious thrills were worth it.

Grandfather Gobbi was the head of the family firm, which sold household goods, agricultural implements, fireplaces, gates, bathroom fittings, and so on. We had a shop in Bassano as well as others scattered about the countryside in the smaller towns, and in my youth it was a very successful business indeed.

The years tend to run together as one looks back and it is difficult to state positively just how far one's memories reach into the past. The earliest event I can date with any certainty must have occurred when I was about three, because it obviously took place during the war. (We called it *The War* in my youth, not knowing that a later and greater one was yet to come.) A bomb was dropped near our house, starting a fire, and I have the clearest recollection of my terror at seeing my father silhouetted against the burst of flame. I thought he had been killed and I rushed to my mother stammering "M-m-m-Mama" in my agitation; and from that moment I stammered continually. This affliction plagued me and was the cause of some teasing during the next few years. Then one day, in jumping too impetuously from a horse-drawn trap, I fell, hitting my head on the iron hub of the wheel. I was knocked unconscious and when I recovered consciousness I had also recovered my speech. The stammer was gone.

I would not exactly recommend a bang on the head as a cure for stammering, but it was certainly a lucky accident for me, considering my future profession. A stammering singer is not likely to make much of a hit in the world except in certain comic roles.

During the First World War my father served in the Army but was invalided out about the time of Caporetto and opened an ammunition factory in Padua. After the war he returned to Bassano and went into the family business, reorganizing and expanding it and becoming my grandfather's right-hand man. One of his brothers, Ettore, also worked in the business but, although a charming man, was not, I think, much more than an agreeable cipher. My father's other surviving brother, Guglielmo, was made of very different stuff. A well-known doctor (who later played a considerable part in the eventual conquest of tuberculosis), he was of such intimidating sternness that I must say I remember him without affection and with a degree of discomfort that I have seldom felt for any other human being.

Of my two aunts on that side of the family it is not necessary to say more than that one married a lawyer in Bassano but died rather early in her married life; and the other—more remarkable for her beauty and humor than her brains, but an engaging woman—eventually married a general of great distinction.

Although I realize now that there must have been more than the usual stresses and strains in our family life, it seems to me in retrospect that I had a wonderful childhood. Relationships with my uncles and aunts were correct if not warmly cordial and, certainly in the days before financial troubles came along to complicate things, life in our big, rambling house—which was part of the family estate—had a warmth and richness and color which belong to an almost forgotten age.

The house was set in a very large garden with trees and a fountain. On the ground floor was our playroom, known simply as "Camerone." It contained all our toys, some generously proportioned furniture, and in one corner a big armchair where Grandfather Weiss would sit and tell us his absorbing stories or carve fresh toys for us. One of these, which I still have and treasure to this day, was an exquisite model of a castle, complete with drawbridge built over a stream. The wood came from a cherry tree—my own cherry tree, which had been planted in the garden but did not, alas, survive a severe winter. I was very unhappy over the demise of my tree, and so my grandfather made me the castle from the cherrywood to console me. He really was a charming old grandad.

Also on the ground floor were the family dining room and a huge kitchen with an open fireplace where both coal and wood were burned. Between these two rooms was a small room where the sewing-woman worked. As can be imagined, she was a very busy woman with five lively children in the house, and I still recall the delicious smell of clean linen which always clung to this room. The washing and laundry room and the pantries completed the ground floor, except for the garage where, in our prosperous days, there were sometimes as many as five cars; for my father was a motor-car enthusiast.

In the house—which was not quite listed as an ancient monument but had a certain historical importance—a marble staircase ran up to the floor above. Here were the principal bedrooms, done in the Venetian style with mosaics, and two bathrooms of enormous proportions judged by modern standards. Since we dealt in bathroom fittings, these were very well furnished in the manner of that period. On the next floor were the maids' rooms, a small darkroom for the photographers of the family, and the storerooms. Chief of these, in my recollection, was the fruit store, which smelled superbly of apples and pears but which was prudently kept locked. There was a man in charge of this room, and under the window there was a little barrel of vinegar—the pride of the house because it was the best vinegar in the whole of Bassano. We made it ourselves and my father was very difficult to please in this respect. It had to be the best wine vinegar, and the man in charge of the apples and pears was also in charge of this. He used to inspect it and taste it and decide if and when anything should be added.

Also on this floor was another large room where we stored old trunks and cases: wooden cases which smelled so sweetly that I think they must have been of cedar or sandalwood. Twice a year when the seasons changed these cases would be brought out. In the spring all the woolen curtains, rugs, and covers would be stored away and out would come the silks and chintzes, and in the autumn the process would be reversed. The same changing and storing would also apply to the family clothes.

It was a tremendous affair each time the house was cleaned from top to bottom. As many as twenty-five people would come from the country or from the estate—always the same people so that they knew exactly what to do—and as they worked and polished, they sang. Meanwhile the woman who did all the washing would have a copper cauldron with a great fire beneath it, and she washed in wooden bowls which took four men to carry. For the last rinsing she would put in some ashes from the wood fire, which gave a wonderful smell to the linen. Like all the others, she sang as she worked, so that this great seasonal cleaning somehow took on the character of a sort of festival.

On my father's birthday—also at Christmas and Easter—the farm people from the estate would arrive in Bassano in their horse- or ox-drawn carts. All the carts would be scrubbed and clean, and animals and people alike would be decorated with colored ribbons. They were on their way to market, the carts piled high with every kind of farm or garden produce in the most wonderful and colorful profusion. The town band would meet them as they entered Bassano and lead the procession, while another procession made up of children from the orphanage which my family helped to support would add to the general festivity. Singing and dancing, laughter and jokes were the order of the day, and then the whole procession would stop in front of our house to greet my father and wish him well on his birthday. Here of course there was an unlimited supply of drinks and great sandwiches of meat and bread available for all, and on the several occasions when my father was mayor of the town there would be official dignitaries to mingle with the throng. There was a sort of exuberant innocence about it all which no longer exists, and for me, looking back, the final touch of childhood magic came when—I must have been about six at the time—I thought I saw a cartload of pure gold standing before our house. In actual fact it was a cartload of silkworm cocoons, but the sun, striking full on the shining yellow threads of silk, made them look like spun gold.

Apart from my parents the people most important to me in my family life were my elder brother Bruno, a handsome, dashing boy to whom I was absolutely devoted, and our nurse, Maria, who was with us for twenty-nine years through good times and bad. I was her favorite and I am afraid she spoiled me somewhat. She was convinced that her poor little Tito was not properly fed at school and when I had occasion to go from one section of school to another and contrived to pass in front of our house she would pop out and press a parcel of food into my hands, to the great satisfaction of my companions and myself.

At school I was neither very good nor very bad—just a normal boy. I was very lively and made a lot of noise, and was involved in my full share of the kind of prank which seems so exquisitely funny at the time but not nearly as funny when one has to explain it or atone for it. I think I was often something of a rebel—but what boy is not?

At one point I was threatened with a serious interruption to my schooling, something which would have made my future career impossible. At the age of ten or eleven I suddenly developed asthma. Not only did I become a poor, weak, breathless little creature, but I also stopped growing. Desperately alarmed, my parents consulted one doctor after another, without result. Then one day one of the employees in the family business said to my father: "Signor Gobbi, my brother is the head of a gymnasium some distance from here and understands so much about physical development. Would you consider consulting him about little Master Tito?"

My father agreed, and into my life came Giovanni dal Sasso, to whom, I say in all sincerity, I probably owe the splendid health and constitution which are the essential basis of any strenuous vocal career. He examined me thoroughly and then said rather enigmatically to my father: "Which would you rather have—a dead professor or a live donkey?"

Naturally my father asked him to be more specific, and the reply was: "If this boy continues his present school life he may acquire a lot of knowledge, but he will die. If you will be satisfied to have him a little less well educated and will turn him over to me, I can cure him."

My father opted for the "live donkey" without hesitation, and Giovanni dal Sasso took over the direction of my daily life. It was a regime of the utmost severity. I still lived at home and even attended school as and when my mentor decreed, but every physical demand he made upon my daily routine had to come first. Since he also had to fit my program into *his* daily life there was simply no knowing when he would arrive. It was nothing for him to come tramping up the stairs at seven or eight o'clock on a cold winter's morning, while I cowered under the warm bed-coverings wishing him anywhere else in the world. He would come into my room, strip off the blankets, pick me up, and toss me out of the low window into the snow, still shuddering in my pajamas; then he would jump out after me and pummel me and rub snow onto me until I was no longer a teeth-chattering lump but a strangely glowing little boy.

This was only part of it, of course. The carefully graded but increasingly strenuous exercises, the varied forms of personal combat which drew tentative but totally disregarded protests from my mother, the subtle stages by which I was taught to relax completely or to resist in every muscle—these were part of a spartan regime which lasted for nearly two years. But at the end of that time I had grown seventeen centimeters and was a big strapping chap without a trace of breathing trouble. God bless Giovanni dal Sasso! He deserved some of the cheers which were to come my way in later life.

The first time anyone noticed my voice was when I was at elementary school, which was the first stage of our education. Our singing teacher was preparing us for an end-of-term performance to take place before the general inspector and our parents. We were to do a sort of chorus of national songs, and at one of the rehearsals our teacher, Maestro Bevilacqua, started going around the class muttering to himself. Finally he stopped in front of me and exclaimed: "You're the culprit! You're shouting like a mad dog—it's terrible! You keep silent. But as we don't want the inspector to know you are not singing, simply open and shut your mouth and pretend to sing."

So my first public performance was in dumb show. But Maestro Bevilacqua was really a very kind man and many years later, when I had already had some success and made something of a name, I went back to Bassano to sing at my sister's wedding. I wrote to him, recalling myself to him, and asked if he would be so kind as to inspect the organ in the church and perhaps try over the items I was to sing so as to hear how they sounded, since I knew the organ to be an old one. I added that I would provide my own accompanist, who would be a very good one.

He wrote back in the friendliest terms agreeing to my request and apologizing for the incident in my schooldays, which he also remembered. I arrived in good time at the church and found him lovingly cleaning and polishing the organ. He was very excited, poor old man, and he looked at me as though I were God when I said: "Could we try over what I am going to sing?" As he asked anxiously where my accompanist was I reassured him: "Don't worry. He's here all right."

When the moment came for the bride to enter the church he again asked anxiously about my accompanist, and again I reassured him. But when it was time for me to start the "Ave Maria" he looked around desperately and asked: *"Where* is your accompanist?" To which I replied: "He's here—I told you. It's you. You were my first singing teacher and in you I have the best accompanist."

At that the old man began to cry, and I was afraid he would be too overcome to play. But he did play—quite wonderfully—and I was so happy to have done this for him; for he was a dear, good man and it meant so much to him.

Well, these are all happy stories of my childhood and my growing-up years. But there are two sides to every coin. In my middle teens, during the great financial crises which engulfed Europe, Italy and Bassano del Grappa were not immune. Financially, the family fortunes deteriorated sharply and my father decided to go to South America to try his luck there. I am afraid I must add that this decision was further enforced by the fact that several husbands in Bassano were after his blood for the very good reason that their wives had responded too ardently to his charming approaches. My father departed for fresh fields—possibly in more than one sense of the term—but before he left he asked his brother Ettore to look after his family's interests.

During these difficult days my mother showed a wonderful side to her character. Hitherto she had been greatly respected for her dignity and quiet authority, as well as her high standing in the town. There was no false pride about her but she had an unself-conscious air of distinction which set her slightly apart from the common run. Now, however, and without hesitation, she went into the family shop, to serve like any humble assistant. If certain ill-wishing people chose to look down their noses or smile maliciously at her fallen fortunes she took no notice at all. She was pleasant and courteous—and dignified—to everyone. No wonder her father-in-law thought the world of her.

This makes it all the stranger that when my grandfather presently fell very ill the other members of the family went to considerable lengths to keep her away from him, on the grounds that he was too weak and tired to see anyone, he had not asked for her, and so on. On the other hand, there was no question of barring the widower of my aunt. He was, it will be remembered, the lawyer. He had gone blind by now but still practiced his profession, contriving to do any necessary writing with the aid of an ingenious wooden frame.

From the manservant who attended my grandfather—and incidentally supplied him with oxygen in his last hours—I heard very much later that there was indeed a family gathering at the end, with the blind lawyer in attendance and my uncle Guglielmo directing proceedings.

Who shall say now what really happened? The practical outcome was that when my father returned hurriedly from South America on the death of his father, it was to find that according to the old man's last will there was nothing for him, nothing for his wife, and nothing for the five children. When he indignantly inquired of Ettore what way this was of protecting the interests of his brother's family, as agreed, he received the shamelessly indifferent reply: "It suited me."

The strange postscript, as it were, to this piece of family history came some time later when one day I met the blind lawyer in town. Recognizing me by my footsteps, he stopped me and inquired solicitously after my mother. Then he insisted on taking me to the finest pastry cooks in the place and loading me with far more cakes than our family could possibly have eaten. He sent friendly messages to my mother, wafted me on my way—and then went home and hanged himself.

2.

AMONG THE CLOSEST FRIENDS we had in Bassano—indeed, they have remained my lifelong friends—were the Barone Zanchetta and his family. As with our family, there were several children and most years we would spend some wonderful months together sharing a house in the Alps, walking, cooking, and camping in the woods. Then as we grew older there were slightly more grown-up gatherings—tennis parties and so on—and it was on the occasion of one of these parties that the first serious notice was taken of my voice, by no less a person than the barone himself, who was a cultured and knowledgeable musician and something of a composer in his own right. Hearing me bawling some popular song, he looked out of his window and called: "Who is that singing?"

I said it was I, and he immediately summoned me and made me sing for him. Then he informed me positively that I was a baritone (and fortunate is the singer who is accurately told by a knowledgeable person what type of voice he or she possesses), and he gave it as his opinion that perhaps I should consider the possibility of singing as a profession.

I didn't take this very seriously; still less did my tennis-playing companions when I returned to them with the news that I might become a singer. They roared with laughter in chorus. But the barone had planted the first germ of an idea in my mind, and he even gave me a few basic singing lessons. On the other hand, I was not at all sure at this time that I did not fancy myself as a painter, having received some encouragement from a well-known fresco painter who was working in the district.

At this point my father returned from one of his South American trips, summarily dismissed both artistic proposals, and ruled that I should go into the family business and learn to make a sensible living there. I cannot recall any bitter resentment at this decision. Parental opinion carried great weight with us in those days, and the artistic rebel was virtually an unknown creature. I went into the business as an under-manager and worked (without salary) as hard and determinedly as I could, with the intention of showing my father that I could make a success of anything. At the end of several months my reward was somewhat meagerly assessed.

But my interest in singing had been growing, encouraged to some extent by my mother. One day she said: "Papa is leaving for Rome tomorrow. I think it might be a good idea if you also got on the train. He can't send you back then, and he will have to take you to someone in Rome and find out if you really are any good."

So, once Father had bidden us good-by and left for the station, my mother and I followed at a safe distance, my luggage having been deposited there beforehand. We made ourselves scarce until the train was ready to depart. Then at the very last moment my mother said: "Go—go now. God bless you. And be sure to write."

And I kissed her and I went.

After the train had been going for some while I went along, looking in each compartment, and finally, in the first-class, I saw my father reading a newspaper. I stood in the doorway for a few moments while he took no notice of me. Then I cleared my throat once or twice, and without looking up he said: "What sort of ticket have you got?"

"I haven't got a ticket, Papa," I admitted.

"You haven't got a ticket? You know you are not allowed to travel on a train without a ticket?"

"I know," I said. "But Mother thought it would be a good idea if—"

"Oh—so Mother thought it would be a good idea, did she? Well, then, it must be. But you will travel third-class. At your age third-class is good enough. I'll come and visit you presently."

"O.K.," I said. "Thank you—" and I was about to go when he called me.

"Come back and sit here. After all, for the first time you have a chance to travel with your father." Then he began to laugh and talk, and I started to enjoy myself, and soon he said: "Now when the ticket collector comes we'll have to pretend you have lost your ticket. Can you act well?"

I thought I could put up quite a good show. So when the ticket collector came my father presented his ticket and then turned to me and said: "You must show your ticket."

"But I gave it to you, Papa," I replied as guilelessly as I could.

"Nonsense. Look again," my father admonished me.

I gave a performance of an anxious and fruitless search, after which my father exclaimed resignedly: "As usual! Always losing his ticket. Now I suppose I shall have to buy him a new one."

This he did and the ticket collector withdrew satisfied.

Once in Rome my father looked up a cousin of his who was a general —a Sicilian—and through his good offices we were introduced to the famous tenor Giulio Crimi, who was also Sicilian. A preliminary meeting was arranged at which Crimi looked me over from shoes to hair, asked one or two questions, and finally agreed to audition me a couple of days later at his own home.

My father and I presented ourselves at the appointed time, and the first thing Crimi asked me was if either of us played the piano. Neither of us did—and nor, it seemed, did Crimi. But after a moment's thought he said: "Never mind. Maybe Tilduzza is here. Come into the garden."

We adjourned to the garden and when Crimi called "Tilduzza!" a girl's voice called back from a tree: "I'm here picking some fruit."

"Well, come down," Crimi said. "There's a young man here who wants me to hear him sing. Will you come and play for him?"

"All right." And a young girl began to climb down out of the tree. I went forward to help her, but she would have none of me. She was a proper Roman young lady and—goodness knows what I was. With great composure she stood beside me at the foot of the tree.

Although this incident may sound suspiciously as though I have "lifted" it from Mascagni's *L'Amico Fritz,* in very truth that was the way I met my future wife, Tilde de Rensis. She—though of course I did not know this then—was the daughter of one of the most distinguished musicologists in Italy and already a fine pianist in her own right. She was very friendly with Crimi's daughter and often at the house, so it was not unusual for her to be called on to play for anyone who wanted to sing for the maestro.

Crimi listened attentively to my singing and at the end said: "Well, I can't promise anything at this stage. But if he would like to stay in Rome and study with me for three months I shall then be able to tell you frankly if it's worth his continuing."

This realistic approach appealed to my father, who arranged for the lessons forthwith and after a short stay in Rome went off once more to South America, leaving me enough money to live modestly and pay for the lessons. At the end of the three-month period Crimi declared that I was sufficiently talented to justify a complete training. But unfortunately very soon after that I received a letter from my father saying that his financial position had deteriorated and he could no longer afford to send a regular allowance. It would be better if I went home to Bassano until things improved.

By now, however, I was determined to be a singer, with or without my father's assistance. So, taking my paint box, I began to haunt the popular tourist spots in Rome; here I would plant myself and paint absorbedly until presently tourists began to ask if they could buy my pictures. I dared not charge much but I sold several pictures—enough for my bare living expenses but not enough for the lessons.

Finally, therefore, I went to Crimi, explained about my father's reverses and admitted that, for the time being at any rate, the lessons could not be paid for.

"That's all right," Crimi replied. "When you have enough money you pay me. Have you got enough for your living expenses?"

Untruthfully I said that I had, for I could not possibly impose on his generosity further, and back I went to my painting. But despite all my efforts I could not make more than enough money for my simple lodging —a long, long walk from my maestro's house—and one meal a day. This almost always consisted of a kind of fried rice ball containing a small piece of cheese or ham. It was called a *supplì* and cost something like thirty centesimi.

By dint of much painting and, even more, of rigid economy, I scraped together thirty-five lire, and then I went to the *supplì* shop and handed over my total assets to the woman behind the counter.

"I'm paying for three months in advance," I told her. "I'll come here every day and you will give me one *supplì*."

"Are you sure?" The woman was amused and impressed. "You may need the money."

"No," I replied, for I had, as we say now, got my priorities right. *"I need to stay."*

The spartan regime was not an easy one. I was soon heartily sick of my daily *supplì*. I also drank a lot of water and soon I knew every fountain in Rome, both by name and by taste. Naturally I began to lose weight, and one day Crimi looked at me searchingly and asked: "Are you dieting? Or have you some problem troubling you?"

"No, no," I assured him airily. "No problem at all."

We went on with the lesson. Then Crimi stopped suddenly and said: "You know, I'm hungry! My wife makes some very good *supplìs*. Do you like *supplìs?*"

I loathed them by now with a deadly loathing but managed to mutter that I did like them. This did not satisfy Crimi, however, and he began to ask more and more searching questions until I broke down in tears and the whole story came out.

"You stupid boy!" he exclaimed. "Why didn't you tell me before? You will come and live here of course. You can share my boy's room. First we will have a little snack—not *supplis*—and then you will go and get your things."

So it was arranged and until my circumstances improved not one penny did that wonderful man charge me for my lessons or my living expenses. Some considerable time later, when I made my first money, I went to him and said: "Maestro, you were so good to me for all those months, teaching me and letting me live here in your house like a son. Now you must tell me what I owe you so that I can show my gratitude and respect by paying my debts."

I really thought he was going to have a stroke. He went quite white and glared at me and then, with true Sicilian intensity, he thundered: "Go away! When did a son ever have to pay his father for anything? You are not my son. Go away."

At which I once more dissolved into tears and apologized profusely, and there was a great reconciliation scene. But he never let me pay for those months. I paid of course for all my later lessons, but for those early vital months when I was truly in need he would not accept anything. Indeed, he took me under his wing in every sense, introducing me everywhere to his colleagues or to anyone who might be of help, and he used to say: "Treat him properly or I will kill you. I am a Sicilian, remember, and I carry a knife."

Beneath this fierce exterior, however, there lurked a sentimental heart and I suppose it did not escape his notice that Tilde and I were becoming more and more interested in each other. Her services as an accompanist at the lessons were frequently required and then Crimi would say: "Come on, let's go. We'll take Tilduzza home and then walk a little."

So Tilde would be most respectably escorted home, with one of us on either side of her. Correct good-bys would be exchanged and Crimi and I would continue on our way. Then one day Crimi stopped in the Piazza Ungheria and asked us to wait while he made a telephone call he had just remembered. He went into a bar and we could see him telephoning. When he rejoined us he said: "I'm sorry, I have to leave you. So you, young man, escort the lady home. Be properly respectful, mind. Look after her. I make her your responsibility."

"Yes, sir, yes," I promised, and off we went, very glad to be on our own for once—until, as we were approaching Tilde's home, she exclaimed: "Oh, goodness! Here's Mother coming!"

"Th-that tall, elegant lady?" I asked.

"Yes. And she's coming this way."

Something in her manner inspired a degree of uneasiness in us, as well it might, for it was really to her that Crimi had telephoned. Very artfully he had inquired if she realized that young Tito Gobbi frequently escorted her daughter home, that they were even now walking together through the streets; and would it not perhaps be a good idea if she found out just what was happening?

"*Ciao,* Mamma," said Tilde with her sweetest smile, while I added: "*Buon giorno,* signora," in my most respectful tone.

"Tilde," said her mother, "you go home. And you, young man, you come with me."

Tilde speedily made herself scarce, and Signora de Rensis addressed me severely: "What is this I hear about your accompanying our daughter home each day, walking with her without our permission, without so much as coming to the house and making yourself known to us? Is that the right way to behave?"

I was dumbfounded, and began to stammer that it was all a mistake —that this was the very first time I had been alone with her daughter because Maestro Crimi always accompanied us, until today when he had been summoned away.

"I never came to your house, madame," I explained earnestly, "because there was no occasion to do so."

"Very well," replied Signora de Rensis, who was, I suppose, beginning to see through Crimi's romantic machinations. "This seems a good opportunity for you to come and make yourself known to us."

So into the house of the De Rensis family I went, thereby taking perhaps the most important step in laying the foundations of my artistic career. Tilde's father, Raffaello de Rensis, was one of the most respected musicologists in Italy. An academician of both the Santa Cecilia Academy in Rome and the Cherubini in Florence, he was a founder and member of the Association of Italian Musicologists. For nearly forty years he was music critic first of the *Messaggero* and then of the *Giornale d'Italia,* and was an acknowledged authority on his subject, highly respected for the objectivity, wisdom, and constructiveness of his judgments. He promoted new operas by new composers and founded the Istituto Italiano per la Storia della Musica. His great pride was to have been able to publish the entire works of Pierluigi da Palestrina.

In consequence, the De Rensis house was frequented by many composers, conductors, and artists of the day, and I found myself in a totally new and fascinating world. I was still very much the boy from the country town, and although we all liked music at home and sang a good deal we were not a musical family in the strictest sense of the term. Nothing like the richness and depth of this new experience had ever come my way before, and I began to absorb it like a sponge absorbing water.

I was still studying singing with Maestro Crimi of course, but now I also studied piano and repertoire with Tilde. I began to meet important people—composers like Wolf-Ferrari, Perosi, and Refice, and conductors like Bernadino Molinari, for whom I sang informally in the De Rensis home in May 1935. When he said that he had not heard such a lovely baritone voice for the last ten years I felt that fame was just around the corner: particularly as I was to make my first (if very modest) stage appearance in about a couple of weeks' time.

My role was that of the count in Bellini's *La Sonnambula*, which is properly a bass role, but not an impossibility for an eager young baritone prepared to seize any chance. Gubbio was the place where I was to startle the musical world, and if the company was rather a scratch affair and some of us even had to assist with the scene-shifting from time to time, at least I was to be onstage, fully made up. Too fully, when it came to the point, for I must have looked about seventy.

Naturally I had arranged for Tilde and her parents, as well as Maestro Crimi, to be present on the great occasion. I sang and played my part with my whole heart, and when it was all over I could hardly wait to take off my wretched make-up and rush out of the stage door, where they were all sitting in the car.

I waited modestly for the compliments, and finally Tilde said, *"Povero Tito, povero Tito"* while her mother looked at me compassionately. Her father, always a man of few words, merely said to the chauffeur: "Home."

In some trepidation now I turned to Maestro Crimi, who was sitting in the back of the car, his hands on the handle of an umbrella and his chin resting on his hands.

"Well, Commendatore?" I inquired rather timidly.

"My address," he replied grimly, "is so-and-so. *If* you think you had better go on studying, come and see me tomorrow. Otherwise—good-by."

And that was my first big success.

3.

DURING THE NEXT MONTH, however, my battered self-esteem received a lift. Another famous conductor—none other than Gino Marinuzzi from La Scala—heard me sing informally in the De Rensis home and said he would like to hear me on a stage. So an audition was arranged at the Teatro Quirino, after which he said frankly to Signor de Rensis: "I can't let this boy out of my hands. Bring him to Milan and I'll see what I can do."

In company with Signor de Rensis I went to Milan to audition at La Scala and, after some discussion, it was decided that I should have a kind of tiny contract—at 1,000 lire a month—to study with one or another of the coaches and attend as many rehearsals and performances as possible.

This arrangement started in November 1935 and lasted until the following April. Within the first month, however, I discovered that all the coaches were much too busy to deal with me. Finally, I found the courage to make a protest and a man called Polsinetti was added to the staff. He was a splendid coach and from the modest beginning of teaching the unimportant young Tito Gobbi he became a highly successful and busy coach at La Scala.

Some very pleasant days followed. My elder sister had a good secretarial position with a big Milan glass factory at that time, and so we lived together in the same pensione and were happy in each other's company. Only twice did I emerge from the obscurity of the unimportant student, neither of these exactly a dazzling occasion.

The first occurred at the opening performance of Pizzetti's opera *Orseolo*. By now I rather fancied myself as part of La Scala. I had still never appeared on that illustrious stage, it is true, but in my own estimation at any rate I could at least cut a distinguished figure among the audience. So, on this particular night, I was sitting in a box, very elegant in white tie and tails, surveying the Milanese smart set assembled in the opera house and occasionally waving a gracious hand to one acquaintance or another. Then into this scene of glory stepped a disquieting figure, who informed me that I was required backstage. Surprised and a trifle disturbed, I followed him as he led me to a maestro standing in the wings, who told me with brutal brevity: "Signor So-and-so is ill, so you will have to take his place."

At this terrible announcement the stars fell out of my brilliant night sky and darkness enveloped me. I protested faintly that I didn't know anything but was immediately cut short. There was nothing to it, I was told: only one easy phrase, all on one note, as I had to announce to Orseolo: "La Signoria del Doge e del Sena-a-a-ato."

I was sent upstairs to be costumed and made up, and all the way I sang under my breath on my one note: "La Signoria del Doge e del Sena-a-a-ato." In a corridor I met what seemed to me to be a wonderful creature, regally dressed and of imposing physique, trying his voice up and down. He looked at me with a patronizing air and asked: "Are you the young man who is going to sing the Herald? You are? Then come here, my boy, and I will make you up. I will do your face because you have no experience in these matters."

Then he sat me down before a mirror and began scratching my face with the most frightful old sticks of make-up. They were worn right down to the metal foil in which they were wrapped, so that in no time my wretched face did have color on it, but mostly my own blood. Looking perfectly horrible, I was then tried out for the enormous costume. At that time I was thin like that famous page to the Duke of Norfolk, so they had to wrap the dreadful thing around me, securing it with safety pins in such haste that they pinned in bits of me too. All this, however, was nothing compared to the glory of singing at La Scala, so, setting my teeth, I accepted all the anguish and made my way to the stage, still repeating my single phrase to myself.

"Who are *you?*" asked the maestro in the wings.

"Gobbi," I whispered back, divided between pride and terror. "I'm the replacement for the Herald."

"Well, keep quiet and wait until I tell you to go," he replied. At that moment I saw my great man from upstairs who had so condescendingly scratched make-up on my face. But now he was incredibly transformed.

Trembling and crossing himself and kissing holy medals before his entrance onstage, he was no longer a demi-god: just a terrified human being.

This metamorphosis in one who had seemed so sure of himself increased my own fears, and I kept on asking anxiously: "When is my turn, Maestro?"

"Wait," the good man told me reassuringly. "I'll tell you when to go."

But he had no idea that I was totally ignorant of anything concerning a performance and had never set foot on a stage before. Consequently I knew nothing about the timing of an entrance. When he told me, "Go!" I leaped forward like a runner at the sound of the starting pistol, flung open the door, and, ignoring the great Tancredi Pasero singing his aria, shouted as loudly as I could "La Signoria del Doge e del Sena-a-a-ato" at least half a minute too soon.

Pasero stopped dead, his mouth open, while the other great man turned a look of fury upon me. Maestro Pizzetti, who was conducting his own work on this important occasion, nearly had a stroke, while the prompter, leaning from his box, hissed: "You idiot! Who sent you here? Go to hell!"

I was utterly bewildered by the insults and furious looks and had no idea what to do next. But somehow I got myself off the stage, forcing my way through the Signoria, who at long last were processing solemnly onto the scene.

My humiliation and sense of injustice were total as I made my way back to the dressing rooms, divested myself of my elephantine costume, and removed at least some of the make-up which disfigured my face. I dragged on my own clothes again just any way—not at all as the handsome young cavalier in the box had worn them—jammed on my hat at a desperate angle and left the famous Scala, telling myself that if this were a sample of an operatic appearance I had had enough of it.

Outside it was snowing, but I started walking all the way back to my pensione, oblivious of the snow soaking through my thin shoes, and as I walked I shed some tears. They stung my cheeks as they trickled over the battle scars inflicted by the demi-god with the make-up stick. But even worse was the pain of disillusionment. The next morning, however, for some reason I have never been able to fathom, I received in the newspapers a few quite flattering lines on my disastrous debut at La Scala.

The second occasion promised better. I had been assigned to understudy the baritone Mario Basiola in an oratorio by Perosi. The part lay beautifully for my voice; there was no stage work, no costume to worry about; and when a day or two beforehand Basiola fell ill no sympathy which I might feel for him could dim my own rejoicing.

The rehearsal went wonderfully, the conductor congratulated me, and Polsinetti was delighted that here at last my great chance had come. On the all-important evening I presented myself in good time: white tie, immaculate suit, my voice brushed up and clean, as we say. I was told to try out my voice, which was pronounced very good, and I was all ready when—Basiola appeared.

There is no way of describing my crushing disappointment. Somehow I managed to swallow my feelings and I went to Basiola and said: "Maestro, I am glad to see you are well enough to come and sing, and I wish you the best."

He looked at me—without favor, I must say, for we did not know each other and to him I was just the young upstart who was trying to push him out—and he replied: "I wish you a good career. But one day you will realize that sometimes it is better to sing not so well than to let someone else take your place. That is why I am singing tonight."

Then two months after I returned to Rome, Maestro Crimi suggested that I should enter the international competition which was held every year in Vienna for the best male and female singer and the best pianist. My entry was accepted and an Italian organization which helped young artists advanced half the entry fee, to be repaid if and when I made some money. There still remained the problem of travel and a place to stay, but a married sister of my mother's lived in Vienna and I wrote to her.

She was away from home, as it happened, but my unknown uncle replied, offering to pay my fare to Vienna and stating that he would meet me at the station if I would let him know by return some way of recognizing me. I replied promptly that I would come off the train carrying my luggage, with the tip of my tie between my teeth, and would he please identify himself in the same way?

At that time I did not know that he happened to be one of the most distinguished architectural engineers in Austria, with a government post corresponding to the head of the Ministry of Works. But he must have been determined to do the right thing by me, for when I marched across the station, the tip of my tie between my teeth, I soon found a bashful little gentleman, effacing himself as far as possible in a corner but with the tip of *his* tie heroically gripped between his front teeth.

We liked each other on sight and got on splendidly. No one could have been kinder to me and with his good wishes I presented myself for the great contest. I sang the "Credo" from *Otello*, "Oh dei verd 'anni miei" from *Ernani*, "Pari siamo" from *Rigoletto* and "Nemico della Patria" from Giordano's *Andrea Chenier*. With this ambitious program I found myself one of the last three contestants, then one of the last two, and finally I was declared the winner.

My prize was substantial in money terms—something like ten or twelve thousand lire, which in those days was quite a sum. Indeed, there was a popular song of the period which ran, "If only I had a thousand lire a month!"—meaning that on this sum one could live. Out of this money I was able to pay for the first flight I ever made—from Vienna to Venice—which took six hours. The plane was a pocket-sized one carrying two passengers only, and my companion was Signor Bodrero, the Italian Minister for Education. As we clung to the small rail which served us both as a seat, and bounced up and down with each rise and fall of the plane, I had the impression that he very much wished himself elsewhere.

Back in Rome, with the realization that I was modestly provided for in the coming year, I first of all tried to pay my debts to Maestro Crimi—with the emotional result already described—and then decided that on the strength of my prize money Tilde and I could announce our engagement.

It was not of course long before I discovered that twelve thousand lire was not such a vast sum after all. And then Maestro Crimi, ever on the lookout for something to help me, drew my attention to an announcement that the well-known film actor and producer, Luis Trenker, was looking for a young man who could not only sing engagingly but leap about athletically and generally fill a role both romantic and active. Through Crimi's good offices I was included among those to be auditioned for the job, and presently I found myself in a dismayingly long queue at the studio.

My turn came late in the day, and the man who gave me brief instructions had obviously already repeated these a stupefying number of times. "Come in from the back of the scene—there. Jump over that group of men sitting at the table, take hold of the guitar which will be put into your hands, and sing something. It doesn't matter what. Just anything," he added wearily.

It was not difficult to see that everyone was now heartily tired of being leaped over and strummed at and sung to, and I realized I had to do something unusual. So, having hastily surveyed the scene, I came running in from the back, planted my foot firmly on a small stool which was handy, turned a complete somersault over the astonished gentlemen at the table, snatched up the guitar, and burst into song. I got the part.

I was then asked what payment I expected and, being completely inexperienced in this world, I replied truthfully that I had no idea but that my maestro, Signor Crimi, would come and speak for me the following day.

Even now I recall that interview with delighted amusement and incredulity. It started with Crimi asking how long the shooting of the film—or at least my role in it—would take and what the suggested remuneration was.

"About fourteen days—say, fifteen," he was told. "And how about five thousand lire?"

Secretly I thought five thousand lire for fifteen days' work not bad. But Crimi said heavily: "You must be joking. You say the filming will take fifteen days?"

"Perhaps fourteen."

"We will say fifteen. For these fifteen days you will pay this young man fifteen thousand lire. And if you should go over the fifteen days—"

"We shan't do that!"

"But *if* you should, you will pay him another fifteen thousand for every two weeks even if you go only one day over."

"All right," I was stunned to hear them say.

"And if," went on Crimi inexorably, "you go abroad to film—"

"There's no thought of going abroad!"

"—you will pay him a thousand lire a day here in Rome and another thousand lire a day wherever you are filming, plus of course first-class expenses and hotel."

"O.K., O.K. But it will—"

"And should you go outside Rome—to Venice say, or Florence—"

"There's no question of that."

"—you will pay him a thousand lire a day wherever he is, and a thousand lire a day here in Rome. Again of course with first-class expenses and hotel."

To my utter amazement there was agreement to all these conditions, with only a few murmurs now about fifteen days' limit and everything being filmed in Rome. In point of fact, they took seven months and twenty-four days in all, and we filmed in Berlin, Venice, Florence, San Gimigniano, the Dolomites, Verona, and goodness knows where else. For every one of those days I received one thousand lire in my account in

Rome, and wherever we traveled—which we did in style—I had my thousand lire a day in each city or country and lived it up in the greatest luxury.

It went to my head, of course. I had never had such a time in my life. In Berlin particularly, where we stayed for two or three months, I had the delicious added problem of being forced to spend everything I earned, because in those days one was not allowed to take any money out of the country. I ate and drank like a lord, I entertained in style, I treated myself to the kind of clothes I had never worn before—including no less than three tuxedos—and every top restaurant in Berlin knew me.

It so happened that one of Tilde's uncles, Signor Montuori, was the leading cameraman, and he sought me out, his face very grave. "What is all this I hear about you, Tito?" he asked. "You are behaving in the most wildly extravagant manner. Drinking too much, entertaining all and sundry. If you are going to marry my niece, this must stop. I hear you even have a motorcar."

I had not, as a matter of fact, but I instantly thought it a good idea. So I hired a gorgeous limousine and the services of a young medical student to act as chauffeur. His name was Franz, and I told him: "Now, when you and I are together in the car we are just Tito and Franz. But do me one favor. When I send for you to pick me up at the hotel or a restaurant, please come in and ask very distinctly for the Herr Baron Tito Gobbi."

Franz thought this was fine. I gave him one of my three tuxedos and he played his part superbly. He would come into the crowded lobby of my hotel, approach the reception desk, and announce very clearly that the car was waiting for the Herr Baron Tito Gobbi. Then I would come running downstairs, all white tie and smiles, bow and wave in all directions, "*Ciao—ciao*" to the admiring audience, who would murmur in their turn, "There goes the Herr Baron Tito Gobbi," and make a magnificent exit.

Once Franz and I were in the car we would roar with laughter and go off to enjoy ourselves. It was one of the most delightfully idiotic roles I ever played and, because we were young and silly and full of high spirits, Franz and I had a wonderful time. I am glad to recall that at the end of the great Berlin spree I still had enough money left to pay for the completion of Franz's medical studies.

Meanwhile, during the filming I got on excellently with Luis Trenker, who obligingly spun out my role to a very useful length. The film, which was called *I Condottieri*, was a splendid hotchpotch of romance and adventure set roughly in the Middle Ages, and I played a troubadour called Nino, who sang his way around the various cities and beauty spots of Europe, trying to trace the heroine on behalf of the hero. Sometimes, well disguised, I took minor roles which were unpopular with others because of the risks they involved. Once, suitably disguised in armor, I led a troop across a river on horseback. And again, with a big mustache and beard this time, I was a soldier climbing the walls of a castle and leaping over the battlements. I was at an age when every athletic challenge was fun.

Finally, in Florence, Luis Trenker said: "You know, Tito, your role is getting almost bigger than mine. I'm afraid it's time I killed you off—with great regret." So I was killed off, with much drama and pathos, in the Piazza della Signoria, and my days of high living were over.

It had all been enormously enjoyable, but I was beginning to feel I had been a playboy long enough and was, indeed, almost exhausted by the exciting time I had been having. Now I wanted to get back to the serious business of becoming a singer. In addition, of course, I had accumulated capital beyond my wildest dreams: certainly enough for two young people to contemplate marriage with some confidence. So, in April 1937, with Maestro Crimi as my best man, Wolf-Ferrari as Tilde's "testimonio," and young Giuseppe Taddei singing in the church, Tilde and I were married.

To say it has been a supremely happy marriage would be an understatement. There was not only our personal happiness but also, from the beginning, the two families got along together beautifully. True, the Gobbis were not exactly a musical family, though both my grandfather and my father had their operatic moments: Grandfather while feeding the birds would sing to them from Verdi's *I Due Foscari* "Questa è dunque l'iniqua mercede," and my father, when we went walking in the mountains, would insist on waking the echoes with "Un bel di vedremo," sung in a rich baritone, replying to our protests of "But, Papa, it's for a *soprano!*" with a careless, "I don't care—I like it."

Basically the Gobbis and the De Rensis family found much in common in a warm, human approach to life, and Tilde formed the perfect link. My sisters found another sister in her, my brothers adored her. She organized the joyful occasions like my sisters' marriages and she supported us in the family tragedies. There was nothing she flinched from undertaking, and her part in my life and career has been immeasurable. Indeed, when I am asked—as I sometimes am—what I regard as the most important influence on my development as a person and artist, I am happy to reply with absolute truth: "The one thing which distinguished me from all my colleagues was that none of them had the good fortune to marry Tilde."

To this, of course, I would have to add the unique training and guidance given me by Maestro Serafin, the unfailing help and advice of my mother-in-law and father-in-law, the first opportunity given me by Marinuzzi, and so on. But as the true basis of any success I have achieved as a man and an artist I would unhesitatingly give my marriage.

This marriage started with a honeymoon in Capri, but within a matter of days we were recalled by an urgent telegram from Wolf-Ferrari. The first performance of his "Canzoniere" was about to take place and, as this song cycle had been dedicated to me, it was unthinkable that anyone else should be chosen to introduce it to the public.

So back we went to Rome, to settle down in an apartment on the ground floor of the house in which Tilde's parents lived. Here we began married life with high hopes but also with the inevitable anxieties attendant on the real start of any career. The film which had provided the wherewithal on which to marry had been a splendid but isolated piece of good fortune. In any case I had no wish to be diverted permanently into films. I intended to be an operatic artist, even if my career so far had been limited to one line at La Scala, the ill-fated Gubbio performance, an occasional modest concert appearance, and a sprinkling of radio engagements.

These radio engagements were organized by Annibale Bizzelli, whom I had met at the pensione where I stayed when I first came to Rome. We had remained excellent friends, and Tilde and I were to number him and his wife Alva among our best and oldest friends for the rest of our lives. No one today would believe the conditions under which we worked. To begin with, my fee was sixty-three lire and twenty centesimi and, as the programs were supposed to be broadcast live to the United States, we had to be present and correct about two or three in the morning. Naturally there was no public transport at that hour and so we walked to the studio, which took about an hour. Incredibly, however, it was all great fun, for we were young and cheerful and full of nonsense. We got bored sometimes hanging about in the studio, waiting for the "go-ahead" signal, but we used to improvise ridiculous songs and backchat, until one disastrous night something went wrong with the signal and for about ten minutes we really were on the air with Bizzelli singing to me something like, "My little flower, you are so sweet—but I wish

I could go home." If that broadcast ever reached the States someone must surely have been astonished to hear the lightning change as I soulfully burst into "O, begl' occhi di fata" as part of the official program.

But what I needed—the ardent cry of every aspiring performer—was the chance to appear in a full-scale opera house before an audience which might conceivably include someone of judgment and influence who could and would give me that vital lift onto the first rung of the operatic ladder.

It was in June 1937 that the longed-for opportunity came. I received a telephone call one morning from the impresario Cappellini (the husband of the famous soprano Iva Pacetti), who wanted to know if I were free to accept an emergency call to sing Papa Germont in *La Traviata* at the Teatro Adriano, the second opera house in Rome. I was of course all too free, but unfortunately I had a severe attack of hay fever at the time, and even as I declared myself available for anything I burst into a volley of sneezes.

"What's that?" cried Cappellini. "Have you got a cold?"

"No, no," I assured him with a careless laugh. "My wife and I—atishoo!—were cooking something and put in too—too—atishoo! much pepper."

"Well, get over that as quickly as you can," was the brusque reply, "and go along to the Adriano and present yourself to Maestro Votto. You know the part of course?"

"Of course—of course," I assured him, stifling another sneeze.

"Have you ever sung it?"

"Sorry—what was that? Well—hm—I—"

"O.K. You haven't. But you don't say that when you get to the theater. You've sung it three times before. Once in Sicily, once in—shall we say Vercelli?—and once in Viterbo. Now go to the theater. And *stop sneezing!*"

"Yes, of course," I said, and hung up the receiver just before a fresh outburst.

Now the one thing which would sometimes stop the sneezing was for me to wet my lips—no more—with a touch of brandy. So I got a small flask of brandy and went to the theater to meet Cappellini. He sent me first to the wardrobe department to try on the costume, which proved to be rather large but not impossibly so, and I returned to him with the cheerful statement that a few alterations would be necessary but nothing that would not be ready by tommorow.

"Tomorrow?" he shouted, "what is the good of tomorrow? The performance is tonight."

"*Tonight?*" I almost fainted, and felt instinctively for the bottle of brandy. Then I started sneezing once more, which infuriated Cappellini. However, I repeated the story of the pepper, vowed that I could manage everything, and hurried to phone Tilde with the urgent request that she take a taxi and come to the theater with my little make-up box and a few necessities.

"I can't come by taxi," replied poor Tilde. "You took all the money with you. But I'll come as quickly as possible by tram."

Meanwhile I met Maestro Votto, who looked me over indifferently and said: "You know this role and have sung it before?"

I assured him I had and faithfully enumerated the three places where I was supposed to have performed Papa Germont. He continued to look at me with that poker face of his: a strangely unexpressive, unfriendly, unsmiling, totally negative face. He knew that I was a last-minute replacement; he must have been fairly sure that I was very inexperienced; but he offered no word or sign of help or encouragement. As far as he was concerned, I could sink or swim. With almost calculated cruelty he said: "So? Then you know the opera well. We do the usual cuts, of course." And he walked away, leaving me still saying: "Yes, Maestro—of course."

The usual cuts! I had not the slightest idea what they might be, but managed to find some little pianist who seemed to know about coaching and asked him what "the usual cuts" meant. He explained briefly, and I frantically committed them to memory along with everything else I was trying to absorb. Then I went to my small dressing room, still sneezing like a maniac from time to time, and still dabbing my lips with the brandy.

Several people looked in and kindly wished me luck, and I learned that the Violetta was Jolanda Cirillo and Alfredo was Voyer. Then Tilde arrived, a good deal frightened by the mad gamble I was preparing to take. But I told her I was determined. I *had* to sing that night. This was the chance I had been waiting for.

"But suppose—" she began.

"Suppose nothing," I retorted. "If I fail then we'll do something else. I'll change my job—complete my studies and be a lawyer; or open a shop and sell—oh, I don't know what—monkey nuts." And I proceeded to make myself up.

I am bound to say I looked more like a young fellow with a dirty face than the distinguished elderly gentleman I was supposed to be. But it passed muster somehow, and at last I made my entry in the second act.

Overwhelming though it was to find myself for the very first time singing with full orchestra, directed by a famous maestro, guided by an experienced prompter, sharing the stage with distinguished colleagues, I somehow managed. Cirillo was marvelously kind and helpful, prompting me with her eyes, so that I moved more or less into the right place on the stage, and our scene together went well. By the time I came to my big aria I was confident and relaxed enough to give of my best.

The considerable ovation I received perhaps made me a little oversure of myself. At any rate, in the third act, in the big ensemble—the first time I had ever been in an ensemble on a stage—I suddenly found myself singing along with the chorus when I should have been an octave lower.

If looks could have killed, Maestro Votto's appalled and infuriated gaze would have slain me, there in the middle of the stage. But at that moment Voyer found a reason to drift past me and gave me the note in an undertone. I seized it, like a drowning man seizing a rope, and got myself back into the right register. But for the rest of my career Maestro Votto never let me live down that elementary mistake. He would refer to it sourly and disparagingly for years afterward, inquiring with a sort of humorless jocularity: "Well, have you learned *Traviata* yet?"

The evening ended in a storm of applause, and I was intoxicated by my success: not only by my success, I might add, for the frequent application of the brandy to my upper lip had encouraged more direct consumption from the little flask whenever my courage sagged. By the time the last curtain fell the flask was empty and I could only smile foolishly at everyone. When I was told to go out on the stage and take my applause, the brandy, the excitement, the reaction from tense nerves all combined to make my legs almost give way. So it was with a friendly Violetta and Alfredo linking arms with me to uphold me that I tottered out happily to acknowledge my first big success.

Votto naturally had nothing very congratulatory to say to me, but another conductor happened to be in the house. The incomparable Tullio Serafin, musical director of the Teatro Reale (now the Teatro dell'Opera), tended to drop into the Adriano from time to time to hear if there were any promising young singers coming along. On this memorable occasion he came to my dressing room where fortunately I had now recovered somewhat from the dangerous mixture of brandy and success.

"Not at all bad," Serafin said with a smile. "Do you come from the Veneto?"

I said I did and Serafin repeated: "Not bad at all. But go on working."

At that, whether from the brandy or the encouraging push which Tilde gave me, I seized the opportunity and said: "Maestro, I should be so grateful if I might audition for you some time."

"Well," Serafin reflected for a moment, "are you superstitious? You're not? Then come to the opera house at five o'clock on Friday the seventeenth, and I will hear you."

This was a reference to the Italian superstition that seventeen is an unlucky number and Friday an unlucky day; five in the afternoon is usually regarded as seventeen o'clock. But for me it was a lucky combination. I went at the appointed time and sang for Serafin. And after some discussion and consultation I was offered a modest engagement. I was little more than a general factotum at first, but my foot was inside one of the world's greatest opera houses, and the opportunities to listen and learn were now unlimited.

4.

THOUGH I WAS not fully aware of it at the time I was starting at last on the perfect training for an aspiring singer. To my knowledge, nothing like it exists anywhere in the world today. I found myself one of a band of young singers who, under the over-all direction of Maestro Serafin, received a training and a degree of practical, carefully graded experience which was unique in its power to develop a talent instead of exploiting it.

The regime of work was severe. During my first six years at the Teatro Reale I learned sixty-six roles, not actually singing all of them on the stage of course but learning them in depth and sometimes "covering" for more experienced singers. It was like working in an academy with other eager, gifted young artists and at the same time having opportunities for professional work. The bridge between studio and stage was always there, ready for the moment when one became qualified to cross it.

No tribute would be too high to pay to Maestro Serafin and the supreme influence he exerted on the development of operatic talent. During the fifty years or more of his great career, there passed through his hands a procession of singers who shed luster on the operatic scene for most of that time. Few there are of us who would not acknowledge our immeasurable debt to him.

During my years in Rome, in varying stages of artistic development or completion there were Caniglia, Favero, Pampanini, Tassinari, Manacchini, Tajo, Carosio, Neri, Del Monaco, Tagliavini, Taddei, Tebaldi, Silveri, Giovanni Malipiero, Cobelli, Rossi-Lemeni, Dal Monte, Gina Cigna, Oltrabella, to mention only a few—in no order of merit but merely as the names spring to mind. Serafin knew what to do with every one of us, guiding—or occasionally driving—us with infallible wisdom and knowledge. His authority was absolute but, unlike a number of other conductors both then and today, he was our friend. He could correct and admonish without wounding and, though terrifying in his rare moments of anger, he never used his position to humiliate or ridicule a singer.

His instinctive knowledge was little short of miraculous. I remember when—*four years* after I had joined the company—I was judged ready to take the role of Posa in *Don Carlo*. I was eager to sing my part through for Maestro Serafin and to show my paces and I studied intensively with one of the finest of all coaches, Luigi Ricci—still my friend and still in my view one of the great authorities on singing. Each time I tentatively suggested to Maestro Serafin that he might like to hear me he would say: "Tomorrow maybe—we'll see," or "Yes, in a little while." Then one day he said: "Tito, this afternoon you come to the studio and I will hear you."

Full of zeal, I went to his studio at the appointed time. He sat down, put his hands on the keyboard of the piano and said: " 'O, Carlo, ascolta—' sing me that phrase." I did so and he said: "Good, good! Now sing me this phrase." Again I complied and he approved. Then he flicked back the pages of the score and said: "Now this one." Again I sang the requested phrase and then he closed the score and said: "All right, Tito. If Ricci says you are ready, you are."

His confidence in Ricci was complete, and rightly so. He needed to hear for himself only that I could sing those three key phrases, and he knew that the task had been satisfactorily completed by both of us.

In connection with that role there was another incident with Serafin which gives the full measure of that wonderful man. I had of course given a great deal of thought to the acting, as well as the singing, and it seemed to me that, since Posa is shot in the back during the prison scene, his lungs must fill with blood and, realistically speaking, his last phrases should be sung *con voce sofferente* (showing his increasing pain and weakness), ending with a choking sound.

I tried this out at the dress rehearsal and was immediately stopped by Serafin and asked what I was doing. I explained my theory but he smiled, shook his head, and said: "No, no. The audience wants to hear you sing in full voice to the end."

I ventured to point out that they would have been hearing me in full voice throughout the evening, so I had no need to prove myself at the last minute, and I boldly proposed that if I sang it his way on the first night I should be allowed to try it my way on the second night.

Rather reluctantly Serafin gave his consent. So I sang it his way through the whole role on the first night and am bound to say that I had a good reception.

"You see?" Serafin said afterward. "What did I tell you?"

Determinedly, I pointed out that we had not yet had the second performance, at which he exclaimed: "You mean, you obstinate young blockhead [*zuccone*], that you still want to do your choking?"

I insisted that I did, so, with a shrug and a skeptical smile, he once more gave his consent.

On that second night I sang to the very best of my ability until my last dying phrases when I allowed pain and weakness to reduce the tone, and then I choked; whereupon the audience stood up and cheered, carried away by the unexpected realism of my interpretation.

Initially I was of course gratified though slightly stunned by the success of my scene. Then, as I went to my dressing room, I began to feel very uneasy. Who was I, after all, to challenge the judgment of the great Serafin and be cheered for it? I was sitting feeling worried and nervous when there was a knock on the door and, when I opened it, there stood Maestro Serafin in company with the managing director of the opera house and the mayor of Rome.

"May I come in?" Serafin asked courteously.

"Maestro," I exclaimed, "this is your opera house!" And as I opened the door fully they all came in.

"I have brought these gentlemen with me," Serafin explained gravely, "because I want them to hear what I have to say. Tonight I discovered that even an old man can sometimes learn from a young one. You are right, Tito. Go on in your own way."

There was the great man! He recognized—and was not at all ashamed to admit—that this relatively unimportant young baritone had broken new ground in the presentation of opera. Until now, largely speaking, that magnificent aria had been sung as a magnificent aria. That night it had also become the expression of a dying man, which was why the audience had responded as they did. Whether my singing had been good or bad was not the most important point at that moment. What mattered was the fact that realism had broken through convention and captured the audience. Serafin was willing to recognize this fact.

The occasion was not only an important step forward for me personally; it was also the first step toward a new kind of realism in the field of opera. I now began to try out some of my other ideas—sometimes against opposition and scornful comment, since I was still a young artist, but usually with Serafin's support. For he was someone who could recognize the seed even if the flower and fruit had yet to develop. Presently colleagues like Italo Tajo came along with similar ideas, and gradually this new degree of realism began to involve every facet of our work, even make-up—indeed very much in the field of make-up where, for instance, we strove to replace the rather obvious beards and mustaches with something that would look realistic even under a microscope. In all this we were to a great extent allowed our heads by Serafin.

He was utterly generous when generosity was called for, but equally he was ruthless if the situation demanded it. I recall an occasion when a leading soprano was five minutes late for rehearsal and rushed in breathlessly explaining how sorry she was but she had been unfortunately delayed on the way.

"We too are sorry, my dear," replied Serafin. "But are you sure you would not have been able to cope with the emergency had you left your bed perhaps fifteen minutes earlier? Anyway, we will begin now. But this is the first and last time it must happen."

By incredible bad luck—or perhaps bad timing—she was late again the following morning: fifteen minutes late this time. When she hurried onto the stage full of apologies the rehearsal was already in progress. Serafin laid down his baton and inquired the reason for the commotion. Then, as she started to explain, he quietly but relentlessly cut across her excuses, saying: "There can be no interruption to the rehearsal. You will go to the office of administration and you will be paid and released. You have already been replaced in the cast." Then, picking up his baton, he went on with the rehearsal.

From my earliest days in the Rome Opera I was made aware of the absolute insistence on punctuality and discipline. During the years 1937, 1938, and 1939, apart from relatively minor roles which came my way, I was studying intensively. The system and timetable were as rigid as if we had been in an office or factory: much more so than in many an office or factory today.

We almost literally "clocked in" and often worked eleven hours a day, not of course singing all the time but learning and studying roles. At the stage-door entrance there was a book with the name of each artist, great and small, in it and a page for his or her timetable for the day. We had to sign in and, taking a copy of the page, we went from one maestro to another with every hour accounted for. As supreme overseer, as it were, of this timetable was a remarkable man called Teofilo de Angelis. A great man of the theater as well as a fine teacher of singing, he was tre-

mendously strict with all of us; and, although he and I became devoted
to each other later, I at first thought him my enemy.

Like a watchdog he would pace up and down the corridor and
pounce on any luckless creature who was doing anything wrong. Indeed,
to this day there are certain phrases which I associate exclusively with
him because they were phrases I found especially difficult but which he
absolutely insisted on my getting right. Equally, it was useless to try to
avoid a difficult lesson by pleading any kind of indisposition.

"What do you mean?—you don't feel well?" De Angelis would say. "I
feel fine, so we will start now. Suppose you have to sing and the theater
needs you; who is interested if you don't feel well? You manage."

And manage we did. That is what is meant by theater discipline.

Then one day some years later, at the end of a season, he called me to
him and said: "Tito, I think you realize now how much you have
achieved and how well you have developed. So, you see, I was not your
enemy but your friend."

I assured him that I was well aware now of how much I owed to him
and that I was deeply grateful for all his guidance and help.

"Very well then," he said with an affectionate air. "Today you may
walk home with me."

As we walked along I noticed that he was carrying the book which
was always at the stage-door entrance, and I asked him why he had it
with him.

"Today I have finished my job," he replied. "This is the end of the
season, and next season I shall not be there at the opera house. I am retiring. But I am taking with me, as a good remembrance of my life's
work, this book which records what you all did as you learned to become
worthwhile artists. It makes interesting reading, and when I die I shall
leave it to you. You can claim it."

He died some time later but the book never came my way. Perhaps,
however, that hardly mattered, for the discipline and habits of good
work which it had recorded had already made their mark upon me for
the rest of my career. For that I have to thank the Watchdog.

Long before those days of security had been reached, however, I had
made my first appearance on the stage of the Rome Opera House in the
part of Lelio in Wolf-Ferrari's *Le Donne Curiose,* in what I can only
describe as nightmare circumstances.

Among my many tasks at that time I was supposed to be understudy-
ing the baritone Manacchini in the part of Lelio. But, confident that
I—the inexperienced student—was never likely to be called upon to sing

the part, I had inexcusably allowed that particular duty to slip to the bottom of my list. The truth was that I knew absolutely nothing about the role, not even the story of the opera, when early one morning Maestro de Fabritiis telephoned and said: "You are the understudy for Lelio in *Le Donne Curiose,* aren't you?"

With a terrible sinking feeling I said I was.

"Then you know the role, of course." It was a statement rather than a question. "You will be singing it tonight."

There must have been a stunned silence at my end, for after a moment De Fabritiis asked: "Are you there?"

I stammered that I was and added feebly: "Wh-what do I have to do?"

"You come immediately to the opera house," De Fabritiis told me briskly. "You will have a coach, Maestro Nicola Rucci, at your disposal. You will work all day with him and sing the role tonight."

On that he hung up, leaving me to fling a few things together while giving some idea of the situation to Tilde, who by now must have been wondering if married life were to be a series of crises.

At the opera house Maestro Rucci was waiting for me, and to him of course I had to explain the real state of affairs. He promptly flew into a great rage and said that the situation was utterly impossible and he must go at once to the director and explain. But I grabbed hold of him before he reached the door and threatened to give him a good kick if he did not allow me a chance.

"Give me until twelve o'clock," I begged, clinging to his arm with desperate determination. "We have two and a half hours in which to work. If by a quarter to twelve you think it's possible I can do it, we work together until the last minute. If you think it's hopeless, you go to the director and say I have only just arrived and you find I cannot possibly do the part."

Either my pleading or my threatening air must have convinced him it was worth trying, so we set to work and never stopped until a quarter to twelve. Then I closed the score and said: "We will go through it by heart now."

This we did and, finding that apart from a couple of small promptings I knew the part, Maestro Rucci conceded reluctantly that perhaps we might risk the gamble. We continued to work until six o'clock, pausing only for a sandwich and a drink sent up from the bar downstairs. Then I was shown the moves on the stage and something of the stage business; my costume was tried on and pronounced a reasonable fit with the assistance of a few safety pins; and I was as ready as I was ever likely to be in the circumstances.

The actual role of Lelio is not a big one, but it is spread throughout the opera, involving most of the very large cast, and the work is an extremely lively one with a great deal of action. Every one of my colleagues supported me throughout the performance. There was no one who did not give me some helpful indication at the right moment. The work ends with a festive banquet in the men's club, interrupted by the entrance of the jealous women. As there is little singing required after this point it was not unusual for real food and wine to be handed around. On this occasion everyone went to town, and the gaiety of the scene was completely genuine. Colleagues were toasting me in real wine, and all joined in the triumphant conclusion of a tremendously successful performance. I had made my debut at the Teatro Reale, and some of those cheers were for me.

Afterward I embraced Maestro Rucci, who had been dying by inches in the wings throughout the evening, and thanked him over and over again for all his help. Then Maestro de Fabritiis came up and wanted to know what all the fuss was about.

"Well," I said, daring to confess at last, "we have a little secret to tell you. At nine o'clock this morning I didn't know a word or a note of this role."

"What do you mean? It's not possible," he replied.

But Rucci supported my statement and explained how we had worked together. In view of the eventual success I was forgiven, but I had had a lesson I never forgot for the rest of my career. Leaving things to chance, believing that somehow it will be "all right on the night"—these are the marks of the amateur.

From this point a variety of roles came my way, something like ten a year during the following three years. Many of them were quite small, but it is a variety of small roles which can provide the very best training for an aspiring singer.

In 1938 I sang my first Puccini role, that of Marcello in *La Bohème* —a much more difficult and important role, incidentally, than many people realize, for Marcello is involved with each one of the other characters. He is in fact the center of that whole Bohemian group. The others are always appealing to him, referring to him in their various crises, and commenting on his comings and goings, so that even if he is not singing he must be very much *there*, a living presence.

Then, in the summer season at the Baths of Caracalla in Rome, I sang my first Wagner role, the Herald in *Lohengrin*. The following year, still with a slant toward Wagnerian roles, I sang Gunther in *Götterdämmerung*, Melot in *Tristan und Isolde*, and the Nightwatchman in *Die Meistersinger*. These were interspersed with the roles of Ping in *Turandot*, Sharpless in *Madama Butterfly* (at the Teatro Flavio Vespasiano in Rieti), and the Father in *Hansel and Gretel*.

Artistically speaking it was a most satisfying year for me, and family relationships were also at their happiest. Not only were Tilde and I a happy, hopeful young couple, but also the family fortunes were taking an upward turn. Our most constant visitor was my brother Bruno, now commander in the airline serving Italy, Spain, and North Africa, and whenever he came to Rome he made our home his. We would go out together, all three of us, to dances, theaters, and supper parties, sharing expenses so completely that he and I tended to throw our money into the same drawer, just as we would swap watches or borrow each other's clothes, since fortunately we had the same measurements.

Since my earliest youth Bruno and I had been exceptionally close as brothers and my marriage to Tilde made no difference to this. It was simply a case of an affectionately united couple becoming an exceptionally united trio. Then Bruno became engaged to a charming girl named Silvia, to the delight of us all. The wedding was to be in Malaga, but unfortunately Tilde and I could not attend as I had a professional engagement which prevented our going. However, I arranged to take part in a broadcast of a light Spanish opera, *Dolores*, on the great day so that at least they would be able to hear my voice.

Then tragedy struck, with the suddenness and force of a bomb. The plane in which Bruno was traveling to meet his fiancée crashed in sight of Malaga airfield where she was waiting, and everyone was killed. In tragic completion of the story the unhappy girl later put on what was to have been her wedding dress and committed suicide. As soon as I heard the news of the tragedy I tried to withdraw from the promised broadcast, but it was too late to alter something which had been prepared and announced. So, on what should have been Bruno's wedding day, I had to go on the air and sing lighthearted music for my brother, who was dead. It was one of the hardest professional assignments I ever undertook, and I still remember Maestro Bellezza conducting the performance with tears glistening in his eyes.

A few days later my dear, good, generous Maestro Crimi died in the street from a heart attack. In Tilde's diary of the period there is a sad little entry: "We feel we have lost a true friend and are very small and lonely."

Many years later there was a strange sequel to the tragedy of Bruno's death which I think I should record. Though some people shrink from admitting it, most of us have had at least one experience in our lives which is totally inexplicable by what are called rational means. In my case, I was driving one day up a steep mountain path with a cliff on one side and a sheer drop on the other. Since by that time I could indulge my taste for fast cars I was probably driving too fast. Suddenly, with a narrow corner ahead of me, I heard Bruno's voice so distinctly that he seemed to be sitting beside me say: "Stop—instantly!" Instinctively I obeyed, coming to a halt on a wide grass verge, practically the only spot of any width in the whole path. A few moments later, around the narrow bend came an articulated lorry out of control.

By dint of practically driving into the cliff wall the driver managed to stop. As he slumped in his seat I went to ask him what had happened.

"My brakes failed," he gasped. "I'm all right, really. I just can't get over my narrow escape. If you are going on up the road, perhaps you'd tell them at the next garage and ask them to send someone."

I promised I would, and went back to my car. Only then did the immensity of what had happened hit me. If I had not been stopped at that vital moment, I would have been swept to my death as I met that lorry on the corner. Even then, the naturalness of my brother's warning and my own instantaneous obedience were such that I almost expected to find him sitting in the car. Indeed, extraordinary though it may seem, I was surprised *not* to find him sitting in the car. For in those few minutes the reality of Bruno's speaking to me was more intense than the reality that he had been dead several years.

As my mental gears shifted once more into what might be termed "normal" I began to shake all over at the realization that something so extraordinary had taken place, and I knew I was incapable of driving for a while. I got out of the car again and went to lean against a great pile of stones in a state of something like nervous collapse; and this time it was the lorry driver who came to ask *me* if I were all right. I said I was but that I too had suddenly been overcome by the thought of my narrow escape. Then presently I was calm enough to drive on.

But I *knew* that Bruno had spoken to me and saved my life. I know it to this day—and it comforts me.

5.

In ADDITION to the steady day-to-day development of my career at the Teatro Reale I was now sometimes given opportunities to do useful work with the Italian radio and also to sing some of my first performances of important roles at lesser opera houses. This is an invaluable part of the development of an artist, and if I had to single out one factor today which militates against young singers becoming real masters of their art I would say it is the scarcity of minor houses in which they can try their professional wings. Nothing is more risky for a young, rather inexperienced singer than to have to make his or her early attempts at an ambitious role in the full glare of an important opera house.

I look back, then, on some of those lesser opera houses with gratitude and appreciation. In October 1939, as I have said, I had sung my first Sharpless at the Teatro Flavio Vespasiano in Rieti. It was here, in the following year, that I was given the opportunity to sing Scarpia for the first time. Not until 1941 did I sing the role in Rome, but right from the outset I was fascinated by the complexity of the character and the tremendous dramatic possibilities of the role.

As always, Tilde and I studied the role together. Her knowledge of the great operatic works was profound and her love for them equal to my own. We would read everything we could find about a character, the historical period and the background, and we would discuss these together. My mother-in-law had even given me a little book on make-up in the early days. It was simply written and a trifle old-fashioned, but studied with intelligence it provided a great deal of basic knowledge.

Make-up, general bearing, the way one walks—these are all part of the fascinating stock-in-trade of a stage artist. On this important matter of walking I had a valuable lesson at my first performance of Scarpia in

Rome. I had given a ticket to a very knowledgeable friend of mine, and afterward I asked him for his frank opinion.

"It was good," he said. "Yes, it was good."

"What was wrong?" I asked quickly.

"Nothing, nothing. It was fine."

But I knew from his tone that he had some reservation and I asked him as a good friend to speak frankly.

"Well," he said slowly, "how old do you think Scarpia was?"

"I don't know," I replied, realizing that I had never thought about that. "Forty-eight, perhaps. Maybe fifty."

"And how old are you, Tito?"

"Still in my twenties," I answered in some surprise.

"Well, I'm afraid I must tell you that you walk like a man in his twenties," was my friend's regretful reply.

I went to my father then and said: "Please walk with me." I walked with him everywhere—indoors, out-of-doors, upstairs, downstairs, uphill, downhill, and on the level, and all the time I studied him and copied him. Then a few nights later, when I was singing Scarpia again, I once more pressed my friend to come, and afterward I inquired: "How is it now?"

"It's all right, Tito," he replied; "you walked like a man of fifty."

No true artist is ever completely satisfied with his interpretation of a role: satisfied, I mean, to the point where he says to himself: "That's it! I've nothing more to add." Although, as I have said, I have sung Scarpia nearly nine hundred times it still interests me to look back and examine the degrees by which I arrived at my full conception of the part and the discoveries which I made even quite late in my career.

The first—and perhaps the most vital—feature of my conception of Scarpia was challenged as early as the rehearsal of that first Rome performance. Maestro Bellezza was conducting and he called up to me: "Here, what are you doing giving yourself such airs? Scarpia is just a cop, when all's said and done."

"I'm no cop," I replied, speaking up for Scarpia. "I'm a baron."

There followed a ding-dong argument, though conducted with good humor, for Bellezza was a dear man and open to argument even with a youngster like myself. Finally he said: "Send for Sanine."

Alexander Sanine was the marvelous resident producer whose opinion was considered final, and when he arrived I started all over again playing my aristocratic Scarpia. At the end Sanine, leaning on the prompter's box, decreed that I was right. He told me never to let the action "die" or the poise of Scarpia falter. He added: "Scarpia is a vulture." In that one revealing phrase he made me see Scarpia *looking down* on people, ready to pounce and therefore regarding them from a height. Sanine then went away, tossing his handkerchief up and down, which was a trick of his, and murmuring: "Titissimo amorissimo! The boy is right."

So I went on building my haughty Baron Scarpia, avidly absorbing all that Sardou has given as the historical background. Was he the lover of the queen? Perhaps; perhaps not. I prefer to think he was, and that is how I play him. He is so inwardly conscious of his social superiority that he has no need to shout or make great sweeping gestures to establish his authority. The cold glint in his eye should be sufficient to quell people from the moment he makes his first entry.

I suppose every Scarpia has struggled to find ways of making that first entry a tremendous moment, but in actual fact, as I realized well on in my career, it is all there in the music. The threatening "one—two—three —four" of the measured notes which bring him to the front of the stage express all the drama and terrifying authority of his appearance. If you walk forward in time to those notes, setting down your feet with the same menacing power given by Puccini to his music, the rest is conveyed by your expression and the elegant arrogance with which you hold yourself. There is no need to rush about and fuss. STAND there! Terrifying power can usually be conveyed more fully by stillness than by a great show of action.

In my idea of Scarpia, once I have disposed of the harsh questioning, I move around the scene unhurriedly but with authority, and I make my black silk cloak flutter—like a bird of ill-omen, if you like, but always with elegance. I don't actually touch anything and all my gestures are fastidious. I keep my voice so also, which gives a wonderful opportunity for contrast when I allow it to vibrate at the arrival of Tosca. Honey is in my voice then, a smile on my face, and the elegant walk goes with the music as I offer her the holy water.

I detest a Tosca who responds almost spitefully or with exaggerated repulsion, thereby suggesting that she already knows what is going to happen in the second act because she has done the part so often before. The conversation with her demands all the colors in a singer's palette. I gossip idly to inflame her jealousy, then realize to my annoyed astonishment that she hardly notices my ardent attitude, and finally my wounded vanity swamps everything else.

As I give my orders over the ominous sound of the tolling bell I lose myself in my thoughts, following her exit with the cold, menacing, "Va, Tosca . . ." Then, gradually warming up my voice, I dream of the success of my plan and, almost exalted, I see her stupid Mario on the gallows and Tosca herself in my arms. At the sudden outburst of the "Te Deum" my bigot's soul receives a stunning shock. I fall on my knees, sincerely repentant in that brief moment, and I strike my breast. *Mea culpa, mea culpa!*

As Scarpia I always take great care over my make-up and my costume, which I do not change between the first and second acts, having decided long ago that his restrained inner nervousness does not allow him to change. My rather small, not very important nose lacks strength, and I put on an aquiline nose which gives me an aristocratic and vulture-like appearance, emphasized by the black eyes and one arched eyebrow. I confess I look handsome thus, and I think I should. Though remaining elegant I have over the years stripped the costume of all ornament and jewelry, and I do not carry a sword or a whip. It is a temptation to wear for that second act a richly embroidered suit, with silk stockings, pumps, and jewels, but I prefer to remain in my morning coat and boots, without decoration. My walk is heavier and stronger in boots and the red sash makes a bloody gash across the black velvet.

There I sit at the richly set dinner table as the curtain rises on the second act, and I meditate aloud. I keep my tone very calm while giving my orders to Sciarrone, but allow an almost sexual excitement to enter my voice as I describe my love for violent conquest and rape. At the peak of the excitement I lift my glass and on the shattering final phrase (with its well-placed powerful E flat) I allow the soliloquy to end in a mood of something like inebriation.

With Spoletta's entrance I regain my self-control and am ready for business once more. I greet him with unusual cordiality, expecting good news. At his frightened confession of failure, however, I run to him in fury, but *I do not touch him,* for he is only a worm; and after that very Sicilian outburst of fury I am in command of myself once more.

That second act requires a very accurate measuring out and control of the voice. Otherwise the vocal strain and dramatic impact can make one very tired before the end and so ruin the performance. It must always be remembered that, following the demanding and multicolored scene with Cavaradossi, there is still the duet with Tosca to come, in two heavy parts. One reason why I love this work is that it becomes a new opera with every change of the name-part. I have had the privilege of partnering most of the fine Toscas of my time, and every one was subtly and fascinatingly different.

The great duet with Tosca is always a marvelous experience. I allow my voice to become smooth and insinuating as I suggest we should sit down and converse like old friends. I laugh almost genially over her offer of money. Corruption? Why certainly—but no money from a beautiful woman! And then comes the explosion of my love and desire as her nearness excites my feelings to an embarrassing degree.

"Quest'ora io l'attendea" (this is the moment I have been waiting for). It is probably the hardest page for Scarpia, coming as it does so near the end after quite a stiff ordeal. Though I try to keep myself bridled throughout the act this moment can easily carry me away. Not only does one have to create a powerful effect with a good vocal display on the phrase itself, but the attack on the next phrase, which soars up in sexual excitement, is very difficult.

Having written the false safe-conduct at Tosca's insistence (I am slightly wounded by this demand, being still almost unable to believe in my own inability to charm her), I rise to claim my price and go literally with open arms to my death. The cry "Tosca finalmente mia" uttered in the fullness of triumph and passion changes to a great shout as the knife enters my breast. Astonishment and incredulity pass over my face as I fall on one knee and then slowly sink to the floor, one arm still flung out in a menacing gesture, and I die with my eyes open. This is the moment when, in my own identity, I feel pure hatred for any Tosca who has permitted herself to smash her wineglass on the floor in one of her outbursts of anger. Not only is this a vulgar gesture quite unsuited to the prima donna of Rome at that period; it is also very unnerving to have to die on the floor among splinters of broken glass.

There remain those tense minutes when I have to lie there dead, not breathing normally but slowly emptying my lungs of air. Out of the corner of my eye I follow Tosca's terror-crazed actions as, with agonizing slowness, she moves around and then toward the door. All the lights are still on my eyes and even now I cannot relax. Strange thoughts pass through my mind—funny things, old stories, images, and dreams.

The first time I sang Scarpia, I remember, I continued to lie there right up to the moment of applause, and in my pride and happiness I thought: "I've done it, I've done it! Oh, how I wish I could tell it to the world, to my maestro, to my friends in Bassano, to all those who believed in me—and even those who didn't!" And then the stage manager was standing over me and saying, "Mr. Gobbi, do you want a blanket?" and presently I found myself bowing to the audience, so light of heart that I felt I could have flown out over the orchestra following my beautiful memories.

It was earlier in the same year of my first Scarpia (1940) that I was approached by talent scouts from MGM in Hollywood, who wanted me for a film which was to be made around the life of a singer. I was not really very much interested, being by now immersed in my operatic career, but as each rejection was merely met by an increase in the terms suggested we finally arrived at the sort of deal no one could really ignore. So, over a celebration lunch with jubilant representatives of MGM I finally signed my part of the contract, and it was arranged for this to be forwarded immediately to the United States for the signatures of the other parties.

We were all in high good humor as we went outside into the streets again. Even an announcement over the public loudspeakers that "Il Duce" was about to address the nation hardly damped our spirits, and rather childishly we all bought ice cream "cones" and stood waiting for the speech. Over the loudspeakers came the voice of Mussolini announcing that Italy had entered the war on the side of Germany.

"Oh, damn!" I exclaimed at this disastrous timing in my own affairs, and my ice cream fell from my hand into the gutter. At once a man standing in front of me turned around and asked belligerently what I meant. Was I questioning the judgment of "Il Duce"?

Fortunately I recovered myself in time to retort: "Wouldn't *you* swear if you'd dropped your ice cream in the gutter?" As I turned away I realized that my prospects of becoming a film star had melted as fast as my dropped ice cream was now melting.

In spite of Italy's entry into the war my contract at the Teatro Reale kept me from immediate call-up and in April 1941, when the company of the Teatro Reale visited Berlin as part of the cultural exchange encouraged under the aegis of the Rome–Berlin Axis, I went with them to sing Ford in *Falstaff*, a role I had already sung in Rome the previous October.

We left Rome in two special trains of immense length with large notices painted on the side to announce who we were. In addition to the many singers the trains carried chorus, orchestra (with their instruments), scenery, costumes, and everything else required for the occasion. It was one of the first times the complete exodus of an entire operatic company had occurred.

It was an extraordinary experience, that Berlin visit, with a great deal of kudos for the company and some strange glimpses of the nightmare world behind it all. On one occasion, I remember, I was walking with a German acquaintance past the Reich Chancellery when a magnificent open car drew up. The driver was an exceptionally fine-looking young man—tall, blond, splendidly made—and so arresting in his impression of vitality and well-being that I slowed down and could not help looking at him. As I did so, he reached into the back of his car and took out a case which seemed to me to contain perhaps a musical instrument.

At the same moment my companion muttered feverishly: "Come on, come on! Don't loiter like that. Come *on!*"

I was not too pleased at being hustled along and took my time, so that I had a complete impression of the almost godlike creature, who ignored us completely and went quickly into the building.

When we were past and on our way again, I asked: "What was the matter with you? Can't one man look at another? Who was that fellow, anyway?"

"That," replied my companion grimly, "was the official executioner. And the case he was carrying contained his ax."

Another experience during that cultural visit was to have a profound impact on me, and was possibly even to save my life at a later date. As is often the case, it started on a seemingly unimportant, and even rather absurd, note. We had all been invited to an official reception at the house of Dr. Goebbels. Many members of the Nazi hierarchy were present, and we filled a number of magnificent rooms. Then, in a moment of irresponsibility, I said to Gianna Pederzini, the mezzo-soprano—and even now I don't know why I said it: "If I stare at someone's back and concentrate on making him look around at me, I can make him do it."

Not unnaturally she immediately challenged me to give a demonstration, so I stared at the broad back of Giulio Neri, the basso, and concentrated for all I was worth on making him look around. Whereat, almost as much to my astonishment as hers, he glanced back at us over his shoulder.

"It's a fluke!" declared Gianna. "Do it again."

Rather pleased with myself, I did it again, with the same result. Then at her amazed and amused insistence I tried it on another member of the company, again with success.

"Try it on Dr. Goebbels," she said boldly, looking up the length of the rooms to where the Party big-wigs were congregated.

This was rather a different matter, but by now I was on my mettle. So I stared at the rather distant back of the Herr Reichminister and, to my mingled horror and triumph, he too glanced back over his shoulder as though someone had summoned him, and his eyes met mine squarely.

"It's not possible," whispered Gianna's awed voice beside me. "Do it just once more, to make sure."

It was impossible to refuse this final challenge, and I repeated my efforts. At that Dr. Goebbels not only glanced around but turned and came slowly through the room toward me. My heart began to beat uncomfortably fast as I searched my mind for something to say. Then as he stopped in front of me I had an inspiration and said in my best German: "Herr Dr. Goebbels, I don't actually collect autographs but, as a memento of this unique occasion, I was wondering if I might venture to ask you for yours."

"I will do better than that," he replied. "I will give you a signed photograph."

I thanked him and began to tell him where I was staying, but he raised a hand to silence me and said: "You have no need to tell me. We know everything about you." This was not the most reassuring thing to be told by such a person, but at least I was out of my immediate dilemma and I rather supposed he might then forget all about me. This was not, however, the case. A few mornings later, before I was fully dressed, someone came pounding on my door calling: "Come down! Come down quickly! The Herr Reichminister Dr. Goebbels is downstairs and wants to see you."

Somewhat alarmed, I threw on some clothes and hurried down. The hotel lobby was crowded, and everyone appeared to be in a state of high tension. In the midst of the crowd stood Goebbels, with his hands behind his back. I approached him, hoping my last hour had not come. Then, as I reached him, he produced from behind his back a large signed photograph of himself, dedicated to me and handsomely framed.

"You told me you would like a photograph of me," he said. "I have chosen the photograph and my wife has chosen the frame. Here it is, and I hope you will like it."

I took the photograph, little guessing what it would do for me in a couple of years' time, and thanked him suitably. He then withdrew—out of the hotel and out of my life. I took the photograph back to Rome with me, and in the fluctuating fortunes of the next two years it alternated between standing on the piano and reposing in a drawer, according to the political situation.

In any case I was now a great deal more concerned with my own affairs. Although I was called up to serve in the Army I was fairly soon released to return to the opera stage. This process was repeated more than once, as though no one could quite decide if I were more useful as a soldier or a singer, and this uncertainty added not a little to the other stresses and strains of wartime existence.

In spite of this, however, the second half of 1941 was a rich operatic period for me. At Spoleto, in August, I had my first opportunity to sing the wonderful character role of Michonnet in Cilèa's *Adriana Lecouvreur*, and in the autumn no less than three major Verdi roles came my way at the Teatro Reale. I was cast as Posa in *Don Carlo* in October and Renato in *Ballo in Maschera* in December; then, because of the last-minute illness of Benvenuto Franci, I was called on to sing my first Simone Boccanegra in November.

For me this was a great challenge and a great opportunity. It was a great ordeal too, for in the tremendous, brilliantly lit council chamber scene, when I came down from the throne and walked forward to the front I could see in the light from the stage that, seated in the center of the first few rows, were not only some of my great contemporaries but also some of the great figures of the immediate past. There were not only Gigli, Cigna, Caniglia, and Lauri-Volpi but De Luca and Stracciari as well.

The simple explanation for their presence might well have been that as Franci was not singing there were an unusual number of complimentary seats available. But they came to my dressing room afterward to congratulate me—all of them—and at this date perhaps I can say without vanity that it was one of the first signs that I was an artist who was beginning to cause interest and speculation. It was not that I was such a marvelous singer compared with some of the people sitting in the first few rows of the auditorium; it was that I was *different*. (Years afterward a highly critical orchestral player put it rather well when he said: "I don't know why it is, Tito. I don't particularly like your voice, but when you sing I forget to play.")

Lest my success should go to my head, Serafin gave me a piece of salutary advice. "Don't imagine," he said, "that because you have sung three major Verdi roles in as many months you have arrived. The good singer who is satisfied with himself *may* remain a good singer, but he will never be a great one. All of us have to go back to the beginning from time to time to re-examine and strengthen the foundations."

6.

ALTHOUGH I TOOK Serafin's admirable advice to heart I was nonetheless gratified to be asked to sing my first Tonio in *Pagliacci* at Palermo early in that same December. By now the dangers and privations of a country somewhat unwillingly tied to Hitler's chariot wheels were making themselves felt in no small degree. On the night of my first Tonio the house was sold out, but when it came to the point many of the audience stayed at home, alarmed by the heavy air raids they had been experiencing.

I sang the Prologue with good effect and to much applause mingled with so many calls for an encore that I finally had to address the audience and explain that for so few people we really could not start repeating numbers. To this someone very properly replied that since they *were* the courageous few who had braved the threat of bombs surely they were all the more entitled to special consideration?

"You are right," I agreed. "And in addition, why don't you all come down and occupy the front seats? And we will start again." So they all crowded to the front and we started the opera over again. By the end the air-raid warnings had still not sounded so Tilde, who had a young friend with her, ventured out on her own to rush the girl back home. She had hardly started her return journey, however, when the sirens sounded and the planes zoomed overhead.

Knowing what my anxiety would be she started to run, avoiding the clutches of people who attempted to drag her willy-nilly into shelter. Soon she found she was lost and alone in dark unfamiliar streets. Then, just as panic threatened to overwhelm her, a figure approached along a dark alleyway. She could see no more than that it was a man. She stopped him and explained that she was lost and had to get back to the opera house.

"I am going that way," he said, and in spite of some misgivings she allowed him to take her hand and lead her. Then, halfway there, in a flash of light from an exploding bomb, she saw his face and almost cried out in horror. He was, Tilde says, the most hideous-looking human being she had ever seen: a figure like Quasimodo, with distorted and repulsive features. Yet underneath all that he must have been a good man, for he led Tilde safely to the opera house (where all the doors except one had now been locked), and after she had gone around knocking on one closed door after another I eventually heard her and dragged her in, to embrace her in an access of relief and thankfulness.

In the following April (1942), in complete contrast to these agitating experiences, I went to La Scala to sing the gloriously amusing role of Belcore in Donizetti's *L'Elisir d'Amore,* and on this occasion found myself in the company of two great operatic artists, Tito Schipa and Mariano Stabile, under the conductorship of Maestro Gino Marinuzzi. In the summer came another milestone when I made my first gramophone records—from *Don Giovanni, Don Carlo, Zazà,* and *L'Arlesiana.* These were the old 78 rpm's made for the home market only. (It was not until well after the war was over that I began the international recording which is so valuable to any artist building up a world reputation.)

Later in the year, in Rome, I was chosen to sing the title role in the first Italian performance of *Wozzeck.* It was one of the most overwhelming experiences of my whole career, and this masterpiece by Alban Berg almost obsessed me, not only then but when I repeated the role much later.

For many years now this opera has been under constant discussion, and there is hardly a composer who has not sought to blacken or exalt Berg or to find some way of reconciling the horror and the fascination which emanate from this work. But speculators, be they ever so attentive and clever, and critics, however profound or competent, must of necessity see *Wozzeck* from the outside. No one to my knowledge has spoken of him from the inside. Not one of these commentators has put on the rough coat of the mad soldier, which burns like the shirt of Nessus. Not one of them has *been* Wozzeck. To talk about him is like submitting oneself to a full and difficult confession. For if an interpreter has the sensitivity to represent Wozzeck, then, in this role more than any other, he becomes the person himself.

In *Wozzeck* Alban Berg's intention is to show with great depth of feeling the drama of the poor humble human being, a simple resigned soul who, jerked from his vague ideas of goodness by the reality of events, is goaded into reacting against the malicious revelations of the people around him. The technical means by which Berg arrives at the artistic realization of this tragic torn-off rag of life are to me not of paramount interest. The important thing is that he has found out how to speak to the spirit with a new voice. Combining logical construction with the lightening caprice of inspiration, he has reached a terrifying power of expression—not in the exterior or melodramatic sense but with an introspective degree of revelation never attained before. His is a world of deluded beings in whom are unleashed the secret forces of nature and the senses—surrealistically expressed, it is true, but all is in proportion there, calculated but at the same time *living*.

For the first performance I spent long days in the wearisome deciphering of what was then the most difficult role in existence, in attempting—often with exasperation—to find the proper fusion of music, words, and action, and in feeling myself slowly but surely being pervaded by the character until I lived inside his tragic, miserable life and came to identify myself with Wozzeck both musically and dramatically.

As an artist who loves his work and resolves his task of interpretation with great conscientiousness, I sometimes find myself carried away into *being* my characters. Normally I can separate myself from them and represent them with the detachment and objectivity which long theatrical experience permits. With Wozzeck that has not been, and never would be, possible. His torments penetrate one's flesh like witchcraft, his madness upsets one like some horrible sight.

And then the music—that music which obstinately denies all that centuries of tradition have consecrated, which obliges one to sing without any real point of support, which presents situations of disconcerting instability, evoking unseizable forms, unexpected rhythms and harmonic combinations which leave one breathless: this music which hangs like an atmosphere of pain and torture over the singer and yet attracts him like inexorable destiny toward the final catastrophe.

I remember the nightmare atmosphere in which I lived for months during those first preparations and the effort I had to make at the end of a performance to shake off the haunting torpor which oppressed me. But when, some years later, it was proposed that I should attempt it again I did not hesitate, though I knew what it would involve. I did not hesitate because Wozzeck has, in spite of the horror, an unbelievable fascination. The martyrdom of his flesh and spirit was still a vivid, living memory within me, attracting me irresistibly.

There were more months of nightmare, the miserable soldier's soul re-incarnating itself within me and throwing a sinister shadow over my normal life. Some time later Tilde showed me a letter I had written to her at the end of the last performance: a meaningless letter in which even the most ordinary subjects seemed morbidly twisted by a soul in torment. At the bottom of the letter, instead of greetings to our child and my own signature was simply the initial "W."

During those war years each country had its own particular miseries, and Italy was by no means immune from them. But whatever the war years brought us, nothing could compare with the dangers and horrors which succeeded Italy's capitulation in September 1943. From the time the Allies landed at Salerno in September 1943 until the Americans arrived in Rome in June 1944 we were virtually under German occupation. Our late allies took the view—understandably perhaps—that they had been let down, even betrayed; and they exerted every effort, brutal or otherwise, to keep their grip at least on the civilian population.

There was a curfew at four o'clock in the afternoon and even those with a pass—which I had since I was employed at the opera house— were forced to go from their place of work to their home by the shortest route. Those were the days when even in broad daylight the dread cry of *"I Tedeschi, I Tedeschi"* would suddenly sound in the street, and everyone would scatter in search of a hiding place, knowing that German soldiers, armed with machine guns, were on the hunt for able-bodied men to be sent to Germany for forced labor. There was no time even to telephone home and say, "You won't see me any more." Without warning or delay, people were rounded up and taken by lorry to the waiting trucks at the railway station.

It happened at least half a dozen times that I was out in the street when the cry went up that the Germans were coming and, like everybody else, I had to make my escape the best way I could. One could be in sight of one's home and still not know if one would ever get there safely; and when one woke in the morning one drew a quick sigh of relief and thanked God one was still alive for another day.

Once I had just left the opera house when I heard *"I Tedeschi, I Tedeschi!"* It was daylight and I was still in the open square in front of the opera house when I saw that soldiers with machine guns were converging on the square from every direction. Only one street was not barred, and along this came four soldiers walking abreast on the pavement.

As it happened, I was wearing a rather military-looking raincoat and no hat. So I turned up the collar of my coat, thrust my hands in my pockets, and, with an authoritative air, marched straight toward the four soldiers, giving not an inch as I came up to them. I knew that if I stepped off the pavement for them my assumption of authority would fall to the ground. Then I raised my arm in the Nazi salute, barked out "Heil Hitler!" as though to military subordinates, and went on my way as they responded "Heil Hitler!" and stepped into the road for me.

The temptation to glance around to see their further reaction was almost irresistible, but I did resist it, for such a man as I was pretending to be would never have looked back. There was, however, a polished window set at an angle to the street and in this I saw that the soldiers had stopped and were looking questioningly after me. I dared not run. I hardly dared even increase my pace. But the moment I turned the corner I took to my heels, jumping over obstacles like a mountain goat instead of a frightened singer. As I went I cried, *"I Tedeschi, I Tedeschi!"* and everyone began to scatter in the familiar way. I slipped through alleyways and around more corners, and finally found myself at home, my heart pumping and my breath almost gone.

In those terrible days one could not help suspecting other people, wondering if they were trustworthy or secretly working for the Germans. One of these was a man well known to us by sight and easily distinguishable because he had a deformed arm. On the whole we thought him suspect and gave him a wide berth, but, as I found out later, he was really engaged in a dangerous double-cross, apparently working for the Germans while using the knowledge thus gained to help people.

One day he overtook me in the street and said quietly: "Don't speak to me—just walk a little ahead of me."

I obeyed and after a moment he went on: "I hope you know that you are on the list of artists who are, so to speak, national treasure." (This meant that one ran the risk of being picked on and taken away to sing for the Wehrmacht, anywhere.) "If," he went on, "you receive a telephone call from the pharmacy one morning and are told that your prescription is ready and should be collected, that is the moment to make yourself scarce for a while."

"Are you sure?" I asked without looking at him.

"Quite sure," he replied. I muttered, "Thanks," as he walked away.

Sure enough, a few mornings later, when I answered the summons of the telephone bell, a voice said: "This is the pharmacy. Will you please collect your prescription? It is ready."

"Any special hurry?" I inquired, as naturally as I could.

"Yes, there is. We have a lot of prescriptions here. Please collect yours today, without fail."

"I will," I promised, and left immediately.

On that occasion I escaped being picked up, but by no more than fifteen or twenty minutes. Just after I had left the SS arrived and proceeded to search the building for any able-bodied men. One young fellow, attempting to escape, jumped from his balcony to the one below and thence to the street. Although he hurt his leg badly he began to hobble away as fast as he could, but the SS followed and caught him. When they discovered, however, that his injury had made him useless for their present purposes they were good enough just to push him to the ground and throw him into a corner like so much rubbish.

By this time I was more than ever anxious to run no avoidable risks, for there was now not only Tilde to care for but also our little daughter Cecilia, who had been born some months before. A man with a wife and child cannot think only of himself, particularly in the circumstances in which we now found ourselves, but sometimes sheer humanity demands that one must take a gamble—as in the case of Salvatore, our runaway soldier.

Salvatore had escaped from his barracks when the Germans were not looking and somehow chose us to appeal to. He arrived at our place out of the blue and said: "Please help me—please help me." So we took him in and gave him some civilian clothing, and he promptly established himself as a devoted member of the household.

He turned out to be the most miraculous cook. He could make a meal —an *appetizing* meal—out of almost nothing. This was something in those days when I would sometimes creep out at night, in defiance of the curfew, to cut a little grass which we would boil next day as a vegetable. Once, when we had nothing but a big pumpkin, Salvatore made a soup which I remember with relish to this day, so whatever we did for him he certainly repaid us in a touching—and tasty—way.

But if Salvatore gave us no anxiety as a member of our household, Cecilia's nurse certainly did—and almost entirely on account of her single-minded devotion to her beloved little charge. To her nothing and no one should be allowed to disturb the routine—and particularly the rest— of her baby. She was a Yugoslav, Maria Crnic by name, and the very sight of a German soldier nearly sent her mad. If a military lorry went rumbling past she would shout: "Damned Germans! Damned Germans! Making all that noise and waking my baby."

One day some German soldiers shot a man in the square outside our home—probably some poor devil who had presumed to run or to cycle too fast, for it was strictly forbidden at that time for anyone to move at more than a slow pace. To disobey this injunction was to risk being shot on sight. At the sound of the commotion Maria flew out onto our fifth-floor balcony (carrying the baby) and, leaning over, shouted in her execrable Italian: "You damned Germans! You damned Germans!"

I rushed out onto the balcony, knowing I must stop her at all costs, and, because she was in a state of near hysteria, I did the only thing I could: I slapped her hard across the face. She blinked, shook her head, and suddenly seemed to come to her senses. She stared at me and said: "Thank you, sir—thank you, sir." And the unnerving incident was over.

The really heart-stopping moment came, though, when I received a telephone call one morning from a friend. All he said was: "We are sending you two blondes."

I knew this meant two escaped Allied prisoners, and I exclaimed: "Are you mad? My wife and child are here and—"

"They are on their way," he cut in, and all I could say was "O.K."

Soon they arrived, one an American and one a South African. They spoke hardly any Italian and we then spoke hardly any English. We welcomed them as well as we could and hid them in a big wardrobe just as a thunderous knocking sounded at the front door.

I answered the door, and outside stood a German officer of a particularly aggressive type. Behind him were two or three soldiers, one of them carrying a machine gun.

"Tito Gobbi?" he demanded.

"Yes, I'm Tito Gobbi," I replied. "What's the matter?" I was a bit aggressive in my turn, as this seemed the best method of defense.

"Nothing's the matter," he answered brusquely. "But you are to come and broadcast to the Wehrmacht. I will come in and see what music you have, and then you will come with me to the radio."

Having no choice in the matter I admitted him, uncomfortably aware that the soldier with the machine gun was almost poking me in the back. At that point Tilde, who had been in the kitchen with Cecilia, came out to ask what was happening.

"It's all right," I managed to say reassuringly. "These gentlemen just want me to go to the radio and sing for the Wehrmacht." And I led the way to the music room, praying silently that the two in the wardrobe would not sneeze or otherwise draw attention to themselves.

Without any direction from me the officer went across, pushed aside the curtain which covered my books and scores, and began to pull them out and examine them. Some he threw on the floor with such comments as: "Meyerbeer—dirty Jew!" "Mendelssohn—another dirty Jew!" "Bizet—filthy reactionary!"

"You think so?" I said. "As far as I am concerned, they all wrote fine music, which is all that matters."

"Shut up!" he shouted, and turned on me. As he did so he came face to face with the signed photograph of Dr. Goebbels, which, since the German occupation of Rome, had been rescued from the drawer and put on the piano.

His reaction was instantaneous, and almost incredible. He clicked his heels, saluted the photograph, and cried, "Heil Hitler!" Then, turning once more to me and speaking in a totally different tone, he said: "I didn't know you were a friend of the Deputy Führer."

"No?" I smiled modestly like one who did not want to boast but could not deny the honor. Whereupon he turned on his wretched soldiers and exclaimed: "Pick up those books and put them back. Quickly!"

"That one too," I said mildly, indicating one which was almost under his foot. This time *he* had to stoop and pick up the score. He did so without question and then, speaking in a conciliatory tone, he said: "I hope you will indeed come and sing for us at the radio. Signor Tagliavini will also be singing."

"Why not?" I shrugged good-humoredly. After a few more reassuring words to Tilde, who was not quite sure even now that I was not being taken off to the firing squad, I accompanied the officer and his men out of the house, and out of the danger zone for our two hidden guests.

At the radio station I found Tagliavini who, seeing me apparently on excellent terms with my officer companion, muttered: "Tito, what's going on here?"

"Nothing," I assured him lightly. "We just have to sing some songs on the radio, you and I. It won't take long. And then we can go away again."

So we sang some songs: Neapolitan songs, an Ave Maria, and so on. Everything went off rather well, and the officer duly informed us that he had received a telephone message to say how well the broadcast had sounded. Smiles and compliments were exchanged, and he said he hoped that we would be ready to do the same thing for the Wehrmacht on future occasions.

"We should like to," I replied, constituting myself spokesman for us both. "But the fact is, you will realize, that Signor Tagliavini and I have a number of engagements, and our time is not our own."

"Of course, of course but—"

"And we may possibly be engaged in filming," I added for good measure, being well aware that this activity was strictly forbidden to Italians at the moment but seeing no reason why I should not take the opportunity of indicating that naturally Dr. Goebbels' friend was free from any such restrictions.

The officer said he quite understood our position, but if we did have some time, etc., etc. I replied that certainly if we did have time, etc., etc.

At this point he took out a notebook and said, "Friday the sixteenth at four o'clock, and we will pick you up," which was his way of showing us that what I had thought to be a clever bit of by-play on my part altered the situation not at all.

I rushed back home, reassured my family and our guests, and gave a grateful glance at the photograph on the piano. The next day I received instructions to take our two to the Swiss Embassy. I was to accompany them as far as the outer gate and ring the bell; when someone spoke through the communication slot inquiring who was there I was simply to reply: *"Amici."*

I explained this to our couple as well as I could adding: "This may not sound very courageous to you, but I must ask that you walk in front of me. I will direct you with an occasional word when we have to turn left or right and I earnestly hope all will be well. But should you be stopped you must not expect me to involve myself further."

They agreed this was reasonable and, with my stage knowledge of how much a walk can betray, I instructed them how to walk more like Italians, abandoning that characteristic swing from the hips which distinguishes some soldiers, particularly Americans. Then off we went—all three of us with our hearts in our throats.

The actual distance was rather less than a mile, but that day it seemed to me like five and to them it must have seemed interminable. Finally we arrived at the outer gate of the embassy, where I carried out my instructions, and when a voice inquired who we were I replied: *"Amici,"* Immediately the outer gate was opened, my two companions stepped inside, and the gate closed again. For the moment at least they were safe.

Several times during the next few months I was collected by my young German officer and taken to the radio station to sing. His name was Niemayer and in some strange way we became almost friendly. Out of uniform he was much more like a normal human being and, one day near the end of the Occupation, he said to me: "Signor Gobbi, I know the end is coming and I know that we have lost. I have the feeling that I shall not live to see the end and I am going to ask you a favor. Will you take this watch of mine and see later that it is sent to my mother and father so that they may have something by which to remember me?"

I pressed the watch back into his hand, assuring him that he must not think he would not survive. He accepted my decision but not, I think, my reassurance. It was the last time we ever spoke to each other and I never saw or heard of him again.

Equally, Tilde and I never expected to hear anything of our escaped prisoners again. But some months after the Americans arrived in Rome I was among a group of artists invited to a big Allied reception, and during the evening I was accosted by an American colonel who congratulated me on having been instrumental in saving a friend of his. This turned out to be our American, who had eventually gotten home safely to the United States. But the colonel had no information about the South African.

However, years later, when Tilde and I were in South Africa for the first time, we met someone who said to me: "You were the chap who saved my cousin's life, weren't you?" After some discussion and delving back into the wartime past I realized that he was speaking of the second of our two guests. He too, it seemed, had gotten back home safely, and again I was congratulated on having perhaps saved his life.

Strictly speaking, I suppose, there was a degree of truth in this. At least Tilde and I had done our best at the time. But how far back in the strange chain of events would one have to go in order to establish exactly what had really saved the lives of those two men? Was it merely that we had been prepared, however reluctantly, to hide them in our wardrobe? Was it that Dr. Goebbels had given me a signed photograph years ago in a Berlin hotel? Or did the whole thing stem from that absurd, unexplained impulse of mine when I boasted that I could make a man turn around merely by staring at his back and concentrating?

It is not only in opera that strange things happen.

7.

MANY TIMES during those months of the Occupation it seemed that nothing which we acted out on the operatic stage could surpass the drama in our everyday lives. Quite apart from the hideous discomforts and dangers of traveling about the country to perform in theaters outside Rome, there were sometimes (literally) guns in the corridors of the Teatro Reale.

On one such occasion in May 1944 our German masters insisted that a performance of *Tosca* be specially arranged for members of the Wehrmacht. Maestro de Fabritiis conducted and Gigli and Caniglia were my colleagues that evening, all of us under strict orders. Even Tilde had to parley with an armed German soldier before being allowed to go to my dressing room.

The performance was a great success in spite of the nervous tension among the cast and the inevitable reflection among us that Scarpia had become a disagreeably topical figure. When it was all over and the audience of German soldiers had stopped cheering, a polite but chilly officer appeared backstage with an order for the principal members of the cast to speak over the radio to the Wehrmacht.

Gigli protested that he was sick and exhausted. Caniglia slipped away without a word and, donning the shawl of one of the cleaning women, shuffled out in this disguise. As she passed me she gave me the shadow of a wink, just in time to prevent my saying: *"Ciao,* Maria." So I was left as the only one of us with no excuse at all, since it was known that I spoke German reasonably well. In any case the form of persuasion was irresistible. With a machine gun actually touching my back I was conducted to a microphone which had been rigged up in the corridor, and here I managed to produce some innocuous generalizations about my role and my distinguished colleagues without committing myself to anything which ran contrary to my own innermost feelings.

In spite of being free from actual army duties I was still militarily obliged to remain in Rome unless otherwise directed by the Ministry of Culture. Nevertheless, so that our little daughter should have a better chance of good food and a healthier life, we arranged that Tilde, taking Cecilia and the nurse with her, should sometimes spend a week or two with an aunt who lived in the country about a hundred kilometers outside Rome. Neither of us felt happy about this enforced separation, but in the circumstances it seemed the best thing to do.

On one occasion when I was alone I received a telephone call from Nicola de Pirro, the general director of opera for the Ministry of Culture. This ministry, although Italian in personnel, came under the strict jurisdiction of the Wehrmacht, as almost everything else did in Rome at that time. It was here that decisions were made about lending artists to other theaters; and if these theaters happened to be in an area of intense military activity that was just too bad.

"Tito," began the director that morning, "you know you are due to sing in *Andrea Chenier* in Sorrento?"

This was true, but as I had heard on good authority that the theater had recently been destroyed I assumed that the performance would not take place, and I said as much.

"Never mind that," I was told. "I think perhaps the theater was not entirely destroyed, so it's better you go in any case."

This, however, was not a journey I was prepared to make for anything less than a certainty, since trains in those days took hours and hours to go anywhere and the few which did operate were so crowded that people even traveled on the outside, tying themselves to the doors, rather than be left behind. Indeed there had been cases where, as the train entered a tunnel, people were swept off and killed.

I therefore said quite frankly that I had no intention of making this journey in the circumstances, but to my surprise and dismay the director said: "I'm sorry, Tito, but you have no choice. That is the order. If you refuse I must send the police to pick you up."

There was no arguing with that, so I undertook to get to Sorrento as best I could. I telephoned a good friend of mine called Unno Armanni. He had a poor little worn-out wreck of a car, and he agreed to drive me and my luggage containing my costume to the station: not the main station but a local one where there might be a better chance of boarding the train at 7 A.M. But we had hardly started before an air-raid warning sounded, followed almost immediately by a plane battle overhead. We scrambled out of the car and took shelter in—of all places—one of the galleries in the Colosseum.

When we finally crept out again the car refused to start. With some effort we pushed it to the top of a hill and then coasted downhill as far as it would go. After that I took my luggage in my hand, said good-by to Armanni, and made for the station where, after the usual struggle, I managed to board the train and started my interminable journey in acute discomfort.

It took us eight hours to get as far as Naples, where we arrived in the middle of a raid of unimaginable ferocity. Bombs were falling out of the sky and shells were zooming in from the sea. Then, in a climax of horror, there was a direct hit on a boat in the harbor which was carrying tanks. The whole thing exploded and bits of tank and caterpillar wheels were projected over the town to a distance of more than a mile, each piece of flying metal carrying death to anyone in the way.

There were sights I shall never forget. In literal fact, I saw a headless man walking. His head had been blown off and yet for a few moments longer the automatic reaction of his limbs had not ceased. With my luggage on my head, in some illogical attempt at protection, I ran and stumbled on my nightmare journey, past collapsing buildings from which the cries of buried people came. Once I stopped someone who seemed to be in authority and cried: "Can't we do something? Can't anyone help them?" He replied: "With what? We have nothing but our bare hands. It would take days to reach them, and they'll be dead long before then."

I went on, wiping my face with my sleeve to remove what I thought was sweat from my eyes. When I looked at my sleeve it was covered with blood: not my blood—someone else's. Then I remembered that a little further back I had felt something slap me in the face. It had seemed to me at the time rather like a big handkerchief, but I realized now that it had been part of some poor creature who had been blown to pieces.

Presently I came across a lorry and, much against the driver's will, I scrambled onto the back of it and managed to stay there until he pushed me off. After that I walked for a while until I found someone with a little broken-down cart, and with this I got another lift to within reasonable walking distance of my destination.

Sorrento seemed like a paradise of peace after my experience in Naples. But the fearful journey proved to have been totally unnecessary. There was no theater left and no performance. Nobody was interested in me and my troubles. There was only one thing to do: turn around and take myself back to Rome.

So the horrible journey started again in reverse—once more the occasional lift in a car, truck, or cart (usually with a scared and reluctant driver); once more the long stumbling walks; and finally the ghastly train journey, and all the while without a drop of water or a crumb of food. All I did manage to get was a little packet of five cigarettes at the railway station. I chewed these in the hope of appeasing my hunger but only succeeded in giving myself a raging thirst and terrible hiccups.

When I finally reached the outskirts of Rome, where the train set me down, I still had a long walk but desperation kept me going. When I reached my own front door I had just enough strength left to push the bell before fainting.

Later, when I recovered a little and had had something to eat and drink, I set off for the Ministry of Culture with rage in my heart—and probably on my face too. I was hastily assured that the director was terribly busy and could not see anyone. I affected to believe this, but as I walked away along the passage I came level with his office door and, kicking it open, walked in.

He rose from behind his desk, turned rather pale, and began: "I'm sorry, Tito—"

"You're *sorry?*" I shouted before he could get any further. "You were ready to kill me rather than risk offending your masters. What do you suppose you sent me to? You are a coward."

Then he sat down heavily and said: "All right. I am a coward, I didn't dare to say 'no.' But I did try to tell you there was nothing else I could do but hand on the order. Perhaps you didn't realize I was trying to hint to you not to go."

Well, there was his side of it too, of course. It was true that his position was not an easy one, so what was the use of maintaining my animosity? In the end we became quite good friends.

Gradually some of the more appalling features of wartime began to lessen, though there were still shortages and restrictions which often amounted to privation. Water had to be fetched in jars and drums from the public fountains, with German soldiers hustling and bullying the lines of people queuing for their miserable quota. Milk was virtually unknown, except for the wonderful occasion when a friend outside the city brought in three cows by night rather than have them commandeered by the Germans. We met him and escorted him silently, grasping the cows around the muzzle whenever they showed a disposition to moo and sweeping up the evidence they left behind as they went. Somehow we got them to our apartment block and shoved them into an underground garage, where we kept them for the short time we dared. Eventually we had to find someone to slaughter them professionally, but were left with the task of dividing up the carcasses among friends and neighbors. It was wonderful to have more meat than we had seen in years, even if some of the joints resembled nothing any of us could remember having seen before. By the time we had finished the great carve-up it looked as if half a dozen murders had been committed.

In our efforts to clean up we had an enormous stroke of luck, however. We came upon a small sealed-up pipe, which proved to be connected to the main water supply of the district. We unblocked this, attached a tap to it and for some time were more or less independent with regard to water, thus avoiding the weary trek to the public fountain.

This was one of the lighter moments of that period, in pleasant contrast to the horrible encounters one was forced to have with the black marketeers inevitably thrown up by the circumstances. Though one tried not to deal with these creatures who, in some extraordinary way, even *looked* as dreadful as they were, one could not be too nice about the origin of the little drop of milk or small supply of flour or fruit which might be vital to one's hungry child.

The black marketeers demanded whatever they might fancy in the house as the price of the wretched bits of food they had to offer. Thus we parted with our treasured radiogram in exchange for a little oil, a little flour, and some salt. But we clung to our small radio set and, with the curtains drawn and the radio turned low, we listened at considerable risk —and against every rule of our German masters—to the news of the Allied advance and the last phases of the war.

Finally, briefly but tellingly recorded in Tilde's diary, came the day for which we had all been waiting:

"June 4. The Germans leave the city! Hurrah! And the Allies finally arrive after a stop of seven months at Anzio. There is no telling what it was for us all. We were up all night. One could see people on every terrace of Rome, and one heard a continuous whispering that sounded like millions of birds chirping."

So the last months of 1944 and the first of 1945 dragged to a close. In April 1945 the Germans in Italy at last capitulated, and a month later the war in Europe was over.

In no country did the cessation of hostilities bring anything like a happy ending. But in the musical worlds of Germany and Italy the confusion which succeeded the end of the war produced one particularly unpleasant feature. Artists who felt they had been unjustly neglected during the previous years now moved into the operatic scene with the determination to oust, if possible, those who had been more successful. It was easy to say, or to hint strongly, that success in their rivals had been due to political rather than to artistic reasons. Tempers understandably ran high and in the general atmosphere of bitterness and recrimination some artists of mediocre attainment took a flying leap up the ladder of success by employing some very questionable means.

In 1946 the Italian monarchy was voted out and the Teatro Reale became the Teatro dell'Opera. There was a great deal of change among personnel and in the style of management, and for a time at least many artists, including myself, found it more agreeable to sing in cities other than the capital.

On the other hand, it was obvious that horizons outside Italy would inevitably begin to widen, and here I must pause to say how much I owe to the fact that I was *forced* during the early part of my career to remain largely within national limits. Unlike so many unfortunate young artists today I had not been tempted to rush about from San Francisco to Vienna, via London, Paris, and New York—overpraised, overworked, overexposed and overrecorded, encouraged (even implored) to sing roles totally beyond the natural capacity of a developing artist.

On the contrary, as a tree grows so had whatever talents I possessed been allowed to mature. Gifted by God, guided and trained by Serafin, loved and supported by Tilde, and exposed to the toughening processes of life in an extraordinary period of history, I was, when the war ended, ready to step out onto the world stage of opera as a relatively experienced artist and, if I may say so, a fairly mature human being.

I was not yet thirty-two years of age.

8.

DURING THE DISTURBED MONTHS which followed the end of the war I sang more in Naples than in Rome, and it was here that I developed my long-standing friendship and association with the Sovrintendente of the San Carlo, Guido Sampaoli. It was also here, on January 30, 1946, that I played Iago for the first time. I alternated this role with performances of Figaro in *Barbiere,* which I had sung in Naples before but which had now come to have a very special association with me and my incomparable colleagues Ferrucio Tagliavini and Italo Tajo, since we had made the first-ever full-length operatic film of this work in 1945.

Film-making and film techniques had continued to fascinate me, right from the days before the war when I spent those seven months making *I Condottieri* with Luis Trenker, and I was happy therefore when the success of *Barbiere* led to the making of many other films. First came one based on *Tosca*—rather significantly entitled *Davanti a lui Tremava Tutta Roma*—in which I played opposite the magnificent, though rather difficult, Anna Magnani (Onelia Fineschi dubbed the singing). This was followed by film versions of such operas as *Rigoletto, L'Elisir d'Amore,* and *Pagliacci* (in which the young Gina Lollobrigida made her first success, as Nedda), as well as such romantic affairs as *O Sole Mio, Souriez Sire, Soho Conspiracy,* and so on. Indeed I am astonished to find that my "film career" comprises some twenty-six films in all. The most famous of them was *The Glass Mountain,* which was made with the delightful Michael Denison and his wife Dulcie Gray, whom we still number among our friends.

Oddly enough—unless a touch of envy accounts for it—my film work earned me small kudos among my operatic associates, who made a number of snide references to "the singing film star." Maestro Santini in par-

My mother and father about the time of their marriage.

An early bit of musical make-believe.

*bove, my father in the garden at home in Bassano.
ight, still undecided about the future, but enjoying
ᶜe.*

Grandfather Weiss with some of the toys he carved, including my cherry-tree castle.

Left, myself as Figaro in the early film of Il Barbiere di Siviglia. *Right, with the young Gina Lollobrigida in the early film of* Pagliacci.

My maestro—Giulio Crimi, the famous tenor.

A scene from Luis Trenker's film I Condottieri, *in which I played Nino, a troubadour, as well as any small parts rejected by others as too dangerous.*

With Tilde at the piano, trying out a number for one of our early concerts.

Above, as Don Giovanni, facing the final challenge in Mozart's opera. Left, Iago, singing the "Drinking Song."

Opposite, clockwise from top left, as Wozzeck, "that tragic torn-off rag of life," in Alban Berg's opera. Tonio in Leoncavallo's Pagliacci. *Michele, the French barge master who is the tragic betrayed husband in Puccini's one-act Grand Guignol masterpiece,* Il Tabarro. *Belcore, the amorous sergeant in Donizetti's* L'Elisir d'Amore.

Rigoletto.

ticular made more than one belittling comment about those who "resorted" to film work for lack of something better. I remember one occasion when I met him outside the opera house and he inquired with a sour smile: "It is true, Tito, that you are giving up singing and taking to being a film star? Someone told me so."

"Quite true, Maestro," I replied. "That must have been the same fellow who told me you are giving up conducting and retiring to the country to grow cabbages."

"All right, all right," he growled. "Better if we are friends and give up sparring in the future." Which we did.

In actual fact, I not only enjoyed my film work but learned some valuable lessons from it which helped me in my operatic career, although the techniques are basically different. For instance, since filming does not follow the plot chronologically, one has to learn how to be instantly in the mood of a scene. There is neither musical development nor dramatic "build-up" to help one, and this is a stern and useful discipline. I also learned not to rely on the support of audience reaction, since there is no audience present, but to train myself to visualize the large audience before whom the scene would eventually appear and to act accordingly. Then there are certain absolute basics to remember, such as economy of gesture, use of the eyes, and so on.

Interspersed with the film-making in those years just after the war were a great number of operatic performances in different parts of Italy. Then in January 1947 Maestro Serafin, who had been appointed artistic director of La Scala a few months previously, personally requested me to sing Mephistopheles in Berlioz's *Damnation of Faust* at that theater.

It was not at all a happy experience. The atmosphere in which we worked was totally and wretchedly different from those great days in Rome when Serafin ruled our artistic lives. I think I cannot do better than quote from my somewhat scrappy diary of the time.

"*Jan. 14:* Milano: From 1 P.M. to 10 P.M. *Damnation* rehearsal. *Really* damnation rehearsal—so much to do in so short a time and I had to study the score in no time. The atmosphere is tense against Serafin. We rehearse without food. What a life! Don't tell me about the heavy work of the cinema. This is hell, it's not art.

"*Jan. 18:* First night of *Damnation of Faust*. I am so tired that my nose bleeds. I worked very hard to go through the performance and did it all right—so they say, at least, and the Press is good."

What gradually reduced me to angry frustration were the working conditions, the managerial disputes, and the first sinister indications of what was to be experienced in one opera house after another in the coming years. By this I mean the dismal shift of power and importance from the artists (who are there to serve the great composers and maintain the real luster of an opera house) to the officials—petty or otherwise—who grew bigger and bigger in their own estimation until they truly thought themselves more important than the great and often ancient house they should have been proud to serve.

If I quote again from that disjointed diary of thirty years ago it is because nothing can show more clearly how this new "system" differed from the hard-working, well-disciplined regime of my early years in Rome. There is also, I am sorry to say, a distressing familiarity in the entries, many of which could be duplicated in describing certain opera houses today. People sometimes ask what has happened to the great operatic standards of the past. Here is at least part of the answer:

"*Feb. 4* [*1947*]: The *Traviata* rehearsals go on with great difficulty and waste of time. Rehearsal at 2 P.M. The orchestra arrives at 4:30. At 5 the choir go on strike—and at 6 everything is O.K. But the dress rehearsal is postponed. The first night is fixed now for the 8th, and the house is sold out. It is disgusting how the Direction behaved—like cowards they complied with the requests of the mob—rubbish.

"*Feb 5:* REST—what a word! I am tired of doing nothing—waiting and feeling sick at my stomach.

"*Feb. 6: Traviata* dress rehearsal.

"*Feb. 8:* No *Traviata*. The Violetta is accused of having collaborated with a German general and public opinion is very much against her. Another soprano is no good—and we go on rehearsing in turn without tenor or soprano.

"I can't stand any more the atmosphere of this opera house. Day after day I am bored and annoyed. Sometimes I go to see some ridiculous performance and get more and more disgusted. All this till Feb. 20 and the *Traviata* is cancelled—and they don't want to pay my fee!

"Anything to get away from here."

Needless to say, this does not mean that the glory had finally departed from La Scala. There were to be further periods of brilliance from time to time, but there were already pygmies in the organization who were beginning to resent the presence of artists of stature because beside them their own smallness could be measured. One world artist after another now began to appear less and less at the great opera house which they should have adorned, either because conditions were made impossible for them or because they were brutally hurried on their way out. And if anyone is innocent enough to ask why a Jack-in-office should actually wish to dispense with the services of a famous artist, the answer is that to the ambitious mediocrity real greatness is unsupportable.

The year 1947, however, brought its rewards as well as its trials, for this was the year which saw the challenge of my first engagement abroad (not counting those which had taken place under the aegis of the Rome–Berlin Axis). I was one of an Italian company invited to Stockholm and I went there to sing Rigoletto.

That first performance was naturally an occasion of great nervous tension, particularly as the King of Sweden himself was present in a house packed with people who had not heard an Italian company for several years. However, everything went well and after the "Vendetta" duet in the third act there was such a storm of applause that the King stood up in his box and, contrary to the rules of his theater, demanded an encore. This delighted the audience who cheered afresh and added their own demands to his. By that time the conductor, the great Maestro Guarnieri, had come around to the stage to make his bow with the rest of the company, and I whispered to him that the King had demanded an encore. But Guarnieri, who was a sick man and in a good deal of pain, replied angrily: "Why should I have to go all that way back? I'm an old man. Why don't you go on and do it without me?"

In rather more urgent whispers I finally convinced him that the royal request had to be complied with, but he returned to the orchestra pit in such a rage that he refused to give me the note to start again. An overzealous member of the orchestra supplied this—only unfortunately it was the wrong note. Nevertheless, I somehow landed on the right one, and the scene was repeated to everyone's satisfaction.

At the end of the performance the whole audience, led by the King, stood up and shouted: *"Viva Italia! Viva Italia!"* That is something for which I shall gratefully remember Stockholm to my dying day, because none of us had heard those words from any foreign audience for many years.

When Maestro Guarnieri rejoined us on the stage I went to help him, but he glared at me and said: "You were sharp all the time."

"Well, sharp or flat, it doesn't matter," I told him. "Come out and enjoy the success with us all." And I more or less dragged him onstage and finally managed for him to be left there alone. I thought the theater would fall apart. The audience cheered and cheered for the man who had led us to triumph. It was such an ovation that Guarnieri began to weep; and when he finally came off stage and I went to help him he fell into my arms and cried like a baby—because we were very good friends really—and he said: "Tito, Tito, it was not true. You were not sharp. I'm a nasty jealous old man. I was jealous of your success."

I hugged him then and said: "Maestro, what does it matter? We'll go out together now." This we did and everything was all right again between us.

I tell that story not as a criticism of someone who was a very fine musician and one of the greatest conductors I ever heard; I tell it merely to show what can happen to any one of us when our nerves are taut, our health not good, and the occasion one of great excitement and tension. Indeed, as far as Maestro Guarnieri is concerned, he would live in my memory for one occasion alone.

This was at a rehearsal of Verdi's *Nabucco*. I was not in the cast but had simply dropped in to listen. They came to the great chorus "Va pensiero" and I thought they were doing pretty well when suddenly Guarnieri flung down his baton and shouted: "Who is the fool who taught you to sing so abominably? Idiots! Dogs! You don't understand a thing. Where is your ass of a chorus master?"

At this Bonaventura Somma, one of the finest of all chorus masters, stepped forward from the wings—a drill sergeant of a man but profoundly respected for his work throughout the musical world. Giving Guarnieri glance for glance he snapped out: "Here I am. Maestro Somma—at your service."

"Idiot!" was Guarnieri's sole comment. Then he went up onstage and ordered Maestro Somma to "stay there, and learn," after which he turned to the chorus and addressed them almost individually. "You, there—yes, that basso. You were much too loud. Keep it down—listen to the next man. And then you have the tenors coming in here—you follow the sopranos—" and so on.

Ten minutes! He spent just ten minutes on a chorus of perhaps five minutes' duration. Then he went back and picked up his baton and they started once more. The opening was a thread of sound, but a thread of purest gold as it spun its way into every corner of the theater; and as the voices gradually swelled to their fullest volume there came a sound like an organ pealing. I sat there hardly daring to breathe lest I should lose one note of it. It was simply miraculous, unlike anything else I had ever heard.

At the end Guarnieri said to the chorus: "That's the way you have to do it at the performance. Remember!" And Somma, walking forward to the front of the stage, addressed him directly: "Thank you, Maestro. You were absolutely right. I was an ass."

Find me two men in the musical world today who will confront each other like that. They were giants!

Later in that memorable first post-war visit to Sweden the company gave an open-air concert in one of Stockholm's beautiful parks. Most of the young voices, like those of Siepi and Del Monaco, had hardly, if ever, been heard outside Italy before. Twenty-three thousand people attended, and at the end the organizer came through the audience laden with flowers and flags in the three Italian national colors and made a speech in honor of Italy and her great contribution to European culture.

We were all in tears. For years we had been, so to speak, in outer darkness; and even if one were not personally guilty somehow one had felt so. This reinstatement, this welcome back into the arms of another nation, was an indescribable moment for all of us. It also set the seal on my happy relationship with Sweden, which resulted in many return visits and in the making of some very warm friendships. Among the Swedish friends we made were the famous publisher Lennart Reuterskiold and his gifted wife Ingrid, and it would be difficult for me to say how much pleasure their friendship has given Tilde and me over the years. Also, to our delight, our friend Fernando Natale—a great music-lover, critic, and conductor—had been appointed ambassador to Sweden, and we were happy to renew the ties which existed between us. Little did I think that —more than twenty-five years later—he would welcome a gifted student of mine to Stockholm!

That first visit to Stockholm in 1947 was, as I have already described, the scene of one of my most memorable Rigolettos, the greatest of all Italian baritone roles. The greatest? Yes, beyond question. The other characters in the work are marvelously real and complete if examined in depth, but Rigoletto *is* the opera, one of the finest creations even Verdi ever conceived.

At the very beginning of my career I remember attending a miserable performance of the work and at the end, as I was about to express my scorn and disgust, I was overwhelmed by the applause. It was inexplicable to me for a moment, and then realization of the truth came to me: *Rigoletto* is, quite simply, indestructible. From that moment I promised myself that I would study this noble work in all its basic truth, never insulting or degrading it by the use of vocal or dramatic gimmicks. I still study it, even though it is now some years since I had to decide, after

370 performances, that I was no longer able to do it the fullest justice either vocally or in the sheer expenditure of energy.

Verdi has perceived, imagined, and described everything. There is not a phrase or a note which is superfluous or without its own meaning. Three words are enough to stamp the Duke as a complete libertine. At his tremendous discovery that Gilda is in fact Rigoletto's daughter he tosses off the moment with a lightly surprised, "Rigoletto? Sua figlia!" but does not hesitate to go on with her seduction. Similarly, when Gilda rushes into the hall of the palace at the end of "Cortigiani . . ." her cry of "Mio padre!" should not be just an expression of her distress but one of horrified discovery. Rigoletto has always refused to tell her anything of his real life and now she sees him—a despised jester groveling at the feet of the men who abducted her. His answering cry must be equally revealing. "Dio, mia figlia" is no mere expression of shock or even of complete realization of her tragic and dishonored state. His first reaction is utter dismay that she should see him thus, and he feverishly tries to pretend that he and the courtiers have merely been joking together: a moment of pathos which, given its proper value, is almost unbearable. These are only a few examples from a score incredibly rich in moments of deep human understanding and musical beauty, frequently overlooked by performer and audience alike.

With his very first entrance Rigoletto is presented with a problem. There are no specific directions as to how he should make that entrance and, particularly today when lavish productions tend to crowd the stage with courtiers, dancers, musicians, and anything else that will take the eye, the unfortunate central character has great difficulty in making any immediate impact. Indeed, I have seen some unfortunate Rigolettos almost overlooked in those first few moments, and there is rather little in the following passages by which significance can be re-established.

This initial problem occupied my mind for a long time, but I finally achieved an effective entrance on a burst of sharp ironical laughter which almost slashed through the scene on the last note of the tenor. From then on every gesture and every word must count. It is Rigoletto's business to amuse the bored Duke and his court, always at the expense of some victim or other. His first attempts fail, and he causes offense rather than amusement when he outrageously dares to suggest that to cut off the head of Count Ceprano would clear the way for the Duke, who is seeking to seduce his wife.

At each failure Rigoletto increases the savage mockery which is part of his unpleasant job until finally, with the entry of Monterone, he stoops to the level of taunting a man whose daughter has been dishonored by the Duke. In those early phrases I always used a clear, nervous, derisive tone, allowing my voice gradually to take on what I call a yellow tinge, full of wicked sarcasm, for the taunting of Monterone. When he replies by calling down a father's curse upon me, superstitious terror overwhelms me and I crawl at his feet imploring pardon without effect.

The make-up for the scene in which Rigoletto is the jester is of special importance, but it is not necessary or even logical for him to be exaggeratedly contorted throughout the evening. He is stunted, of course, and has one shoulder higher than the other, but, as I found when I studied the subject at the Palace of the Dwarfs in Mantua, it was the custom of that period to increase the deformity of poor, badly formed creatures by the way in which they were costumed. This I applied to my own get-up. With artfully used padding and string I made my legs look short and misshapen, and I used to wear a huge hump inserted in my jester's costume and attached under my wig to the nape of my neck, so that I was obliged to keep my head tilted to the right. The result was an oblique look upward, the left eyebrow lifted and the nasal partition out of straight, giving to my face a derisive sneer.

For the scene when Rigoletto returns to his home I did exactly what he himself would have done. I divested myself of the deforming addition to my costume, emerging as a stunted, slightly crooked man, lovable to my devoted daughter and offering her no evidence by which she might guess my shameful trade.

As he nears his home in that second scene Rigoletto's voice precedes him, and this should be the lamenting—the howling almost—of a man who has lost all hope as he recalls the curse of a father which Monterone has laid upon him. If the stage is a shallow one, which is often the case in this scene, he should advance with short, slightly wavering steps, which will give the effect of his wearily approaching from a distance, weighed down by care. The beautiful scene between him and his daughter affords every opportunity for a variety of coloring in the voice, but he must not yield to the temptation to slow down too much at the emotional points as this checks the natural flow of the melody.

At the very end of the scene, when Rigoletto returns to discover his daughter's abduction, there is always an urge to find a fresh way of expressing the drama and his despair. I remember once at the Teatro Reale in Rome that the stage set had a flight of fifteen or sixteen steps running down toward the audience, and it occurred to me what a marvelous effect it would make if I sang my final, "Ah-ah-ah, la maledizione," from the top and then rolled to the bottom. It so happened that we had a similar flight—but of marble—at home, and I decided to try it out there.

I uttered my anguished cry from the top, tucked my head between my legs and rolled down the steps, ending up against the radiator half-stunned, my back so striped with bruises that I must have looked like a zebra, but obstinately determined to try again. By the first night of the production I had perfected my fall and did it with great effect, but I felt constrained to add to the stage directions on my score, *"Fortissimo— precipitato—molto doloroso."* To be worthy of a role like Rigoletto, however, one must be ready for a few sacrifices.

Vocally, the role of Rigoletto is one of the hardest in the repertoire, requiring a tremendous amount of dramatic power to be superimposed on the tender, almost sacred feelings of a father. The music is by turns impetuous, brilliant, and moving, describing in a masterly way all the contrasting emotions of a human soul. Every bit of physical as well as vocal strength is called for. I shall never forget how, absolutely drained by the demanding scene of "Cortigiani" and almost panting with agony, I would plunge into the pure bliss of "Piangi, fanciulla" and then warm up again into the madness and triumph of "Si, vendetta!"

As for the text, to know the value of every word and the cause and origin of each character's every action is the least that is required. On the subject of this vital "marriage" of word and action I should like to emphasize that one of the most important things for a singer to remember (not only in *Rigoletto*) is that the legato of singing will be better expressed if it is accompanied by legato of action. The identical timing of the two will often be difficult of course, and then it may be necessary, as it were, to stretch the one to accommodate the other.

If, for instance, a short musical phrase requires a smile and a gesture of the hand to add significance to its expression it may be advisable to allow that smile to dawn and that hand to start rising fractionally before the accompanying sound. Equally, if the musical phrase is a long one it may well be most effective to start the accompanying gesture fractionally later, adding point and significance to the conclusion of the phrase. Admittedly this is a difficult thing to learn and to make an instinctive part of one's art but, once perfected, it will add to the whole presentation of a role a smooth oneness which will transform it.

One word of warning, however, to anyone adding these refinements to his or her presentation: if any of these moments is missed or bungled, never look back on it until the performance is over. The moment has gone and can never be recalled. To dwell on it will only increase a sense of confusion which can quickly lead to disaster. To let even part of your mind be preoccupied with what has happened is like tossing the stone which starts the avalanche.

The final scene of *Rigoletto* requires a very special atmosphere, provided initially by the magical sonority of Verdi's chords, enhanced—if the producer is intelligent—by the dreary wastes of the Mantuan swamps glimpsed from time to time as the lightning flashes, but conveyed above all by the attitude of Rigoletto and Gilda. As they come slowly into view they move almost like automata, two tragic figures representing not only their own resigned misery but the misery of all poor human beings crushed between a threatening heaven and an indifferent earth.

There is no longer any savage fight left in Rigoletto. He has come to the end of the road. Even his revenge will give him no satisfaction. And all this one must endeavor to convey in the acting and the voice. It is no moment to pour forth a beautiful healthy tone. I used to strive to produce a weary, almost squeezed tone, heavy as the weight which is settling on my soul. Then comes the celestial melody which ends Gilda's tragic young life, and when it has ebbed to its close I used to allow a pause before, rising to my feet and gathering all my remaining strength, I utter my last despairing cry, "Ah, la maledizione!" and fall dead beside the body of my child.

That last effective A flat and B flat are not written in the score and today there is much discussion about them. Were Verdi alive now it is possible that he would permit this variant, but somehow I doubt it. I wish I could believe he would for, beautiful or not, those notes come with an impact of such stunning force that the audience is invariably carried away. I almost always used to include those notes, though with a slight sense of guilt. Then on one occasion, in an access of artistic virtue, I omitted all the embellishments which tradition and custom had allowed throughout the opera; whereupon friends and audience registered not only disappointment but alarm, some of them coming to me afterward to commiserate with me upon my not being well and even praising my courage in singing when in poor shape.

So much for artistic integrity!

9.

THE SWEDISH VISIT, although the highlight of 1947, was not the only foreign excursion in prospect. Doors were beginning to open on every side and horizons were widening to take in one country after another. Early in 1948 we were invited to London for discussions on the proposed film of *The Glass Mountain* and at the same time I received an offer to undertake an extensive concert tour of England and Scotland under the management of Lynford and Joel.

There are several references to this in John Joel's own book, entitled with somewhat rueful wit *We Paid the Piper*. Even though their bold venture into management eventually collapsed I am glad to say that my tour was a profitable undertaking for them, and certainly in these young men we found two of our first real English friends.

Our arrangements had been conducted entirely by correspondence, but they promised to meet us at the station. So, as on that long-ago occasion with my uncle in Vienna, I wrote to ask how we were to recognize them and received the reply that one of them was tall and the other was short, and that they would both be dressed in "typical English style."

Tilde and I scanned the waiting crowd on our arrival and, on spotting two young men, one tall and one short, both attired with a strict formality more suited to a funeral than the reception of a stage performer, I exclaimed: "There they are!" However, the formality dissolved in the first few minutes and we got on splendidly from the start. Indeed, some years later I was to be John Joel's best man at his wedding, and his family and ours have ever since remained on the warmest terms.

On that first visit I began what was to be for Tilde and me a life-long love affair with the London audience by giving a concert at the Albert Hall. In her diary Tilde comments on our first sight of that beautiful but intimidating place: "My! What a hall! We were terrified by its immensity. Tito rehearses a little and feels all right." Then, after the concert: "Fantastic success. So many people in the dressing-room we thought we were going to be suffocated; going out, we were positively assaulted and were afraid to be torn to pieces."

During the concert John Joel had come to me at the interval to say he had just heard that the artist for his next Albert Hall concert had had to cancel owing to illness; would I consider doing another concert in his place? I agreed gladly and at the end of the concert he made an announcement to this effect, adding that the box office would be open for an hour for the purchase of tickets. The stampede that followed still remains one of my most gratifying memories.

Tilde's diary of that time, though not always in impeccable English, is full of delighted impressions of our first discovery of England and the English. On visiting the theaters and cinemas: "Even if we hardly understand we want to get acquainted with the country and the people. We went to see *St. Joan* at the Old Vic; gosh, what a performance! All the actors are terrific, especially Alec Guinness and Harry Andrews. Fabulous directing, fantastic lighting, and a sense of unity and spareness that was really a delight—even for us who could not catch the long talk in English. The way these people wear their costume is amazing. They all look *grands seigneurs*. After every show or performance the national anthem is played, everybody standing still; very moving and beautiful; shows respect for the country as well as themselves."

I also sang at a Promenade Concert while we were in London, and Tilde, writing for both of us, reports: "The Promenade is an extraordinary performance; never seen anything like that; the hall is emptied of the seats and the people standing for hours on end. We were absolutely stunned by the love and enthusiasm this audience shows. We dined inside the house and went out after an hour, but the people were still waiting to see Tito and have a signature."

In the provinces these scenes were repeated, and of Leeds Tilde writes: "The enthusiasm is not to describe for fear to sound very boastful. Even in the street, under a constant rain, we were for an hour, Tito signing, smiling and talking to everybody."

No wonder our first English visit delighted us. Incidentally I also made some records—"Organization perfect!" Tilde comments—and gained my first experience of television both as performer and audience.

Back in Italy I added the part of Jochanaan in Strauss's *Salome* to my repertoire, singing this at the Scala in May 1948. But undoubtedly the most challenging experience of the year was still to come—our visit to the United States, where Tagliavini, Tajo, and I were to make our American debut in *Barbiere di Siviglia* in San Francisco.

We said a tearful good-by to our beloved little Cecilia, though she herself remained unflatteringly cheerful. She had no conception, of course, of the kind of journey we were undertaking. In her experience we always came back, suitably laden with presents, and I suppose children usually enjoy the excitement connected with rather dramatic comings and goings.

This was long before the arrival of the jet plane, it must be remembered, and travel delays were much more frequent. Though we set out for Stockholm we were forced down by bad weather in Nice, where we were stranded for two days. Finally, by way of Geneva and Copenhagen, we reached Stockholm where, in spite of frantic cables explaining the reason for our delay, we found Maestro Dobrowen tense and irritated by the hold-up. (Indeed, there is a photograph—much prized by both of us in later years—which shows us greeting each other with false smiles while obviously being ready to erupt like a couple of volcanoes.) I was rushed immediately into rehearsal with hardly time to draw breath. But God was good to me and for some reason my voice was in excellent shape in spite of everything. We ended the rehearsal very good friends and remained so until Dobrowen's death.

Concerts and opera kept us in Sweden for most of September, when we set out for the United States. We were forced back to Oslo by a violent storm and delayed there for six hours before flying to Glasgow to start our first Atlantic crossing, then a scheduled flight of fifteen hours. We paused briefly in New York—but long enough for our first experience of the high-powered publicity campaign which is the delight, or terror, of most visiting artists—and then flew on to San Francisco.

At that time, and for some years previously, the opera was under the direction of Merola, an American of Italian extraction who soon found himself the unwilling buffer state between two warring factions. On the one hand were the Italians—young, ambitious, and eager to conquer new worlds after having been pent-up in their homeland throughout the war years. On the other hand were the well-established American artists whose supremacy had been unchallenged for several years. We were all on our mettle and therefore reveled in our undoubted success. In particular, Tagliavini, Tajo, and I (soon dubbed the Three T's or the "Three Flying Musketeers of La Scala") caught the popular fancy to a degree that was dangerous to the other faction.

Finally one of the principal American artists stormed backstage and cried: "We've had enough of these damned Italians!" Whereupon Mr. Merola discovered that deep down he was a damned Italian too and promptly tore up the American's contract. There was a great to-do in the best operatic tradition before an uneasy peace was restored. But it was a peace which brought more disillusionment than satisfaction to me personally. In my contract I had been listed to sing in *Otello,* but when I went to the opera house to savor the pleasure of seeing my name down for Iago I found another name there. On making angry inquiries I was regretfully told that I had been engaged to sing *in Otello,* but not specifically the role of Iago. If I cared to accept Roderigo I was welcome, but . . .

It was the classic case of not having "read the small print," but I was never caught that way again. In all competitive professions—and particularly those connected with the stage, where rivalries must of necessity be very personal and intense—such unhappy incidents are not uncommon. At this particular time, it must be remembered, everybody had had their nerves at full stretch during the war years and afterward. We Italians, as I have said, were determined to show what we could do; but equally it could not have been pleasant for those who were used to a safe position in their own country to find themselves challenged on ground which they must always have regarded as their own preserve.

Also it must not be supposed that shabby behavior occurs only between rival nationalities. I am not, I am sure, singular in being able to recall some quite astonishing experiences with certain compatriots. In South America, for instance, a year or two after the San Francisco fracas, I found myself among a galaxy of singers chosen for their star potential. The director, Barreto Pinto, had a disagreeable tendency to pit one soprano against another, one tenor against another, and—as I found to my cost—one baritone against another. Jealousies and competition ruled throughout the opera house, and I cannot recall any other time when the atmosphere was more unpleasantly electric.

After several distinguished baritones had shown their paces in *Barbiere di Siviglia* I was called in unexpectedly to take my turn at the role. Immediately before the performance all my baritone colleagues, dear fellows, crowded into my windowless dressing room to wish me luck, every one of them puffing an enormous cigar. Within seconds we could hardly see each other and I was half suffocated when suddenly the director looked in, burst into roars of rage, and drove them all from the room. For my part I rushed to the nearest exit, took several gulps of good clean air, and managed to acquit myself satisfactorily when I appeared on stage caroling joyously. Afterward, a good deal to my astonishment, the director—who was principally responsible for the situation arising—insisted on doubling my agreed fee on the grounds that I had been "sporting" over the incident.

Later in the tour I was singing the elder Germont in a broadcast performance of *Traviata*. In the second act I had just started "Pura siccome un angelo" when the lady playing Violetta—really a good friend of mine—moved gracefully across the stage and swung her crinoline over the floor microphone, thus reducing my part in the broadcast to a distant whisper. When her own part came along she naturally swung her crinoline clear of the microphone.

It was during the same performance, if I remember rightly, that the Alfredo embraced me with excessive emotion at the end of my aria "Di provenza," shaking me with such filial fervor, that I had great difficulty in not quavering into silence. However, if I could not manhandle Violetta, at least I could tackle my operatic offspring on his own ground. Grasping him firmly by the wrist I forced him to his knees with a great show of parental feeling, and there I held him.

In the opera world, as in life generally, the sooner one learns to show indifference to pettiness, the sooner one escapes such attacks. I was fortunate in realizing comparatively early that it is a mistake to give spiteful people the satisfaction of knowing one is hurt or dismayed, and this ability to rise above events confers on one an inner strength which is well worth cultivating. I know this is the counsel of perfection, and I cannot claim that I have always followed it myself, but at least I have tried.

I think perhaps I learned this from my mother, who had immense dignity and poise. One instance is stamped on my memory: my good-looking father had been playing the Don Giovanni and my grandfather—who had a patriarchal tendency to summon the family together when advice or reproof was called for—did so then. I think he principally wished to assure my mother of his support but before he could say anything *she* addressed *him,* together with the rest of the assembled family.

"Thank you very much for your concern for me," she said, "and I hope what I am going to say will not lessen your affection for me. But one thing I must ask you to understand. I am proud of my husband and will not have anything said against him."

In point of fact I suppose it might be said that my wise mama was the winner in the end. For the last twenty years of her life my father never left her side and he adored her to the end.

At the conclusion of that first operatic visit to the United States in 1948 Tilde and I said good-by to our colleagues and set out once more on our travels, this time to South Africa where a lengthy concert tour awaited us. We flew from San Francisco to Johannesburg, a journey of seventy-four hours, in which we passed through every graduation of temperature until we finally arrived in a heat wave. We tottered down the steps of the plane, weary, bedraggled, and feeling scarcely human, while the press photographers waited there expecting us to smile.

However, we at once found ourselves in the kind and capable hands of Alex Cherniavsky, who had a splendid tour arranged for us. The South Africans, being rather far removed from the usual concert circuit, were particularly avid for the kind of Italian singing which had been missing from their lives all the war years. Everywhere we went—Johannesburg, Pretoria, Port Elizabeth, East London, Cape Town, and back to Johannesburg—we were feted by enthusiastic audiences. On the last evening in Johannesburg the concert hall was sold out and every emergency seat crowding the passages and anterooms was taken. And still there were thousands outside, their faces pressed to the glass doors, calling for entrance.

"I think you'll have to make a start in spite of the shouting outside," Cherniavsky said dubiously at last. But I was determined no one should be disappointed if I could help it. "Fix up a microphone in the hall," I suggested, "and some loudspeakers out in the street, and ask to have the streets immediately outside cleared for an hour or two."

With the permission of the police this was done, and the scenes of delight and enthusiasm which followed were among the most heart-warming I have ever experienced. Indeed, I was so moved by the South African audiences in general that I declared we must make a return visit. Cherniavsky at first shook his head doubtfully, saying that usually there was one successful tour and that was it, but in the end he yielded, and in actual fact I toured South Africa five times in all.

Later, when Cherniavsky was in Rome I asked him why he did not boldly take an opera company out to South Africa. I suggested he should aim for the best and ask Beniamino Gigli, who was still in excellent form. Cherniavsky thought the idea too ambitious and was sure Gigli would not be prepared to go so far for the sort of fees he could offer.

"Let me try," I said impulsively. "Tell me your top terms, and let me talk to Gigli."

So it was arranged, and I played the part of go-between and impresario for the first and last time in my life. Cherniavsky spoke no

Italian and Gigli virtually no English, so that I was able to exercise all my tact and persuasion in passing on to each of them just as much as was advisable. In the end we fixed up a splendid contract for both opera and concerts, to the utmost delight of both parties. Then, after the last business talk, when Cherniavsky had departed with the completed contract, Gigli went to his desk and began to make some calculations.

"You made an excellent contract for me, Tito," he said, writing busily, "but as you're not really an impresario shall we say 5 per cent on the total instead of the usual 10 per cent? That comes to one million—"

"What are you saying?" I asked indignantly.

"It's not enough?" Gigli glanced across the room at me. "Well then, say—"

"Say nothing!" I cut in rather angrily. "I don't want to be paid. It was nothing but a pleasure for me to do this for a great colleague."

"You don't want *anything?*" Gigli was obviously astounded. "But a little money is often useful for a young fellow like you."

"Maybe," I agreed. "But this was done solely for the honor and pleasure of having you for a colleague again."

"Then in that case," he said, getting to his feet, "I think we must embrace each other and in future you call me 'Beniamino' and we give each other the 'tu.' "

This we did, and I think I was one of the very few people ever allowed to call him "Beniamino" by his own invitation.

Then he took from a side table a beautiful little ivory carving of a mouse eating a piece of cheese, and said: "I would like you to have this as a remembrance of today. And if ever you need me for a performance —concert or opera—for any charity in which you are interested, you have only to tell me the date and if I am free I shall be there."

It was, as I recall it, about two years later that I was asked to do a concert for the combined charities of my hometown, Bassano del Grappa. Remembering Gigli's words I said: "Give me a little time. I might be able to do better than a concert of my own."

Then I telephoned Gigli and asked if, for a very modest fee, he would consider coming and singing something at our concert.

"But it seems to me, Tito, that you and I have a special arrangement about this," he replied. "Did I not promise you a full concert without fee any time you wanted it? What is the date?"

I gave him a tentative date, and having consulted his secretary he said: "You can rely on me. I shall be there."

We put heart and soul into making all the arrangements perfect, but we soon found it would have to be a concert without seats. It was going to be "standing room only" with loudspeakers fixed up everywhere. Accommodation was booked at the hotel, a dinner was arranged in the ancient castle, notices were sent out all over the countryside.

On the day before the concert I called in at the hotel to check the last arrangements and was informed that Commendatore Gigli had not yet arrived. Then, as I turned to retrace my steps through the vestibule, I saw a gentleman in a funny white peaked cap, sitting in a chair reading a newspaper. It was Gigli, who had slipped into the town unannounced and without fuss.

The next day the great trek began. Throughout the afternoon and into the evening there came winding down from the hills hundreds and then thousands of people from the countryside. Every square, every street was packed with waiting people, and not a scrap of traffic was allowed to stir. One young motorcyclist who revved up his machine three squares away from the central point of interest was very properly jumped on and nearly lynched by the crowd and his offending motorcycle flung into a doorway.

Then Gigli walked from the hotel to the square and began to sing. He sang and he sang and he sang—every aria they asked for, every favorite song. He would pause and say: "What would you like now?" and the audience called their requests and he sang them as though he were at a family party.

Finally, when the time came to rescue him and take him back to his hotel and his room on the first floor, crowds stood outside calling for him as though he were a king. I went out onto the balcony and explained that they really must let him go, that he was tired and needed rest. But they pleaded for him to come out and show himself.

So I went in and said: "I'm terribly sorry, Beniamino, but they say— if they could just *see* you for a moment—"

"I understand, I understand," the old tenor said, getting slowly to his feet, and he climbed the two steps to the balcony and went outside.

Tilde always says that it was a sight none of us will ever forget. The people stood so close together that you could see only their raised faces— thousands of them—white in the moonlight. Then he flung out his arms to them and began to sing again, the voice as perfect and seemingly as untired as ever.

The next morning I came down early to make sure that our exalted guest went off in style, but Gigli was already downstairs and ready to go. Even earlier, however, were the people who wanted to say "thank you."

When we went out to the waiting car there was hardly space for Gigli to sit in it. From the floor to the roof, from the back to the front, it was crammed with little offerings: fruit, vegetables, ceramics, a bottle of wine, a loaf of bread baked by the local baker, who said: "It's all I can do, but I hope it's a good loaf." There were pens from the factory nearby, flowers, woven materials, jams from the housewives—everything one could think of. At the very last minute, almost as the car began to move, a little old lady rushed up with a tray of ravioli covered with a cloth.

"I've just freshly made it," she cried. "You only have to put it in boiling water for five minutes."

Gigli said, "Give it to me here," and took the tray on his knee, for there was nowhere else in the car to put it; and the car drove off at walking pace, the people following alongside calling their love and their blessings.

For the rest of his life, whenever we met, Gigli would recall the occasion and say: "I am sure it made you happy but, Tito, it made me very happy too." He had a great understanding of simple people, which was probably why his singing went straight from his heart to theirs. His was the art which conceals art. Perhaps only a connoisseur would appreciate *what* an artist he was, but when he opened that miraculous throat and sang no one needed any special training to know that one of God's greatest gifts was being spread before them.

Before leaving the subject of this unique artist and colleague there is one more story I must tell. It happened, some years before the Bassano incident, that Gigli, Maria Caniglia, and I were singing a performance of *Un Ballo in Maschera* in Lecce. The opera ended very late, as is often the case in provincial towns, but one restaurant remained open for us and after a long and enjoyable meal some of us walked back through the sleeping town to our hotel. The first touch of dawn was in the sky when suddenly, as we walked along, the silence was broken by the sound of a wonderful tenor voice singing. We stared at each other, and then the voice stopped and I said doubtfully: "It must be a record."

"That's no record," Gigli replied. The voice started again—"Amor ti vieta—" and around the corner came a good-looking young fellow pushing a barrow piled high with vegetables.

We all stood and stared at him, and then Gigli addressed him: "That's a very fine voice you have."

"You think so?" The young man paused and smiled while someone quickly murmured: "You know who these are? Signor Gigli, Madame Caniglia, Signor Gobbi."

The young man acknowledged the introductions with a friendly nod, and Gigli went on: "You ought to have that voice trained. And," he glanced at the rest of us who indicated our agreement, "it wouldn't cost you anything. We would see to that."

"Oh?" The young man looked mildly interested. "What would I have to do?"

"Well," Gigli explained, "we would see that you went to the right teachers, and as soon as you were ready you would go into the theater and start with small parts and then later big parts."

"And what then?" the young man asked.

"Why, then you would travel the world and make a lot of money and be very happy," Gigli assured him.

"I'd be happy?" The young man considered that. Then he asked suddenly: "Signor Gigli, are you happy?"

Somewhat taken aback, Gigli said: "Yes, I think I am. Yes, certainly —I think I am."

"Signor Gigli," came the smiling, almost indulgent reply, "you *think* you are happy—I *know* I am. Thank you, but I will sell my vegetables." And the young man went on his way once more, pushing his barrow, while we all looked after him in amazement.

We were so deeply impressed that we felt we could not leave the matter there, and the next morning we went to the market. We could not find him but we made inquiries of one or two people and some of them said: "Oh yes, we know whom you mean. No, we don't know his name and he's nowhere around just now."

"Tito," Gigli said solemnly, "you know what it is. He's just one of those angels you see once and never again."

10.

FOLLOWING the first American visit and my first South African tour I began to find myself increasingly in demand in the international field. In 1949, during a trip to Cairo to sing in *Rigoletto, Barbiere,* and *Pagliacci* with an Italian company, I received the first somewhat startling evidence that I had become important enough to merit intrigue on the part of a rival baritone.

Cairo had for some time been virtually the preserve of Gino Bechi, who was tremendously popular there. His was an immense talent, his voice in those days being large, beautiful, and intensely dramatic, his stage presence nothing short of magnificent. When he had first appeared on the Italian scene it had been like the arrival of a blazing comet.

It was not easy to have to follow him in a place where he was regarded as a sort of king, but I was not unduly perturbed, being determined to do my best. Shortly before my first performance, however, when I was already in my dressing room making up there arrived at the theater and in certain newspaper offices telegrams bearing the shocking news that Bechi had died suddenly in Trieste.

I was overwhelmed by dismay. When Pino Donati, the husband of Maria Caniglia and one of the best of artistic directors, appeared in my dressing room, I said: "We'll have to cancel the performance. Such terrible news—and he's such a popular figure here!"

To my shocked surprise Donati, whose theater experience was much more extensive than mine, replied callously: "Nonsense. There's no problem. I guarantee there'll be another telegram tomorrow contradicting the report."

The performance went ahead and, sure enough, the next day there arrived a reassuring telegram from Bechi to his devoted Cairo public. Having heard of the extraordinary report of his death he wanted to assure his friends and supporters that there was no truth in the story. Far from being dead he was very much alive and well and singing in Trieste. If he were suffering from anything it was only deep nostalgia for his faithful Cairo public.

Naturally this brought him well into the news again and very soon, prompted by who knows who, a kind of competition was started in one of the newspapers to decide who was the most popular singer among the Cairo audience. Presently it was announced in big headlines that Bechi and Gobbi were heading the list, with Gobbi about two hundred votes ahead. Finally I was pipped at the post by three hundred votes which arrived for Bechi—almost all of them from Italy, for some unexplained reason.

A couple of months later a friend of mine managed to trace copies of the original telegrams announcing Bechi's death and reassuringly contradicting the report. They both emanated from the same place in Italy, but the curious thing was that the date of the contradiction preceded the date of the announcement.

During a long career in such a competitive profession I have learned not to entertain too many hard feelings about this sort of thing, even though straightforward artistic rivalry is one thing and backstairs manipulation something else. The trouble perhaps was that Bechi, though at the top of his profession, had to be the center of interest. Good-humored and a bit of an exhibitionist in private life, he had a talent for capturing attention wherever he went. On the stage this quality told in his favor. He was superb—a marvelous actor and a marvelous singer— and I could bear him no animosity for that bit of nonsense in Cairo. Indeed, when he ended his career I realized that it was a great loss to my career as well. At the risk of sounding pompous I must say that, though I admired and appreciated many of my baritone colleagues as very good artists, with Bechi I felt I had a rival worthy of my own mettle. It was a rivalry which brought me the stimulus of real competition—something of inestimable value to any serious artist.

After the Cairo visit Tilde and I joined forces in a concert tour of Malta. My wife, being very modest, is sometimes a little too anxious to stand back in my shadow but, having come into my life in Crimi's garden as the girl who was asked to accompany me at my very first audition, she developed into an accompanist of wonderful sensibility. In the early part of my career we frequently partnered each other in concerts and here, as in everything else, her musical knowledge and artistic understanding were of immense support to me.

Then, in 1950, came an unexpected invitation to sing Don Giovanni under Furtwängler in Salzburg with a highly prestigious cast including Ljuba Welitsch, Elisabeth Schwarzkopf, Irmgard Seefried, Erich Kunz, Anton Dermota, Josef Greindl, and Alfred Poell. As long ago as 1943 Serafin had asked me if I had ever studied Don Giovanni. I said I hadn't but that I was ready to start work tomorrow if he wished, and when would he think it a good time for me to sing it?

"Maybe in fifteen years' time," Serafin replied. "But it's quite a good idea for you to start studying it tomorrow."

In the seven years which had passed since then I cannot say that I had studied the role intensively. Indeed, when the Salzburg invitation came there was a great deal to be done. In particular a tremendous amount of work would be involved in the sheer committing to memory of the endless passages of recitative which "carry" the plot. For the experienced singer there is no insuperable problem in tackling several arias in the course of an evening. But those all-important recitatives of the divine Mozart can be for Don Giovanni a foretaste of the hell which awaits him at the end of the work.

My old friend "Bibi" Bizzelli (who had accompanied me in those far-off radio programs of my youth) now came to the rescue. It happened that we had both become avid stamp collectors, so with our stamp collections and our scores of *Don Giovanni* we retired to the Gobbi seaside home in Santa Severa, determined to cut ourselves off from our normal world. In this we were immediately assisted by such a heavy fall of rain and snow that we would have had to remain virtually housebound in any case. We had plenty of wood in the place and so, with roaring fires everywhere and surrounded by stamps in every stage of being detached, dried off, cataloged and reattached, we studied *Don Giovanni* together.

From time to time, in what I freely confess was my artistic immaturity as far as Mozart was concerned, I grew bored with the task. At such moments Bibi, who was a humorous and ingenious person, suggested that we should lapse into our native dialects. So I would sing Giovanni with a strong Venetian accent and Bibi would sing everyone else in Tuscan dialect. For some reason or other we found this highly amusing and it helped to lighten the hours of heavy study. By the time I transferred to the more solemn atmosphere of Salzburg I was ready to tackle my first Don Giovanni—as far as anyone can be described as "ready" when first attempting this work of towering genius. I have reserved my detailed views on what is one of the most controversial of all roles for a later point in the story. I will only say here that I still regard it as a privilege and a matter of singular good fortune that my first approach to this role was under the guidance of Furtwängler. The great German conductor's reading of the score was perhaps less sparkling than the usually accepted Italian one, but it was highly dramatic and of great depth and insight. There was no question of Don Giovanni's being just a gay philanderer who came to a deservedly nasty end; under all the charm and ingenuity he was a killer, and one was never allowed to forget it.

Fresh from the thrilling Salzburg experience I went to London in September for the first visit of the Scala Company. Once more the "Three T's" scored a happy success, creating a still warmer bond with the London audience. I was also asked at a moment's notice to sing Ford to Stabile's incomparable Falstaff.

Then, while Tilde and I were once more in Stockholm, I received a telephone call from Maestro Serafin asking me to sing in *Falstaff* in Florence during the following January. Naturally I supposed I was to sing my familiar role of Ford but, when we returned to Rome, I found it was Serafin's intention that I should now undertake the name part—the great Verdi baritone role not yet in my repertoire.

"But do you think I am ready, Maestro?" I asked doubtfully.

"Yes. You're ready," was Serafin's brief reply.

If Serafin said so I was willing to accept this, but there was little time in which to prepare, particularly as we were both committed to engagements in Rome and Naples which entailed our commuting between the two cities. I pointed this out to Serafin, who considered the point and then asked: "Do you drive the car yourself—and safely?" (He was a rather nervous car passenger.)

I assured him that I did. "Then I shall accompany you," Serafin informed me. "You will drive and I shall sit beside you and teach you how Falstaff should be sung."

Improbable though it may sound, that was how I learned all the magical nuances, the ever-changing vocal coloring, the many subtleties required for the interpretation of Falstaff. I sang and he sang on the road from Rome to Naples and back, and he showed me exactly how to tackle those phrases which were the most difficult for my voice. I would not claim that when I sang the role for the first time in January 1951 I was already presenting a rich, mature reading of the part—it takes many years to become a real Falstaff—but at least I had made a good beginning on a role which was to afford me some of the happiest hours of my career.

Verdi himself takes pains to emphasize the intimate quality of the work, fearing that in a large house the rapid dialogue and ever-changing expressions of the characters might be lost. Certainly it is the most difficult of his operas to follow and pretty difficult to perform, freed as it is from all previous conventions. The music grows out of the beautiful libretto, perfectly conceived by both composer and librettist, producing what is undoubtedly one of the most extraordinary masterpieces of all time.

Its musical prose appealed to me from the very beginning, enabling one, as it does, to look at life with a certain sense of detachment—with an indulgent bonhomie peculiar to a man who has lived life to the full. Whereas at the beginning of most operas I felt nervous and excited, with the big belly of Sir John I put on in addition a sort of beautiful calm.

In his own realm of the Garter Inn, supremely regardless of the protests of Dr. Caius, Falstaff proceeds to write his two identical love letters. Presently, incensed by his rascally servants and by the size of the innkeeper's bill—which he chooses to repudiate—he launches into his dissertation on the meaning of honor: a homily which, though totally without any moral content, is tossed off with such an air of grandeur and with such gloriously varied musical coloring, that it causes a sensation both on the stage and in the audience.

To me there are three sides of his character clearly described by the music: humorous and ironic, lyric-idyllic, and fantastic-romantic. He is totally indifferent where he himself is not concerned, barely condescending to Quickly but obsequiously unctuous with the wealthy "Signor Fontana." A strong man, as sensual as he is daring, he possesses a spirited humor which helps him to extricate himself from the most difficult situations. If he has his moments of depression, he is able to throw them off with a mixture of cynical indifference and lively fantasy. His vanity is immeasurable.

In person he must tower over everyone and everything on the stage—tables, chairs, benches, people. I once saw a performance at the Metropolitan in which my friend and colleague Geraint Evans played Falstaff, and in the first scene there was a gigantic innkeeper who dwarfed everyone, including the central character. This giant, well aware of his own importance, was all over the place, even cornering the unfortunate Sir John when he was meditating alone, until I think poor Geraint must have longed to throttle him—as I did. My surprise was complete when this "actor" actually took a bow at the end of the act.

The delightful little aria "Quand'ero paggio" is a vaguely ironical self-portrait. With this and the two great monologues from Acts I and III Falstaff's character is completely defined. In my view it is in the monologue of Act III that the real Falstaff is revealed. Alone, with no one to overhear him, he rails against the women who have really gone too far in their mockery and he recalls his dreadful experiences almost as if he were in a nightmare. His usual fantasies about himself are powerless to comfort him and he is about to sink into genuine depression when he remembers the reviving power of wine. He calls loudly for a tankard of wine—*hot*—and then delivers himself of an ode to the powers of drink. At the first sip the little devils dozing in his brain wake up and exhort him to take pride again in his own superiority and the fact that he is once more the bold and accomplished cavalier ready to triumph over all the insults of the common people.

The entrance of Quickly brings him back to earth for a sad moment; but as she unfolds a new and tempting proposition he is ready to be involved again. He does have some fearful foreboding as, in the beginning of the magical last scene, he walks heavily to his rendezvous at the haunted oak, wearing the horns of the ghostly hunter, but once more his vanity betrays him to the tricks of the Merry Wives, joined now by Ford and the other characters and many of the townsfolk of Windsor. Yet even after he has taken quite heavy punishment he still comes out the winner: "L'arguzia mia crea l'arguzia degli altri" ("My quick wit sharpens the wit of others").

The work is filled with episodes involving the different characters, like a Flemish painting in which each group of figures has its own life but remains a vital part of the whole. Every role must be drawn as clearly as the next one, with everything combining to give a living picture of minute exactness. This is a matter of considerable difficulty, for no one performer should stand out against another nor detract from the completeness of the ensemble. *Falstaff* is a problem of delicate balance, which changes from moment to moment around the figure of Sir John. His is the one dominating role, the pivot around which everything turns. But if even one minor character were to be removed the loss would disturb the delicate balance of the whole.

Nannetta and Fenton provide one episode, and they paint the lyric-idyllic side of the story. The Wives in their episode display, each in her own way, an almost diabolical liveliness—Quickly in particular showing a genius for comedy which would fool the devil himself. To all three of them the arrival of the duplicate love letters presents a welcome diversion from their everyday life.

Ford—a role I played many times in my early days—is full of rich opportunities. In the guise of the rich "Signor Fontana" he arrives at the Garter Inn with the intention of ridiculing Falstaff but becomes a victim of his own trick when Falstaff complacently informs him that he is about to cuckold Master Ford. Almost mad with terror he becomes, in his own belief, a tragic betrayed husband. But inherent in this misconception there is irresistible comedy for the audience, and it is by accentuating his dramatic reaction that the comic element is increased.

The romantic-fantastic element of the work is provided by the last scene. Heralded by the sound of the poetic horn preceding Fenton's exquisite sonnet, and concluded by the beautiful comedy, it spreads itself like a great fresco, while the music enchants the ear by its sheer magic. In spite of the lively action it is the music which dominates to the very end.

Remembering always the composer's insistence that the work is a comedy, one should take the final fugue not as the moral to a fairy tale but as the "congedo" (farewell) to the Commedia dell'Arte so genially re-created by Verdi. Yet, as Eleonora Duse wrote to Arrigo Boito, *"Com'e' triste la tua commedia"* ("How sad is your comedy"). And indeed it is true that, even in the midst of so much gaiety, there is the faintest touch of melancholy.

11.

ALTHOUGH THE YEAR 1951 had started well for me it continued badly. While I was singing in *Un Ballo in Maschera* in Calabria a badly built bridge collapsed on stage and my leg was severely injured. Not only did this launch me on a dreary lawsuit which lasted for years but it also meant the cancellation of engagements abroad and very nearly compelled me to abandon the South African tour which I had arranged with such care for Gigli and myself. In the end I went—on crutches—and our enthusiastic reception must, I think, have contributed toward my eventual recovery.

The most treasured memento of this trip was a lion cub we acquired for Cecilia, who received him with open arms. He was christened Figaro and became a devoted member of our household, striking up a particularly good relationship with our cat, from whom he learned how to open doors. He was with us for a year before he became too big for domestic life and had to be presented to the Rome zoo. We visited him there as often as we could but he soon became indifferent to our presence, except for one occasion when I called Cecilia loudly by name and he turned his splendid head and looked at us as though something stirred far back in his memory. His interest and affections were now centered on a beautiful lioness by whom he had several cubs. He was devoted to her and when she fell ill and died he retired to a corner of his enclosure, refused all food and drink, and pined away. He attained a sort of fame by being written up in one newspaper as "The lion who died from love," and I am inclined to think that poor Figaro really did merit that description.

Not long after Figaro's acquisition we all went to South America—to Rio and Sao Paolo—during which time our friend Madame Wolf-Ferrari, the widow of the composer, took over the job of what might be called lion-sitting. This was the unfortunate trip when there was so much bad feeling generated among the artists, and the only person who seemed to derive great fun from the whole affair was Cecilia. She was on splendid terms with Gigli, who was one of the company, and when she became too much of a nuisance in my dressing room and I irritably told her to go away and stop worrying me, she would reply: "Then I'll go and see Gigli instead."

Very soon I would hear roars of laughter coming from Gigli's dressing room, and finally he would lead her to the door where I would hear him say: "Go along, Cecilia! If you make me laugh any more I shan't be able to sing."

He also indulged her in another way, which was a great novelty at the time. He was the only one of us who had a television set in his apartment, and he used to say: "If you will sit very quietly and watch the screen while I rest in my room you can come in." So there she used to sit, swinging her legs which were too short to reach the ground, and Gigli seemed to like having her around.

It was on this tour that I sang for the first time with Maria Callas, who was to become the greatest of all my colleagues. Tilde and I had already heard her once in *La Gioconda*, with which she had made her first impact on the Italian audience. Now I sang with her myself in *La Traviata*.

Looking back, I cannot believe that anyone else in the whole history of the work ever sang that first act as she sang it then. Later perhaps she looked the part more convincingly, later she may have added certain refinements to her characterization of the role, but I find it impossible to describe the electrifying brilliance of the coloratura, the beauty, the sheer magic of that sound which she poured out then. And with it—perfect diction, color, inflection, and above all feeling. It was something one hears only once in a lifetime. Indeed, one is fortunate to hear it once!

In 1953 I joined her in the recording of *Lucia* under Serafin in Florence and then, later the same year, came the first recording of *Tosca* under De Sabata. This was the beginning of a long professional association in both recording and stage work, an association so complete in its integration and understanding that I think I may claim the right as well as the privilege to write at some length about what was one of the most amazing appearances in all opera.

I think of Maria—and I venture to believe that she thought of me too —as a friend as well as colleague; and, as far as one can say one understands a fellow-artist, I came to understand something of her. First and foremost she was a diva, in the sense that she was set apart: not just in the top rank but beyond even that—something unique. This meant that people demanded the impossible of her, so that she forever carried the burden of having to reaffirm her supremacy or else be regarded (by herself as well as by others) as in some sense failing. Such a unique position creates a great loneliness and a sense of responsibility so crushing in its weight that it is almost more than a human being can bear.

For a singer this striving for eternal perfection is particularly cruel, for the singer—unlike every other musical performer—is his or her own instrument. If the singer is sick, so is the voice. If the singer is under a great strain, so is the voice. If the singer is shaking with terror, only the most reliable technique will save the voice from doing the same.

Self-appointed critics tend to say: "If you have a good, well-trained voice you should be able to sing well." But it really is not as simple as that. There are so many other factors, particularly in the case of an opera singer who has to act as well as sing. And it is not acting in the sense of straight stage acting. All must be contained within the musical form. You cannot pause on a word for added dramatic effect. The music does not allow you to declaim, "To be"—pause for effect with hand on brow—"or not to be." The integration of acting and singing must be absolute. In Callas this integration became nothing short of miraculous. Her musical and dramatic instincts were faultless, and her dedication to her art was total. In consequence she did not suffer fools gladly, particularly in her earlier, less patient days, and I am bound to say—why should she? For she never demanded from anyone else a standard for which she was not herself prepared to strive.

It would be absurd to pretend there were not times when she behaved badly—when she was, as people loved to say of her, highly temperamental. Sometimes she was undoubtedly in the wrong, sometimes the stories were complete invention, and sometimes she was fully justified in her reaction—as on the much-publicized and photographed occasion in Chicago when some fellow without even the manners to take off his hat tried to serve a writ on her as she came from the stage. She was perfectly justified in thrusting him from her path with words of furious contempt. How dared this oaf lay a hand on someone who had just given 99 per cent of everything she had and was, in her effort to serve her art and her public? Suppose she did owe money—the matter could have waited for a couple of hours. To attack any artist at such a time is contemptible.

My own single serious brush with Maria also occurred in Chicago, in 1954, and perhaps deserves a full account since I can personally vouch for the truth of it. I also give it as an illustration of what sometimes happened in the highly charged atmosphere in which this controversial figure moved. It was during a performance of *Traviata*. The second act, with its superb duets between Violetta and the elder Germont, had gone splendidly; she had left the stage, the short scene between Alfredo and me had taken place, and I had sung my final aria which practically closes the act. Then, as the curtain fell, something went wrong with the mechanism so that one half of the curtain came down while the other remained up and then vice versa, all to the amusement of the audience. As the technicians struggled to sort things out people backstage were saying desperately: "Go out and take another call, Mr. Gobbi, until we get this damned thing right."

I looked around, inquiring once or twice for Maria and the tenor to join me, but was forced to take several solo calls—to considerable applause. Out of the corner of my eye I saw Maria's husband, Battista Meneghini, go off in the direction of her dressing room and presently she joined me for the last call and, the curtain having decided to behave by now, we went off to our respective dressing rooms.

As the interval lengthened out extraordinarily someone came to me to tell me that Madame Callas was very angry with me and wanted to see me in her dressing room. I went along there, passing Meneghini in the doorway.

"They tell me you are angry with me, Maria," I said. "What is the matter?"

"Shut the door," she ordered, as though I were a servant. And then: "You must understand that I will not allow anyone to interfere with the success of *my Traviata*. If you ever do such a thing again I will ruin your career."

As will be imagined, I took a deep breath at this. Then I replied very calmly: "You were right to suggest that we close the door. Now—first I have always understood that it was Verdi's *Traviata*. As for what happened with the curtain, I did what seemed best at the time, with no thought of harming my colleagues. Your saying you will ruin my career is just a piece of nonsense. It is true you are a power in the opera world, but I also have some power and don't forget that I arrived on the scene ten years before you did. I give you three minutes now to go on the stage and continue the performance. Otherwise I go out and explain to the audience exactly what happened—and you know I will do it."

I left her then. Two minutes later she passed my door on her way to the stage.

The third act went beautifully and just before the last act I went onto the stage to check the layout, as I usually do. Only the work light was on and suddenly from the shadowed bed a rather subdued voice said in Venetian dialect: *"Tito, s'i tu rabià?"* ("Tito, are you angry with me?")

"Oh, Maria," I replied. "Are you already there?"

"Yes. Are you still angry with me?"

"No, Maria, I'm not angry," I said more or less truthfully, for there was something so silly and childlike and touching about this tentatively offered little olive branch that it would have taken a harder man than I am to reject it. "We all have our nervous explosions at times. Now forget about it."

I never had any real trouble with her again, and in later years there were times when she would not take on certain engagements unless she had my support.

This is a rather extreme case of temperamental behavior, but when I told her that we all have our nervous explosions it was true. I can myself recall a few times when I kicked things around the dressing room. I hope those occasions will never be chronicled but, if they are, may they be recorded with a little charity.

On the subject of Maria's total dedication to her art, of which I have spoken, there were some interesting personal results, none more so than the dramatic change she made in what might be called her public image. It was, I remember, during the 1953 recording of *Lucia* in Florence, when we were all lunching together, that Maestro Serafin ventured to tell Maria she ate too much and was allowing her weight to become a problem. She protested that when she ate well she sang well and, anyway, she was not *so* heavy.

With a lack of gallantry which surprises me now, I remarked that there was a weighing machine just outside the restaurant door and suggested she should put the matter to the test. We went there together and, after the shock of reading what the machine recorded, she gave me her handbag and her coat and kicked off her shoes. All the palliatives that most of us have tried in our time! The result was still somewhat dismaying, and she became rather silent. In one's middle twenties—which was all she was then—it is not pleasant to have to face the hard facts of excessive overweight.

I saw her only briefly later that year, when we recorded *Tosca*. In the following year, when we were to record again, I was coming from the theater one morning when a voice called: "Tito!" And I turned to see a lovely, tall young woman in a long coat. She flung open the coat and demanded: "What do you think of me now?" And I realized that it was Maria, completely transformed.

"Maria," I said with all my heart, "you—look—beautiful."

At which she gave me a smiling, sidelong glance from those lovely long eyes of hers and said, with an enchanting touch of coquetry: "Tito, are you courting me?"

"Of course!" I replied. "May I join the queue, Maria?"

To myself I said: "She is really awakened now; she knows she is a woman and a beautiful one at that."

I think it was her absolute determination to channel everything into becoming a world star which had induced her to make that dramatic change, and for good or ill it made her a world figure overnight. Now she was not only supremely gifted both musically and dramatically—she was a beauty too. And her awareness of this invested with fresh magic every role she undertook. What it eventually did to her vocal and nervous stamina I am not prepared to say. I only assert that she blossomed into an artist unique in her generation and outstanding in the whole range of vocal history.

Later when we frequently partnered each other in *Tosca* we worked marvelously together, deeply respecting and considering each other for the sake of the performance. During the rehearsals we would study and arrange everything together. Then at the performance we threw ourselves into an exciting adventure, in the absolute certainty that each of us would complete successfully any sudden change. This bold and inebriating freedom gave us moments of supreme excitement rarely experienced on stage. We were never Callas and Gobbi. We *were* Tosca and Scarpia. In some indefinable way we would sense exactly what the other was going to do and even if—as is bound to happen from time to time—something went wrong we would not only work it into the action so that no one guessed there was an emergency, we would even sometimes turn it to an advantage.

I remember once, in the second act of *Tosca,* at the moment when Cavaradossi is dragged away with Tosca clinging to him, one of the men (as the action demands) pushed her away and, as she staggered back, she either forgot or did not notice that there was a small step behind her and she fell heavily. From the other side of the stage I asked her with my eyes, "Are you hurt?" and with an answering glance she was able to reassure me. But, realizing what a fine piece of stage "business" we could make of this, I went over to her and disdainfully extended my left hand to her. Immediately, also realizing what could be done, she almost clawed her way up my arm on the pleading word, "Salvatelo!" ("Save him!") To which I replied ironically, "Io?—Voi!" ("I?—No, you!") and let go of her, whereupon she dropped back despairingly on the ground with such apparent helplessness and pathos that a slight gasp of indignant sympathy ran through the house. She needed no instructions, no hint of what was in my mind theatrically speaking. She *knew* and made the perfect completion of what I had started.

With Maria it was not performing but living. Today I could not say with certainty what happened here or there, at a rehearsal or a performance, so intense was our commitment. But on one occasion at Covent Garden—I think it was at a dress rehearsal before an audience—I suddenly realized that, when she had backed against Scarpia's desk, her head hanging backward, she had put her wig in the flame of one of the candles and smoke was beginning to rise from the back of her head. I went over and took told of her, putting my hand on the back of her head as though to draw her into an unwanted embrace, and managed to put out the smoldering curls.

Fully confident and relying on me, she never made a false movement. We simply went on acting and singing. She waited for my help and just whispered, *"Grazie, Tito,"* when the chance came. *That* was Callas.

On another occasion, in Paris in 1959, we were invited to take part in a big gala. We were to do the second act of *Tosca* with only one rehearsal. When we arrived for the rehearsal we found no one in charge or with the remotest idea about what was to be done, and the actors for the minor roles were wandering about aimlessly, most of them loaded with irrelevant theatrical props. There was a good deal of talking and no action: whether from inefficiency or sabotage I am not quite sure.

Suddenly Maria stood up and demanded silence and everyone's attention. She flatly declared that the performance must take place and that, in view of the total lack of organization and co-operation, she had arrived at a final decision. Then she turned to me and said: "Tito, please will you be the producer and try to organize this performance? And from this moment everybody will obey you!"

So authoritative was she that no one queried this decision and, although I had not had any real experience of producing, it never occurred to me to refuse her request. Everything went smoothly from that moment. Everyone obeyed my direction, including Maria herself. At that time she had not yet become the great Tosca of her later years and when in the stabbing scene she raised her hand menacingly with the knife I said: "No, no Maria! If you lifted the knife as high as that I would be able to see what was coming and would take evasive action."

She accepted my instruction like the humblest member of the cast; and her perfect example of professionalism and dedication to the work at hand made everyone else give to me the unquestioned obedience they would have given to the most experienced producer. And that was Callas!

In contrast, I remember one day in New York she was alone and I asked her to join us for dinner. She gladly accepted and played like a young girl with Cecilia, but when we took her later to the hotel lift she suddenly turned to us and said: "I feel so lonely. I haven't even my little dog with me here. Wouldn't you like to offer me just another ice cream?" And that was Maria.

Again, much later—indeed, as late as October 1967, when she was virtually in retirement—Tilde and I were celebrating my birthday in London with a small group of friends at the Savoy Grill when suddenly Maria appeared smiling in the doorway, her beautiful eyes shining. As she made her way toward our table she said, without raising her voice but with that effortless projection of words which was one of her great gifts: "Tito, I remembered it was your birthday today. I have just flown over from Paris to wish you a happy birthday. May I join the party?"

It can be imagined with what delight we welcomed her. The next morning I wanted to send her flowers but the hotel staff informed me that she had already left for Paris. She had truly come just for my birthday. And that was Maria.

When in January 1964 she made her great comeback in *Tosca* at Covent Garden (after two or three years of semi-retirement) it was an event of worldwide interest. It is impossible to describe the sensation it caused and, to a creature of Maria's sensibility, it must have been sheer torture. I suppose there are few more appalling ordeals than to make a stage comeback when you are headline news; far worse than any debut. Mercilessly caught in the crossfire of public searchlights, you hang there suspended for all to observe and criticize. Triumph or crucifixion? You are battling for the one, but fate may deal you the other.

Everyone at the Royal Opera House was frantically afraid that she would cancel at the last moment. Sander Gorlinsky, her manager, had no time for anything else. The strictest orders were given that no one should be admitted at any rehearsal and the only reports issued were brief ones to the effect that everything was going well.

One charming incident in connection with this secrecy is worth recording. Maria stayed away from a rehearsal of Act II one day because of a slight cold, and John Copley stood in for her. On this occasion it so happened that a distinguished titled lady came to the box office to pick up her tickets and, realizing that a rehearsal was in progress, she implored Sergeant Martin to allow her just one glimpse of the diva: if he would just open the door a single crack . . . The poor man, with all the solemn authority for which he is famed, explained that he simply could not do so, not even for such a distinguished lady. Well, would he just for one moment open the little window connected with the house so that she might at least hear a note or two from that famous voice?

With this request Sergeant Martin complied and at that moment John Copley, lying in my arms with beard and glasses, let out an excruciating shriek: "Ah piu' non posso, ah che orrore."

"Ah, the unmistakable voice!" whispered the delighted lady to Sergeant Martin. "Thank you, thank you." And she went away quite satisfied.

But there were not many of these lighter moments for any of us as the first night drew near. To some extent David Webster had put Maria in my care—to coax, to reassure, to support her insofar as one colleague can support another; and never, I think, did I prize a trust more highly. We worked very hard, since Maria was always a tremendously disciplined artist, but after the long rehearsals she would phone me at great length to discuss our parts and go over them all again. At the dress rehearsal, looking a mere girl in the beautiful pale pink dress which Zeffirelli had decreed for her, she was scared to death but sang resolutely and acted superbly. The clicking of cameras backstage made the place sound like an office with twenty typists and, in the atmosphere of nervous tension, even David Webster must, I feel sure, have had some difficulty in maintaining his slight customary smile.

January 21, 1964. Here is Tilde's description of that never-to-be-forgotten night, written in her diary next morning.

"What a night! A beautiful performance, though for the first time in my life I heard the 'Vissi d'arte' go without applause." (My own view is that the audience was too spellbound by the drama to interrupt with ill-timed applause.) "The second act was unbelievable: two giants, and they bowed to one another before the curtain like two gallant opponents. The stage was invaded after the endless ovation. I have seen for myself the self-controlled English people go mad, take off their coats, scarves, or whatever and wave them in enthusiasm. Tito was great and it was wonderful to see the perfect reactions of the two of them. Maria certainly gave a big shake-up to the character of Tosca, making her much more human and extrovert. But this can be done *only by her*. Others who would try to imitate—beware!"

In spite of her tremendous, unparalleled triumph she remained desperately nervous. On each day of performance she would phone me to say she could not sing—she had no voice left, or else she must change everything in the second act. I would be half an hour on the telephone consoling the poor girl and encouraging her. "All right," I would say, "you don't sing. It is enough for you to appear. You just act and I'll do the singing. . . . All right, you change whatever you want. You know we understand each other—" and so on.

In the evening she would come by my dressing room before going onstage and I would take her to the wings, holding her icy hand and whispering encouragement while rivulets of perspiration would be running down her neck and the edge of her dress. Yet when she came off stage after her exquisitely sung duet with Cioni she would clasp my hand and wish me luck and stand there waiting until my first phrase had been sung. Indeed, there was something utterly touching in the way she would show endearing flashes of concern for others however deeply absorbed she might be in her own ordeal. When Cecilia arrived in London it was Maria, not I, who said to her: "Tonight your father and I are going to sing for you."

We gave six performances in London and we repeated the same teamup in Paris and New York. I doubt if anyone who was present at those performances will ever forget them. I know I never shall—not only for the artistic peak which they reached but for the extraordinary rapport and understanding between us.

Probably millions of words have been written about La Callas, and quite a few about the vulnerable, lonely, elusive creature who was Maria. There is little I can add. She shone for all too brief a while in the world of opera, like a vivid flame attracting the attention of the whole world, and she had a strange magic which was all her own.

I always thought she was immortal—and *she is*.

12.

ANY ARTIST attempting to give an account of his life and career faces the constant danger of lapsing into lists of dates, places, and performances. Nothing, alas, is more boring. If the account is verbal one gradually realizes that, although the listener still wears a glazed smile of polite attention, his thoughts are clearly elsewhere—and small blame to him. If the attempt is being made in writing the enterprise is haunted by uneasy recollections of those many memoirs which are lavishly sprinkled with, "I sang So-and-so in such-and-such a place with immense success" (or even "without much success," though this admission is less frequent) "but when I came to Somewhere-else the reception was even more enthusiastic."

On the other hand, any history, whether of mankind in general or of the humblest individual in particular, becomes confusing and imprecise without signposts of some sort. So one must try to steer a careful course between the Scylla of endless dates and the Charybdis of confusion. The early years of a career usually merit some detailed consideration since it is then that the seeds are planted and to them that later developments can be traced; which is why I have dealt with my own beginnings rather fully. By the middle 1950s I had become an international artist of some standing. For Tilde and me the days of hard struggle were virtually over and we had moved to the beautiful apartment in the Via Asmara in Rome which was to be our home for many years to come.

Undoubtedly one of the outstanding influences to enter our lives at this period was Sander Gorlinsky, who became—and has remained ever since —my agent and impresario. At first I was not overenthusiastic about accepting any management, having decided, after some disillusioning experiences in the United States, that I would manage my own affairs. (Our friend John Joel had already given up management in England.) I knew that Gorlinsky was the man who had masterminded the visit of La Scala to Covent Garden in 1950, though it was not until years later when we were close friends that he told me the fascinating story of how this was done on an almost nonexistent bank balance, a cool nerve, and quite extraordinary vision. So when it was first suggested that I should become one of his artists I hemmed and hawed and said, "Discuss it with Tilde," or "Get me an engagement with the Covent Garden Company and we'll see."

Sander still laughs about this as my first appearance with the Covent Garden Company turned out to be the easiest thing to secure. I was singing in a provincial concert—in Manchester, I think—when Sander telephoned to say that a last-minute replacement was required at Covent Garden for Renato in *Ballo in Maschera*. I drove at top speed to London and arrived just in time to scramble into my costume and rush onstage. No one even had time to tell me that at Covent Garden they did what is usually called "the Swedish version," that is to say the version in which the period and country are those in which Verdi originally set the work as distinct from the earlier period and the Boston setting to which he had to alter the story for the sake of sensitive political feelings at the time of composition. I coped fairly well with the alteration in names but nearly tripped up over the fact that I was used to stabbing the hero when I assassinated him in the last act. I was just groping for my dagger when one of the chorus thrust a pistol into my hand.

"What do I want a gun for?" I muttered.

"We shoot him here," replied the chorister out of the corner of his mouth. And so I dispatched my victim with the correct weapon.

While I was still procrastinating over the possibility of Gorlinsky's taking over the management of my affairs, he, it transpired, was willing to go to great lengths to clinch the deal. It so happened that Tilde and I were visiting my hometown that summer, and when we arrived in Bassano who should be walking patiently up and down outside the principal hotel—eating an ice cream—but Sander Gorlinsky? So we sat down and discussed plans then and there and came to an amicable arrangement, which has never been regretted. Sander and his delightful wife Edith became two of our closest friends and subsequently joined us on many holidays together. To give a final glimpse of the sentimental streak in one who is usually regarded as the toughest of businessmen: it was Sander who remembered the twenty-fifth anniversary of our historic meeting and who wanted to arrange for every child in Bassano (about five thousand of them, I believe) to have an ice cream like the one he had been consuming when we finally met and settled our agreement.

This was also the period when I was making contacts and forging links with various cities and managements which were to have a lasting influence on my life and work. Of these perhaps the most important, and certainly the most regular and longstanding, was my relationship with Chicago.

In 1954 I was invited by Carol Fox to take part in the star-spangled fall season which she was promoting at the Lyric Theatre, and late in October Tilde, Cecilia, and I flew to Chicago for my first appearance there. Carol was then a brilliant, lively young woman with the most ambitious plans for bringing back opera to Chicago in a big way. In little more than twenty years she has succeeded in bringing the Lyric Opera to a very high standard and has won for it world renown. During the first years the late Lawrence Kelly (who presently left to manage the Dallas Opera) and the conductor Nicola Rescigno worked in association with her, but subsequently Carol herself became general manager in charge of administration, artistic policy, finance, and pretty well everything else— and proceeded to show that her over-all grasp of the various aspects of management was extraordinary. Our old and valued friend Pino Donati was also to contribute his unrivaled judgment and experience in the matter of season-planning, and the gifted Maestro Bruno Bartoletti became resident conductor.

The whole remarkable achievement is something of which America can well be proud (particularly, I would say, American women), for they have in Chicago an opera director of outstanding quality who is purely American. I myself am proud to have taken part in the growth of this fine enterprise, as singer, producer, and (unofficially appointed) general adviser. I have even been called the Lyric's godfather, though not in the Marlon Brando sense. During my long working experience with Carol I have had every opportunity to appreciate her clarity of vision, courage, and immense day-to-day capability. But this is to accord only professional appreciation. What is unique in my experience is the warmth—almost the exuberance—of the friendliness with which she can enhance her working relationships. We have had our differences, of course—what else in so long an association?—but these drop away when I recall the birthday parties she planned with such affection, generosity, and humor, her sympathy in moments of distress, her appreciation of extra efforts made, and so on. No wonder all the Chicago "Ins" gather around her, making the Lyric a great cultural center in the city, and I am happy to have been part of the Chicago Lyric family for more than twenty years, working in the friendliest association with so many Chicagoans.

That first season opened with Callas' incomparable Norma. A week later Simionato, Simoneau, and I sang in *Barbiere*. Two days after that Callas and Simoneau appeared in *Traviata* in which I sang the elder Germont, and later in the month Eleanor Steber, Di Stefano, and I sang in *Tosca*. Few opera enthusiasts, I imagine, would quarrel with the fare provided in those three weeks.

Before we left for Europe again it was arranged that Carol, Lawrence Kelly, Rescigno, and I should meet in Rome early in the year to discuss plans for the following season. I did not fancy myself as official talent scout but when I went to Florence in December 1954 to sing Nabucco under Serafin it seemed to me that I had found a soprano well worthy of Carol's consideration. The Abigaille was a relatively unknown girl called Anita Cerquetti: a somewhat large and unromantic figure, I have to admit, but she had a beautiful "stage" face and her voice was absolutely stunning.

When Carol arrived early in the year I tried, not very successfully at first, to interest her in my discovery. She said she was not thinking of engaging anyone unknown; she was not prepared to travel around, and so on. But I assured her that she could hear the girl right there in our drawing room. So, with Carol's rather reluctant consent, I telephoned Anita and asked her to come immediately.

When she walked into the room Carol gave me a rather disparaging glance, but when Anita opened her mouth and began to sing Amelia's first aria from *Ballo in Maschera* she nearly jumped up off the sofa with excitement. Then, containing her enthusiasm and prudently remembering the opera company's finances, she leaned toward me and asked in an urgent whisper: "Do you think we could get her fairly cheaply?"

"Don't be mean," I retorted, well pleased with the reaction. "You pay her what she's worth."

So Anita Cerquetti was added to the list of singers for the next Chicago season, and later in the year she made her American debut there with great success. Hers was a splendid talent, and it was indeed a tragedy that ill-health cut short her career before she arrived at her full powers.

Life seemed very good to Tilde and me during those early months of 1955. We were settling down in our new home and installing my parents in the home I had bought for them quite near us. Interesting engagements were crowding in upon me, including my first Michele in Puccini's *Il Tabarro* and my first Jack Rance opposite Caniglia's incomparable Minnie in *La Fanciulla del West*. I don't think anyone else ever played the card scene in Act II in quite the way she did. It was so tense that one could feel the breathless excitement coming out of the audience, and when she finally flung the pack of cards into the air with a glorious peal of triumph there was a roar of applause and approval for her successful piece of card-sharping.

Both Michele and Jack Rance are among the most fascinating of Puccini's creations and a joy to any singing actor. Among certain rather anemic gentlemen of the musical world it was customary to speak and write with a touch of condescension about Puccini, that great man of the theater. But the simple fact is that if anyone today could conceive—and then carry to musical and dramatic completion—any one of the great gallery of Puccini portraits, the world would be his.

Sander Gorlinsky had been as good as his word, and in June I came to London to sing with the Covent Garden Company in *Tosca* with Tebaldi and *Aïda* with Antonietta Stella, Stignani, and Penno. In addition I had the fascinating experience of undertaking my first sittings for the marvelous Scarpia portrait by Leonard Boden which is reproduced on the jacket of this book.

As an amateur painter I have always had a deep regard for those who bring to perfection what I myself so earnestly strive to accomplish, and I was already happy and proud to number among my friends the great Italian artists De Chirico and Gregorio Sciltian. To find in Leonard Boden and his equally gifted wife Margaret not only fine and sensitive artists but also friends for life was one of the happiest discoveries for Tilde and me that even London could provide. Not only that. It was at their studio that we first met Betty Eliot, without whom no London visit thenceforward would have been complete. To Betty we turn in every emergency, by Betty we are driven to almost every professional assignment in England, from Betty we receive a wealth of friendship which expresses itself in such kindness and efficiency that we would be hard put to it to name any aspect of our lives in which she has not been a friend and a blessing to us.

During the sittings for that Scarpia portrait I followed with the utmost appreciation every stage of the work. Today it hangs in our home just outside Rome, and even now I often pause before it to marvel afresh not only at the artistic beauty and skill of the painting but at the psychological penetration into the character of Scarpia, which is yet also somehow me.

That summer visit was not to be our only one to London that year, for in October I was to sing Iago. Although I would hesitate to list any of my roles in order of preference, there is no question that Iago is one of the greatest and most glorious challenges in the whole baritone repertoire. The psychological insight required is at least equal to the musical demands, and I admit that I was particularly eager to play this role before what I regarded as the discriminating London audience.

When I first began intensive study of the role of Iago I tried to see through the eyes of Verdi and Boito what they had taken from Shakespeare and how they had then built the character with words and music. Basically Verdi wants Iago to be a handsome, pleasant-seeming man in whom everyone has confidence and to whom everyone therefore talks freely. He must appear to have a frank disposition, though in fact his soul is devious and satanic; and this apparently honest fellow, with his distorted view of life, acts differently toward each person in the drama. He knows only too well all the people around him, and he despises them all. Because he is so different in his attitude to each person it is more than usually important to consider their various characters and reactions.

Otello is a general of the Venetian Republic, a strong and loyal soldier and a passionate lover. But he is a Moor, and in the "Love Duet" Desdemona refers to the fact that he is a freed slave. So we accept the idea of his being brought up in Venice with a smattering of "civilization" which easily rubs off under the stimulus of violent emotion. To me this clearly explains both his jealousy and Iago's success as he seeks to expose the primitive man behind the glorious façade of the hero. If one asks what is Iago's motive in all this, the answer is that he has no motive in the accepted sense of the word. He simply enjoys being evil—is indeed a supreme artist in evil—and revels in the destruction he causes as he instills jealousy into the ingenuous soul of Otello. Dramatically speaking, the change in Otello when it comes is sudden, but the transition has already been prepared in the music.

Desdemona, though she is essentially romantic and sweet-natured, is not, as is often supposed, a stupid little woman. On the contrary, she is quite a complex character, passionate and with the courage and strength to oppose the whole city and nobility of Venice to get her man. Musically speaking, her melodic line is never broken from the beginning to the very end. Her character is rather barely outlined and a fine artist must fill the gaps with grace and femininity, taking always as her best guide the music itself. On a casual assessment it may seem illogical that an intelligent and loving woman should put up with her husband's insane jealousy, but the fact is that she is taken completely by surprise. This white and gold goddess is used to getting whatever she wants from him, which is why she presses her pleas for Cassio beyond sense and safety. In the furious Otello she finds herself confronting a man she simply does not know.

Emilia is deeply attached to Desdemona, who has probably shielded her more than once from Iago. She is aware of her husband's malevolence but is too cowardly to reveal her knowledge until the end, when it is too late. Cassio is a brilliant captain, handsome, gay, elegant, always busy with love affairs and ready to talk about them, a good swordsman, jealous of his honor. Roderigo, a young Venetian gentleman, is secretly in love with Desdemona, who remains unaware of it.

With all these people Iago gets to work, varying his attitude to each of them and finding sheer delight in manipulating them for his own ends. So he goes his wicked way with no one suspecting him. This being so, it is a great mistake to play him with a sneering, Mephisto-like air. He should be gay and charming—a rather captivating fellow—as he moves around with an apparently natural simplicity, totally unsuspected. Far from being an obvious stage villain he is able by his genius for treachery and plotting to cover his tracks while throwing suspicion on others.

The costume, make-up, way of standing, moving, and walking are all important in the build-up of his personality. Whenever I had a say in my costume I kept it simple, for it should be remembered that Iago is only an ensign. In my view a dark costume is best with no more than modest braiding, black tights and short black boots giving length to the legs. The boots should be soft-soled, enabling one to adopt a panther-like tread suggestive of an animal stalking its prey. For my make-up I would use a fair foundation, with red lips and large eyes—rather engaging—and a reddish wig which left a careless quiff of hair over the forehead, giving a youthfully attractive air to an otherwise dangerous face.

In the first act I liked to wear a short cloak, the fluttering movement of which gave point to the busy way Iago moves about, pushing people around and contriving to make Cassio drunk. In the second act I would discard the cloak, concentrating on great elegance of posture as Iago gradually takes command of the scene. I would bow respectfully to Otello, until at the end of the second act, having gained my hold on him, I would bow less and less, ceasing to care about any seeming respect. To Desdemona I bowed profoundly, even when she took no notice of me. During the "Credo" I mostly remained still, thinking my thoughts aloud, for absolute composure is required here. The lightning change to action with the entrance of Otello is then all the more effective.

Although there must be no movement for movement's sake Iago must register his *presence,* particularly when he is not singing, always showing interest, taking the limelight without fussing. He drives the plot in the fullest sense of the term for it is, after all, *his* plot.

The musical portrait of Iago is by far the most vivid characterization in the opera, right from the masterly first sketch in his dialogue with Roderigo: "Ed io rimango di sua Moresca Signoria l'alfiere," the ironic trill terminating the phrase, with that quick leap an octave lower describing his nonchalance.

There are three principal moments in which he reveals himself: the "Drinking Song," the "Credo," and the "Dream"—three marvelous aspects which are a joy to perform. In the "Drinking Song" he shows himself as pleasantly frank and friendly, but the descending chromatic scales betray his insincerity. In the "Credo" (the "Credo scellerato" as Boito called it) he states his outlook and his philosophy of life in a soliloquy addressed not to the audience but to himself, as he thinks about and analyzes himself with excited cynical vanity.

How I enjoy performing the "Credo"! Before the tremendous vitality and genius of the Grand Old Man, the fearful words and impressive instrumentation, one must feel awed—even reverential. I avoid as much as possible any emphatic tone, for the words, wedded as they are to the musical phrases with harmonic precision, say all. Each time I feel as though I have been entrusted with the responsibility of revealing the soul of Iago, the words and music expressing with supreme eloquence his mocking and bitter wickedness.

Between the "Credo" and the "Dream"—the third and most subtle of Iago's solos—the ground is magically prepared by the great duet between him and Otello in Act II: one of the most exciting in all operatic literature, both for its powerful expression and the simplicity of the means used by the composer.

I carefully study my inflections. It would be wrong for instance to sing "Mio Signore" in a strong, solid tone, so I adopt an almost unctuous sound, sweet and insinuating, regretful and servile. Tonal quality has always been for me the most fascinating part of interpretation, so that over the years singing has become interesting to me almost entirely insofar as it gives new life to a character, good or bad.

In one of his letters Verdi writes: "It is impossible to perform Iago without a clear pronunciation . . . he must not sing loudly or raise his voice except on a few occasions . . . If I were an actor-singer I would 'speak' the whole part right on the lips." Significantly he puts the word "actor" first, for Iago is a mighty role for an actor, even more so in the opera than the play, I think. He is never simply bold or cynical or subtle, but a mixture of all three. His personality is marvelously outlined, sculpted, revealed from the little phrases of his dialogue, from his small hints, from the peculiar intonation of a word. I venture to say that even without the three arias he would still stand forth magnificently.

The great second act duet opens as Iago sends Cassio to Desdemona and then, pretending not to see Otello coming, speaks aloud but apparently to himself, choosing his words carefully.

"Ciò m'accora . . ." I say softly. ("I'm sorry to see that . . .")

"Che parli?" Otello asks rather abstractedly.

"Nothing—" Then I give a start of apparent surprise and exclaim, "You here?" and add almost too hastily: "I was talking nonsense."

"Was that Cassio just leaving my wife?" Otello inquires.

"Oh *no!*" The tone of this makes it a clumsy and palpable lie. "He—just ran away like a guilty man when he saw you."

That is the first dangling of the bait. But now I must make sure that Otello takes it, and so I say, "Mio Signore . . ." hesitantly and then speak smoothly, almost casually, as I begin to ask about the earlier friendship between Desdemona and Cassio. This scene is so true and intense that I almost lose myself in it, putting questions in a mellifluous tone, answering with apparent reluctance, maliciously repeating Otello's own questions as though playing for time, thus conveying the impression that something significant is being concealed.

That malicious echoing of Otello's phrases is pure gold to a subtle performer: "Nol credi onesto?" "Onesto?" "Che ascondi nel tuo core?" "Che ascondo in cor signore?"—and the orchestra echoes too. By now Iago has brought Otello where he wants him, and his own character is complete so far as the audience is concerned. The Moor is restless but not yet really alarmed. He still needs a fatal word, which Iago now supplies: "Temete, Signor, la gelosia" ("Beware, my lord, of jealousy") —an apparent warning against the very emotion he is carefully instilling in Otello's heart.

Otello is now roused, but demands evidence. Iago indicates that this is not absolutely available but advises watchful caution, repeating the word "vigilate" three times as Desdemona, serenely unaware of anything amiss, enters and proceeds to add weight to Otello's dawning suspicions by interceding earnestly for Cassio's pardon. This brings the first outburst from Otello, in which he seizes Desdemona's handkerchief and throws it on the floor. Although it is Emilia who picks it up, Iago wrenches it from her. He had not planned this, but instantly his genius suggests to him how the handkerchief might be used as evidence.

The women gone, Iago enjoys Otello's desperation as his conviction of Desdemona's betrayal grows. He looks at Otello, exulting in the ruin he has caused. Then, going close to him, he falsely begs him not to make so much of a trifle. This provokes such fury that Otello actually lays hands on Iago, who immediately falls to the floor, exaggerating the force of Otello's attack and assuming a half-frightened reaction. But he quickly regains control and recalls a strange incident when, he pretends, he overheard Cassio in a dream speak of love passages with Desdemona.

In the famous (or infamous) "Dream" I feel as though I am suspended on a very fine thread as I begin to instill poison into Otello, calculating the effect on my victim of every word, every note, every nuance. The opening phrases are innocuous; there is still time for me to retreat if I produce a reaction beyond my intention. But as I feel my way and realize that I am succeeding I increase the intensity of what I am saying; and the intensity of the music increases too until the description of Cassio's ecstasy has the rhythm and thrust of a sexual encounter. Within the space of a few bars, and by the subtlest of means, Verdi creates a sense of eroticism which makes nonsense of the puerile obsession with breasts and buttocks and reproductive organs that afflicts so many producers today. The insinuation is so graceful, the elegance of the music so compelling, the accent on the word "Moro" so exquisite and deadly that the wretched Otello almost feels himself present at the scene of his own betrayal.

Then for good measure his tormentor refers to the famous handkerchief which he claims to have seen in the hands of Cassio. Otello's conviction of his wife's guilt is complete, and Act II ends with the famous "giuramento" duet in a scene so dramatically beautiful and so powerfully expressive that I doubt if it has ever been equaled and certainly never surpassed.

By the beginning of Act III I am totally at one with Iago; his words and actions are my words and actions; almost, I could say, his thoughts are my thoughts. Busily preparing the final trap I remind Otello to ask Desdemona about the handkerchief, whispering the fatal word "fazzoletto" on the very threshold of the room before taking my leave and bowing deeply to Desdemona as she enters. The dialogue between husband and wife subtly alternates between affectionate appeals on her side and bursts of fury and bitter irony on his until, brutally insulted by him, she runs from the stage, both of them now in a state of utter desperation. Left alone Otello breaks into the magnificent "Dio mi potevi scagliar," the orchestra accompanying the voice like a lament, rising into a lyrical phrase and ending in the outburst of vengeance.

At this point, perfectly timed, I make my entrance, announcing the approach of Cassio. Without ceremony I push into hiding the man to whom I had been bowing only a few hours ago and turn to welcome the rather doubtful Cassio. I start the brilliant conversation with reference to his loves and adventures and soon have him laughing and ready to talk. At that point I start spinning a web for my captive flies with elegant phrases going from stage to orchestra in a marvelous display, punctuated by the sobbing interjections of the hidden Otello. The episode of the "fazzoletto" is so skillfully prepared and handled that Otello is completely convinced of Desdemona's guilt. Cassio, though slightly puzzled about where the "fazzoletto" comes from, willingly continues to discourse about his conquests. And I? I just enjoy the game, singing with warning mockery, "Questa è una ragna" ("What a spider's web").

Broken though he is, Otello must still go on and receive in state the Venetian ambassador, though he hardly knows any longer what he is doing. In a delirium of fury he insults his wife, throwing her to the ground, before turning threateningly on everyone and finally collapsing. Iago, only temporarily shaken by the news that Cassio has been named the new governor of Cyprus ("Inferno e morte!"), immediately begins to gather up the loose ends, setting Roderigo against Cassio and inspiring Otello to kill Desdemona. During the great ensemble, in which everyone else is still, he moves around from one to another, prompting to action and completing the trap he has devised.

After the final collapse of Otello, when Iago and he are alone together, I believe in playing Iago with the minimum of movement. The Lion of Venice, indeed! I look at him sardonically. I do not push him with my foot—I just sneer, for he is of no interest to me any more. I have destroyed him. Nor do I furtively climb the throne as though I wanted it. That is quite wrong. Iago, who is wicked for the sheer pleasure of being an artist in evil, has completed what he set out to do. Everything he has planned will now happen without his being there, as usual.

It is not his intention that he and Otello should exchange any other words, and what they have to say over the dead body of Desdemona is brief in the extreme. "Discolpati!" ("Clear yourself!") Otello says almost imploringly. But there is no reply, no justification to be made. Iago flings at Otello the one contemptuous word "No" and runs away.

In a note by Giulio Ricordi which I found he says: "The tremolo in the orchestra in this scene must be prolonged as far as needed before the word 'No.'" Then the world narrows down to the tragic couple, the final bars depicting the great love story in a celestial atmosphere.

Loving the role of Iago as I did, and believing—I hope not too arrogantly—that there was something rather special in my presentation of it, I looked forward to that London visit in October 1955 with an excited eagerness which I had seldom felt in my life before.

Tilde and I arrived in London rather late in the evening on account of fog, and I immediately telephoned from the airport to the opera house inquiring about the rehearsal schedule. I learned to my relief that only the last act was in process of rehearsal that evening and, as Iago has no more than an explosive phrase or two before his final exit, I congratulated myself on not having missed anything vital.

Next morning I presented myself at the opera house, full of enthusiasm for the long-awaited task, and was informed that Maestro Kubelik, the musical director, had already replaced me as I had failed to attend the rehearsal the previous evening. Explanations about the fog, about the realization that my two or three phrases could hardly have been missed, about anything that I had done or not done were of no avail. Kubelik did not want me and did not intend to have me.

Someone else would be singing Iago.

Macbeth.

Clockwise from top left, as Marcello in Puccini's La Bohème. *Jack Rance, the ruthless sheriff in Puccini's* La Fanciulla del West. *The Babylonian king Nebuchadnezzar (Nabucco) in Verdi's opera. Count Almaviva in Mozart's* Marriage of Figaro.

Opposite, as Amonasro, the savage chieftain who is the father of Aida in Verdi's opera.

With Amy Shuard in the London production of Verdi's Macbeth. *Below, close-up of Rigoletto taken from the prompter's box.*

Above, Brothers-in-law Boris Christoff and Tito Gobbi in Don Carlo (1963). Left, Gianni Schicchi, in Puccini's opera, assesses his chances of cheating the rascally relations of Buoso Donati and enriching himself.

Baron Scarpia, the aristocratic villain in Puccini's Tosca. *Opposite, Act II with the incomparable Maria Callas in the famous Zeffirelli production in London.*

Leonard Boden's studio in London, where a portrait of Queen Elizabeth II is flanked by the Pope on one side and Baron Scarpia on the other.

13.

I AM NOT, I think I can claim, a man to nurse grievances, and only three times in my whole career do I remember feeling a sense of raging resentment. The first occasion was when I was quite young, and it marked the painful transition from the rather happy-go-lucky fellow who expected everything to go right to the disillusioned young man who was forced to realize that the world could sometimes be a very unfair place. I had been engaged in 1937 to sing in the summer season at the open-air theater at Castello Sforzesco in Milan, as the Herald in *Lohengrin*, under Maestro Failoni, and as Silvio in *Pagliacci*.

From the beginning of the *Lohengrin* rehearsals I realized that for some reason Failoni disliked me. Even now I am not quite sure what it was about me which irritated him. It could have been that he thought I was more sure of myself than I really was or that I dressed the wrong way, having adopted a slightly informal attire suitable to the very hot weather but not perhaps to the demands of a rather formal maestro. Anyway, whatever the reason, I obviously found no favor in his sight. When at one rehearsal I had delivered myself rather well of the Herald's first announcement and the orchestra accorded me friendly applause by tapping with their bows on their music stands, he broke off the rehearsal in a fury and said it was for him to accord or withhold approval. He then made me repeat the announcement again—and again—until I made an error, at which he dismissed me from the cast, saying he did not wish to see this idiot again.

At this Manacchini (whom I later replaced as Lelio and with whom I was good friends) came forward and said that if the maestro wished to dispense with his Herald he could also count himself without his Telramund, and arm in arm we left the stage together.

Much though I appreciated my colleague's loyal defense I now began to find myself in a very awkward position. I sang my performances of Silvio (not under Maestro Failoni) with quite good success; but not only were my fees for the Herald withheld, I also could not get hold of my money for the Silvio performances. Tilde and I had not been very long married at that time and were having to count our money very carefully indeed. Our landlady at the modest pensione where we lived kindly accepted my shamed and stumbling assurances that as soon as I was paid we would settle our bill, but we saw our small reserve dwindling at an alarming rate.

The summer season at Castello Sforzesco was run by the City of Milan and had nothing whatever to do with La Scala, so I took myself along to the appropriate office—situated about an hour's walk from our pensione—and tried to get the money which was owed to me. Each time I was told that Signor Colombo (I remember his name painfully to this day) was out or too busy to see me.

For Tilde and me any riotous living was now reduced to a refreshing drink in the local fountain, long walks, and surreptitious glances at newspapers and magazines on newspaper stands—until one day the indignant woman in charge of a stand popped out and demanded why we didn't *buy* a paper. I was so taken aback—being rather a shy youth—that I blushed scarlet and stammered out the explanation: that we had no money to buy a paper.

"You can't afford a *paper?*" She was astounded that these two young things in their grubby white attire should have sunk so low, and she generously undertook to lend us some of her wares from time to time provided we would bring them back in good condition. This we agreed to do; and for years afterward whenever I visited Milan in more prosperous days I would call in to see her, with a bottle of wine or a *panettone* to commemorate her kindness to us.

Still my fees were not forthcoming; only the familiar excuses. One day, in a passion of fury quite unlike the easygoing fellow I had been until then, I affected to accept the usual excuse but slipped past the doorman instead and, kicking in the door of Mr. Colombo's office, stood over him with a heavy ruler snatched from his own desk and demanded my money—in cash and at once.

I got the money all right, but the sense of injustice which had prompted this uncharacteristic action and the bruises inflicted on my self-respect remained for a long time. If in the days of my maturity I had been asked about the incident I suppose I would have said I had forgotten about it long ago. But on that terrible day at Covent Garden in 1955, when I was told I was no longer required for Iago, I was suddenly once again the stupefied, disillusioned Tito Gobbi of eighteen years before.

Tilde shared my unbelief and dismay—and pain. The disappointment was all the greater for the high and happy hopes with which we had arrived. There was also a bitter sense of grievance at the unfairness of the decision and at the silent co-operation of the artist who replaced me. I am proud to say that in all my career I myself have never agreed to replace somebody without his personal consent or a convincing explanation from the opera management. I would commend this course to all artists from the very beginning of their careers.

David Webster, with whom I was on excellent terms, could do nothing except insist that I was paid for the whole contract—a generous gesture which I appreciated, though it was really a case where money hardly mattered. All I wanted now was to shake the dust of London from my feet, but unfortunately this I could not do, for two reasons. One was that I had to stay for a concert to which I was committed. The other was that Walter Legge, my ever-good friend from EMI, insisted that I attend that first night of *Otello*—if not on the stage, then at least in the audience, as evidence that I was not ill but had been replaced by no wish of my own. I did what was required of me, for common sense told me that Walter was right, but it was a most unhappy experience despite the expressions of indignation and sympathy I received.

At the concert, where I had the support of Ivor Newton as my accompanist, my reception was such that it seemed everyone was anxious to show their friendly sympathy in the warmest terms possible; and when we left two days later for Chicago we felt that London was dear to us still, in spite of the bitter taste in our mouths.

The Chicago season included a sensationally successful Rigoletto, which did something to soothe my wounded feelings, and then came *Ballo in Maschera* in which Cerquetti, with Björling and myself as colleagues, scored a triumph, thereby justifying all that we had predicted for her.

This checkered year ended on a note of unexpected comedy. On our way home from the United States Tilde, Cecilia, and I went to Caracas where I was to sing in performances of *Rigoletto, Pagliacci,* and *Tosca.* Neither conductor nor orchestra was exactly distinguished, but the reaction of the audience was extraordinary. After the Prologue they covered the stage with a rain of gardenias and orchids. At the end of our one-week visit the manager came to me and implored me to stay for another *Rigoletto,* but we all three wanted to get home by now and the artistic situation was not exactly tempting; so I politely refused. He pressed me further, however, and then I said frankly: "If you offered me twice my fee, tax-free, I would not stay."

"But that is exactly what I am offering you," he replied. "Twice your fee, tax-free, and a piece of jewelry for your wife and another for your daughter."

Well, that was really too good to refuse! So the Caracas audience had their second *Rigoletto,* I had my inflated fee, and Tilde and Cecilia had their jewelry.

By now I was well set on the operatic merry-go-round. No sooner were Christmas and some performances in Rome behind me than we were off to New York for my debut at the Metropolitan as Scarpia, with Zinka Milanov as Tosca and Mitropoulos conducting. This was of course at the Old Metropolitan, shabby perhaps in those last years but possessing an atmosphere beyond description. Ghosts from the glorious past lingered on stage and in the great cavern of the auditorium, and only the totally insensitive could remain unaware of them.

Frankly, the production was dreadful and made one sigh for some honest little provincial house in Italy. For one thing, during the first act no one onstage registered the slightest fear of Scarpia. He might have been any harmless fellow who happened to occupy an official position. Then in the second act, just before the "Vittoria" outburst, the young tenor who was singing Cavaradossi rushed over, seized an armchair, and, raising it threateningly above his head, advanced upon Scarpia. No one else on the stage reacted at all, except me. With no more than a black look I stopped him in his tracks, at which he lowered the chair and murmured in confusion: *"Scusi, Commendatore."*

When I inquired the reason for this inappropriate piece of stage business he replied apologetically that this was what he had been told to do. Immediately there broke out among the small army of producers and sub-producers an offended babble of discussion, mostly in German. As fortunately I had quite a serviceable knowledge of German myself I contributed a brisk comment or two which produced a somewhat disconcerted silence. I pointed out, slowly and fairly patiently, that Scarpia is surrounded by what amounts to an armed bodyguard, and the moment the prisoner raised that chair from the floor Spoletta or one of the others would have shot him dead. It was obvious that this practical explanation was not at all acceptable, but I firmly went on to make other alterations, at least insofar as my own part in the drama was concerned.

At the performance the next evening the audience's reception was delirious and, with great generosity, Zinka Milanov—who was undisputed queen of operatic New York at that time—left me alone before the curtain at the end of the second act, which was her way of adding the mark of her approval to the ovation.

Milanov did not have a reputation for being lavish with her compliments, but when she made them they had a flavor all their own. Many years later, when she had been long retired and I was myself becoming aware that all careers have to end, she came to a performance of *Madama Butterfly* in Newark, New Jersey. I was producing the opera and I had also undertaken to play Sharpless, a part I had not played for a very long time. Afterward among the people who came backstage was Milanov, and she walked up to me and said in her forthright way: "You are quite simply the greatest Sharpless I have ever seen. I only wish I were young enough to sing Butterfly." It may not be very modest of me to repeat this, but such a tribute from such a quarter is something to be cherished. I count it one of the finest compliments I ever received and so I allow myself the indulgence of putting it on record.

After that first *Tosca* at the Met, Mr. Bing sent for me. I supposed he wanted to congratulate me on the success of the performance, but I could not have been more mistaken. When I arrived in his office I found him sitting more or less in state, flanked on either side by what looked like most of the production heads of the opera house. I was not quite sure whether I was being regarded as a prisoner in the dock or an anatomical specimen. Then Mr. Bing explained with a rather severe expression on his face that it seemed I had made something of a revolution in the *Tosca* production, and this could not be permitted. The production was not a new one and any artist brought into the cast was expected to fit himself into the existing idea of the work.

I replied, with some sharpness, that this was indeed usually the best arrangement. "But," I went on, "in this case I think you invited me because I am already an acknowledged Scarpia. I don't want to teach anybody, but certainly there are few people who can teach me anything about this role. As for the chair attack in the second act, which you all seem to think is such an effective idea, I must tell you that it is simply absurd. As I have already explained to these gentlemen Scarpia is surrounded by an armed bodyguard and *anyone* raising a chair against him would be shot immediately. Maybe if you like it that way we will do it that way and finish the performance at the end of the second act. I don't mind."

There was a certain amount of throat-clearing and foot-shuffling at this, in the middle of which I said mildly: "As a matter of fact when you called me here I thought it was to congratulate me on the success of the performance."

"Of course, of course." Mr. Bing then not only offered warm congratulations and thanks but began to talk of other roles in which they would be happy to have me. I managed not to smile too broadly, but I have an idea that my friend Baron Scarpia chuckled sardonically.

It was during this New York visit that a rather sad little incident occurred. One morning Tilde arrived at the stage entrance of the opera house to find a small, agitated, elderly gentleman repeating plaintively, "But I want to see Tito Gobbi, I want to see Tito Gobbi," while the official at the desk firmly shook his head and declared that no one was allowed in to the rehearsal.

Tilde approached the desk and was shocked to realize that the man being turned away was none other than Tito Schipa. Divided between anger and dismay she took him by the hand and said to the man at the desk: "Do you realize who this gentleman is? Signor Tito Schipa, one of the greatest artists who ever sang in this opera house. He is coming with me now. My husband will be pleased and proud to see him." And she led him to my dressing room.

On our return to Rome the time had come for me to complete my study and rehearsals for my first *Macbeth*. I had already spent a good deal of time on the work for this, but I had not yet found my answer to the basic problems. I was eager to penetrate to the heart of this new role, but I was also afraid; for although *Macbeth* is in some senses "typical Verdi" it presents vocal and dramatic problems which are peculiar to itself.

To begin with, in this first of Verdi's Shakespearean operas the composer has yielded more to the great dramatist than in the later ones. The declamation is highly dramatic, the tessitura of an almost giddy height, the thrilling duets reduced at times to little more than a whisper yet so full of meaning that not a syllable must be lost, the last cry of desperation of such intensity that it must stab the audience with a sense of pity and terror. No wonder I trembled before the task!

But it was a fascinating task too. Gradually, as I realized that the frightening tessitura and the demanding declamation could be dealt with by the coloring of the voice, I began to feel the role coming within my grasp. In my rough diary of the time I recorded: "Very heavy work, but *how I love it*. Tremendous character. I remain terrified of myself for hours!"

We operatic artists have our rough times, as I have shown, but the discovery and pursuit of a great new role can make up for everything. Possibly I am particularly fortunate in this respect for, as I virtually never go to the opera unless I am myself performing, my discovery of a role has all the fascination of an adventure. I do not start with any preconceived notions at the back of my mind about the generally accepted interpretation. I start, as it were, from the core of the character, working outward by the light of my study, my own experience, my understanding of people which life has taught me, and finally a sort of instinct which I cannot exactly define. In a sense I virtually become that character, so that his gestures, vocal inflections, and conduct stem from my already acquired inner knowledge of him.

I had studied the actual character of Macbeth for a long time before I began to rehearse the work. I was completely convinced of the way he would react and therefore I could convey that conviction to the audience. Other artists might have a somewhat different idea of him—for there is no such thing as an absolute interpretation of any role—but in my view unless an artist has his own inner conviction that *this* is how a certain character ticks he will not be able to win total acceptance from the audience of his interpretation of the role.

To give in any sort of detail my crowded program and itinerary for 1956 would be to produce a typical example of those lists which I firmly eschewed in an earlier chapter. What stands out for me above all else in that year was our visit to London in July, not only because there were five beautiful and successful performances of *Rigoletto* but because of what happened at a party given for us by David Webster in his own home. Many of our good friends were there, heaping congratulations upon me for the *Rigoletto* performances, and then suddenly Maestro Kubelik entered the room, and silence fell.

Count Zoppi, the Italian ambassador, murmured to me: "Here is the enemy!"

As I stood there, rigid and nonplused, Kubelik walked across the room with his hand out and congratulated me in the warmest terms on my Rigoletto. Then he added, for all to hear, how deeply he regretted what had happened the previous summer, and that if anyone had been the loser by it it was he, since he had missed having my collaboration.

It was a gesture of generosity which I shall never forget. I accepted his hand with all my heart and said that this called for a toast together. Then, taking two glasses from a nearby shelf, I filled them with champagne. As I did so I realized that David Webster's beaming smile of approval had become a trifle strained, for it seemed that I had in my enthusiasm selected two cherished items from his magnificent glass collection and, delighted though he was to see Kubelik and me bury the hatchet, he could not hide his anxiety lest we should clink his precious glasses too heartily.

Exercising due caution, we drank to each other, and, although it is true that I still had to wait some years before I finally sang Iago at Covent Garden, the sense of bitterness and injury had gone.

Naturally this is one of my favorite "conducting stories," and usually when I tell it someone or other is prompted to ask about other conductors with whom I have sung. I think this particular interest is largely due to the fact that my years in opera have spanned a period of great change. I have, so to speak, one foot in the secure, traditional, perhaps rather conventional world dominated by the immensely knowledgeable old maestros and the other foot in the more adventurous, experimental world of today, where much is interesting and worthwhile and much merely trashy. Perhaps because of this I have learned that nothing is intrinsically valuable just because it is old, and still less is anything intrinsically valuable merely because it is new. It takes time and patience— and a certain degree of humility—to develop a sound judgment of one's own, but it is important to do so; otherwise one tends to fall victim to the confident, loud-mouthed amateur who loves to tell the other person what to think.

Among the conductors to whom I look back with gratitude and admiration are Bernardino Molinari (who first praised my still uncultivated voice and gave me the courage to press on), Gino Marinuzzi, who gave me my first chance at La Scala, and—above all—Tullio Serafin, to whom I owe more than I could possibly describe.

Molinari was a simple, straightforward, unpretentious man, fond of saying: "I am the son of a cook, so what do you expect?" But in the field of music he was a man of great determination, commitment, and vitality, the resident conductor of the Santa Cecilia Orchestra.

He was not by nature a theater conductor. His approach might be described as somewhat mathematical, but when he was transported by a work he communicated an extraordinary degree of fire and excitement to both his orchestral players and his singers. I became genuinely fond of him, although in rehearsal he was subject to fits of nervous rage which resulted in a flow of picturesque abuse that had to be heard to be believed. At the same time these scenes subsided as suddenly as they had blown up, and he then lost all recollection of them.

I remember once when I was to sing under him at La Scala in a performance of Perosi's *Risurrezione di Cristo,* everything had been agreed, the contract had been signed, rehearsals had been satisfactory and I went to his house in Rome to have a final run-through. He simply said, *"Buon giorno, Gobbi,"* in an abstracted sort of way, and I knew that he was already absorbed in the work, tense and nervous as usual. However, we went through the work well (in those young days of mine even the beautiful, fiendishly difficult high mezza voce passages were no problem).

"Good—very good—marvelous!" he said approvingly. "Now do it again."

This was a special weakness of his, for he could never resign himself to the fact that enough is enough. So, much against my will, we started again, though I knew this was pushing the voice too hard. Sure enough, one particularly difficult passage did not come off as well as the first time, at which he nearly jumped out of his skin, shouted all kinds of abuse at me, and declared that it was quite impossible for him to risk his own reputation by having such an idiot, dog, etc., etc., for his soloist. There was only one thing to do: he would have to send a telegram to La Scala to say that I was impossible and they must find someone else.

I let him rave on for a few minutes; then with all the calm I could muster I said: "Maestro, I agree. You are absolutely right. If you will write out the telegram now I can easily send it off on my way home."

"What telegram?" he demanded, stopping dead in the middle of his tirade.

"The telegram to La Scala," I reminded him. "The one saying that I am no good and that they must find someone else."

"You want to send a telegram to La Scala?" He blinked at me incredulously. "Why? Why? Don't be a fool. If you're so stupid you can't do it twice, it can't be helped. You do it once. You did it marvelously. You have to sing this performance, and by golly, you shall!"

Away from the scene of his work he was an entirely different man—kind and amusing, his delightful wife Mary and he being close friends of the De Rensis family and of course of mine too. He was a great conductor, no question of that, strong and very forceful; there might be room for a minor criticism here and there, but I would like to have another like him today.

No greater contrast to Molinari could be imagined than the charming, rather aristocratic Marinuzzi. A born opera conductor and man of the theater, with both strength and poetry in his approach, he had a wonderful flexibility and a deep understanding of the problems of a singer. He was also someone with whom one could sometimes venture a joke, though I doubt if I would have tried it in anything other than a comic opera. One day when we were rehearsing *L'Elisir d'Amore* at La Scala I said lightly that I thought the finale after the departure of Dulcamara would be much more exciting if Belcore were to throw off a top note one octave higher than his usually accepted one.

"Tito, don't be mad," was Marinuzzi's good-humored reply. "You couldn't possibly do it."

I agreed that it was only a joke. But when we came to the actual performance I realized I was in very good, easy voice and as the moment came along I turned my back, tried out the note under my breath and, having gotten it, turned once more to face the audience and let it rip with full force. Marinuzzi's expression was a study of astonishment and amused reproof. But he said to me afterward: "Don't you ever dare do that again." And I knew he meant it.

If he was indeed a singer's conductor, so too was Serafin in a different way. Serafin was like a rock. The ground never shifted under your feet when Serafin was in charge. You were sustained by the absolute certainty that he would be equal to every situation or emergency—almost that no ill-wind would be allowed to blow upon you. He also was flexible as far as the reasonable needs of a singer were concerned, but always within the most miraculous timing of the whole work. There was never any suggestion of rigidity about a Serafin performance, and yet I think that for the whole of his long and glorious career his total timing for the standard works remained constant; which gave one an incredible sense of security.

In my early days in Rome we had at the opera house a marvelous man called Antoni. Appointed by Serafin, he was in charge of the stage in the sense that it was his responsibility to see that each performer was in his or her place at the right time, that everything went with the smoothness of clockwork, and that the strictest discipline was maintained. This extended to the fact that no one was allowed to cross the stage with his hat on before, during, or after rehearsal. The stage was to us like a church or a temple. If anyone forgot, Antoni simply said, "Hat off!" and the offending article was snatched off at once by the abashed wearer. To Antoni also fell the task of timing everything not to the minute but to the second, from the moment the curtain rose until its final fall.

It will be remembered that I sang Rodrigo in *Don Carlo* for the first time in Rome under Serafin in 1941. It so happened that something like twenty years later I sang it in Chicago, again under Serafin, and I was fascinated to recognize a familiar sense of such security—such an operatic "coming home," if I may put it that way—that I felt I had to discover the underlying cause. I wrote to Antoni, who was still in Rome, and asked if he could supply me with the timing of each scene and act in *Don Carlo* as we had done it in 1941. He had kept his records and promptly sent me the information I requested. I compared the 1941 timing in detail with the timing twenty years later, and *in the whole work* there was a difference of slightly less than thirty seconds.

Within the total timing of a scene, however, Serafin was always ready to discuss slight variations if he considered them reasonable. A singer might say: "Maestro, may I take it a little more slowly here?" To which he would reply: "Why? Tell me why, and if it is a good reason we will do it." Then, after the singer had explained himself, Serafin might well say: "Yes, yes, I think we can do it. We shall have to move a little more here and here. But—yes, we will do it."

With very, very few conductors was this possible. They all differed in the qualities which earned them the description of "great." With De Sabata, for instance—a genius of a conductor—there would be brilliant extravagances unthinkable with anyone else, but by them he would obtain the most stunning effects. One of the most memorable of these was the opening scene of *Otello* at Covent Garden when the Scala Company made their first visit there just after the war. The brilliance and drama, the terror and excitement of those opening minutes were such that the audience almost literally cowered before the storm. And I believe someone was heard to mutter afterward: "We did everything but put up our umbrellas."

In rehearsal De Sabata had an unrivaled talent for breaking down the score into its component parts so that he had each group of instrumentalists playing like individual soloists. Once, in Florence, I slipped in at the back of the theater when a De Sabata rehearsal was in progress. He was drawing from each group of players a ravishing sound, but not until he put them together did I realize why the sounds were familiar and yet not quite identifiable. It was the second act of *La Bohème*, but now the effect was like a familiar painting glowing afresh in all its original colors.

Apart from the outstanding figures of my early years it seems to me that there was an almost unlimited supply of fine operatic conductors, musically and vocally knowledgeable *in depth*. Always good, occasionally great, knowing their job from A to Z, they served the work and the composer with all their heart and brain; and the fact is that within the sort of framework these men created one could often do some of one's best work.

Then at a later period came people like Mitropoulos, Von Karajan, Giulini, Gavazzeni, Solti, Santini, and so on, with all of whom I have worked most happily and to all of whom I would attribute varying degrees of greatness. With the exception of Santini (with whom I did a great deal of recording) and Mitropoulos, those I have mentioned are, happily, still there for the audience to hear and judge for themselves.

I had the pleasure of working several times with Mitropoulos, who was an extremely fine conductor and an unusually sympathetic man. At least one orchestral player at La Scala had reason to bless his generous spirit. The poor fellow lost his valuable violin, either by robbery or accidentally—I have forgotten which—and when Mitropoulos, who was conducting there at the time, heard about this he himself put up the money to have the instrument replaced with one of equal value.

He handled his players admirably, even in moments of great stress or difficulty, as on one occasion when we were rehearsing *Wozzeck* at La Scala. Part of the time the orchestra is divided, some of them playing onstage, and at a very taxing point one of the wind players panicked and said it was impossible to play a certain passage so fast.

"Oh, but I'm sure you can do it," Mitropoulos told him soothingly. "Let me come and see." He went up on the stage, addressed the man by his first name (he had a great talent for remembering first names and establishing a friendly atmosphere), and began to explain the passage afresh. But the man only became more nervous and said brusquely, "I can't do it. Maybe you can think *you* can!" and he held out his instrument to Mitropoulos almost insultingly.

"Well, let me try," Mitropoulos said in a good-humored way, and taking the instrument, he put it to his lips, and played the passage perfectly. "There, you see," he said, smiling, "even I can do it, and I'm not a real expert. I'll slow down a little for you, and I'm sure you will find you can do it."

Then he went back to his desk, leaving the man speechless with amazement but suddenly able to do what the conductor required of him.

When firmness of a more ruthless kind was required, however, Mitropoulos was quite capable of displaying it, even toward the most distinguished person. During the same *Wozzeck* rehearsals De Sabata, who was the artistic director of La Scala and very conscious of the importance of his position, put in an appearance. What followed had more than a touch of professional jealousy about it. De Sabata wandered about onstage for a few minutes, glancing over the shoulders of some of the players and generally giving the impression that his was a position of overriding authority. Then, with an affable but patronizing air he addressed Mitropoulos: "Well, Dimitri, I am sure everything will go well tomorrow but you must be very tired now, so I think we should bring the rehearsal to an end for today."

This was, of course, an insufferable challenge to the authority of Mitropoulos, who, however, was quite equal to the occasion. He gave De Sabata a perfectly pleasant glance and replied: "No one here is tired, Maestro, and we will continue the rehearsal. But if you yourself are tired we will not keep you."

Visibly shocked by this unexpected though well-deserved snub, De Sabata left immediately and the rehearsal continued. In point of fact this incident not only represented a trial of strength between two conductors, it also pinpointed our whole position at La Scala, where we were not accepted as friends but as rather unwelcome necessities. For a specialized work like *Wozzeck* it had been necessary to call in outsiders—Mitropoulos, myself, and one or two other members of the cast. To men like Ghiringhelli, Oldani, and even De Sabata this was an affront to their pride. For some time they had come to believe that their personal importance and the greatness of La Scala were one and the same thing. Everyone performing there must be made to understand that they were secondary to the greatness of the house and the men who ran it.

Mitropoulos and I could afford to be indifferent to day-to-day pinpricks and we enormously enjoyed working together. When he discovered how well I knew and appreciated the work he was not at all above asking me for confirmation on some point or other at rehearsal. Under his guidance we all—cast and orchestra alike—felt pretty sure that we would give a good account of ourselves on the first night.

When that first night came it proved to be a veritable battlefield. It was Milan's first experience of *Wozzeck,* and the audience's reaction was terrific. Throughout the first act there were whistles and boos, interspersed with an occasional expression of approval and much loud discussion. Twice Mitropoulos turned and gestured with his hand for silence, and at the end of the act there was a storm of mingled protest and applause.

Then Mitropoulos came forward on the stage, appealed for silence, and said: "I concede that you have the absolute right to judge this opera. But we have been working very seriously, with devotion and respect, in order to present this work to you in the very best way we can, and it requires a lot of concentration. Please will you be so kind as to express your judgment at the end of the performance. In this way we shall be able to give you the best of our work, and we will accept at the end whatever comment you care to make."

During the second act there were a few boos, and the third act was not a triumph; the audience left the theater slowly, arguing passionately and with a degree of interest accorded only to a worthwhile work. We, for our part, took off our costumes and make-up and repaired to the Biffi Scala to be entertained at supper by the directors of La Scala. The principal artists as well as the heads of the various departments, the chorus master, and so on were all present, and after the supper came toasts and speeches of restrained congratulation from one or two of the directors: then Mitropoulos rose to reply on behalf of the performers.

As he glanced at me I knew from his expression that he was going to congratulate me publicly and I shook my head in warning. He took no notice, however, and proceeded to thank all the La Scala staff and management who had made the evening possible. "But," he went on, still ignoring my telegraphic signals, "though all this reflects the greatest credit on so many people, there is one person without whom this great occasion could not have taken place. Without Tito Gobbi it would have been nothing. *With* Tito Gobbi we can play *Wozzeck* anywhere in the world today."

There were some heartfelt, "Hear, hears" from various parts of the room, but those on my left, where the directors of La Scala sat, had a hollow ring. I cannot swear that I actually saw anyone turn yellow, but I knew that I had joined the glorious company of those who would never again be really welcome at La Scala.

14.

THE DEMANDS of my career were now such that I constantly felt grateful for the fact that I am by nature a healthy and energetic person. This is largely due, I think, to my having many interests outside my career. To relax over my painting or modeling or to deal with some mechanical or repairing job in my home—these are to me as much of a rest as two or three hours of sleep might be to another person. On the other hand, the balance between one's personal and one's professional life is not always easy to maintain.

Romantically minded people tend to imagine their favorite artists pursuing a strangely glamorous life in which they progress from one exciting occasion to another with little or no involvement in mundane, day-to-day happenings. Perhaps a much-publicized love affair might be permitted in this scheme of things, but more ordinary griefs and problems—the loss of a parent, boring illnesses, trouble with a teen-aged child who is being just as tiresome as any rebellious youngster in the gallery—these are not the things to be associated with "stars." But they happen all the same and must be dealt with somehow, possibly at the same time as some crisis in the more public side of one's life.

During the second half of the 1950s the operatic pattern was fairly constant: Chicago in the autumn, Rome at intervals throughout the year, London once or twice a year for both opera and concerts, Lisbon very often around about April, Salzburg in the summer, and perhaps Verona too, with a variety of other engagements stretching from Madrid to Tokyo. If I could have imagined such a life when I was a boy in Bassano, knowing little of the operatic world . . . ! Which recalls to me with a sense of amused nostalgia my very first encounter with a famous operatic figure when I was indeed a boy—not in Bassano but in Padua, where I was for a time a student in the high school. I usually spent my free time on the weekends in company with another young student, and together we walked, played chess, and talked endlessly, as one does in one's teens. One Saturday as we walked through the streets of Padua he suddenly said:

"Look who's coming! You know who that big man is on the other side of the street?"

"No." I shook my head.

"Aureliano Pertile."

"Who's he?" I asked without much interest, though the name sounded familiar.

"Oh, I say!" exclaimed my companion, a little shocked at my ignorance. "He's one of the most famous tenors in the world; and incidentally he is my uncle. Do you want to meet him?"

I said I didn't mind and we crossed the road and introductions were made, the famous tenor offering a friendly if rather flabby hand while remaining muffled up in a thick woolen scarf. Then he said good-naturedly: "Are you boys doing anything tomorrow afternoon? You're not? Well, would you like to come and hear me sing in Giordano's *Fedora?* Here are my two tickets if you like."

We took the tickets with appropriate murmurs of thanks, but when we had gone on our way I asked: "Do we really have to go?"

"No, of course not," replied my friend. "Who wants to waste a fine afternoon at the opera?"

However, it happened that the following afternoon was anything but fine. So, after some consultation, we decided to look in at the theater for half an hour, though we agreed we need not stay for the whole afternoon if we found it boring.

I still thought of my friend's famous uncle as the large, muffled-up gentleman in a scarf, when onto the stage came what seemed to me an almost godlike figure who proceeded to sing as I had never heard anyone sing before. My companion, the audience, the very theater itself almost ceased to exist. I sat there riveted, with never a thought of leaving, until the curtain fell for the last time. Then, after the final ecstatic clap, we found our way around to the stage door, from which eventually emerged the god—now transformed once more into the large, muffled-up gentleman—and to him we stammered out our thanks in a daze of rapture. That is what one's first great tenor should do for one!

Years afterward I actually sang with him in *Pagliacci* in the great open-air theater of Caracalla, he playing Canio and I singing Silvio. He was past his splendid best by then and, sadly, at the end of the famous "Vesti la giubba" he made the mistake of overdoing the sobs so that it sounded curiously as though he were laughing. At once the audience began to laugh too, destroying the pathos and drama of the scene.

The next day I ran into him in the street. We paused to exchange a few words and I said how fine the performance had been—which it had. But he slowly shook his head and said: "No, the audience don't like me any longer. It is time I went." And suddenly I could not emphasize the passage of time by telling him that in the days of his glory I had once waited for him outside the stage door when he was in his prime and I was a boy.

During our many operatic journeys Tilde and I always looked forward with special eagerness to our visits to Lisbon, not only for the pleasure of the performances, the people, and the opera house itself, but because there we almost invariably had occasion to meet our exiled King, Umberto. He was a devotee of the opera and, as he always came backstage to offer his congratulations, Tilde and I became friendly with him and were sometimes invited to visit him at his villa. He would ask us many questions—the questions which any exile must want to ask of his home. Though we were happy to be asked it made us sad too, for he is one of the most interesting and knowledgeable people I have ever met. A man of immense culture and intelligence, he has a frank, warm-hearted charm which establishes an easy relationship between him and anyone he comes to regard as a friend.

He also has an impeccable sense of diplomacy, and I remember this being put to the test in an intriguing way on one occasion when I was playing the title role in *Simone Boccanegra*. In the interval before the last act the King came backstage, and it so happened that the Italian ambassador, who was also in the house, chose the same moment to come. As the ambassador told me later, the two men met at the door which separates the auditorium from the stage—the representative of republican Italy and the exiled monarch.

It was the King who stepped back and said: "As the official representative of Italy, you have the prior right, I think."

"Oh no, Your Majesty!" replied the ambassador. "Will you please go first?"

For a moment or two they exchanged compliments about the matter of precedence and then the ambassador insisted on withdrawing.

My own special recollection of that evening is that when the King arrived in my dressing room he said jokingly: "So now we're in competition! As Doge of Genoa you also are a head of state." And then suddenly, with a quick change of mood, he sadly quoted Simone's words from the previous act when, after the poison scene, he says: "Even the clear water from the fountain tastes bitter to the man who wears a crown."

Later some of the others in the company said: "You have had a lot of hospitality from him. Couldn't you invite him in return to meet some of the company?"

I made this suggestion the next time we visited him and he accepted with obvious pleasure. The party was an unqualified success, our distinguished guest setting everyone at ease and making us feel we were all friends drawn together by mutual interests. I think that evening remained in the memory of us all as an occasion to be treasured.

Among the many performances in which I took part during the late 1950s some naturally stand out above others. Pride of place might well be given to the famous Visconti production of *Don Carlo* at Covent Garden in May 1958. The cast included the lovely Dutch soprano Gre Brouenstijn, Jon Vickers, Boris Christoff, and myself under the inspired musical direction of Maestro Giulini. But it was the genius of Visconti which irradiated the whole performance. The superb stage sets were a delight to the eye and to the intelligence (not always the same thing). The lighting was miraculous, satisfying to both heart and mind in its romantic beauty and its sense of reality. The grouping and movement of the characters on the stage imparted a masterly impression of complete naturalness, and there was not a gimmick in the whole evening—the final test of a great production.

It was during this production that Boris Christoff and I fully developed our presentation of the wonderful scene which Verdi has given to King Philip of Spain and the Marquis of Posa. It is one of the greatest character confrontations in the whole range of opera, and to have been privileged to take part in such a fine performance is in some way to have fulfilled oneself as a singing actor.

Boris and I had been not only artistic colleagues but brothers-in-law for some years, since he had married Tilde's lovely sister, Franca, and it is difficult to describe the satisfaction of playing opposite a protagonist of such mettle. I think both of us would agree that we first reached a high peak in our careers with the 1957 Rome performances of *Simone Boccanegra* during the superb duets which Verdi wrote for Simone and his old enemy Fiesco. Boris and I have it on the authority of Tilde's diary that there were on this occasion "five beautiful performances; our two boys *so* wonderful. My sister and I bursting with pride and crying together. It is going to be difficult to find such a pair—their duets matchless, each one so good in his own right!"

Undoubtedly a certain degree of family prejudice can be detected in this verdict. But in those duets, and subsequently when we sang together in *Don Carlo*, we seemed to establish a unique rapport and did, I think, set a sort of standard against which most later performances have been measured.

Boris and I have not always agreed. What two lively, positive artists ever do? Indeed, one occasion received much unwanted publicity when we quarreled badly in Chicago. It is always much more "news" if there is family friction rather than family solidarity, but it can truthfully be said of that occasion that it is all water under the bridge now and was based at the time on a complete misunderstanding. There are strong ties between all four of us, and nowadays if I am cooking lunch at the Casale (which I enjoy doing) there is no one I would rather have with me in the kitchen as critic and appraiser than my brother-in-law. For his part he is kind enough to think that my take-off of a Russian singer giving a dramatic recital is one of the funniest things he knows.

In every career—indeed, in every life—there are periods when everything seems to go wrong and, as a family, we struck a very difficult patch during the years 1959 to 1962. To all appearances 1959 opened well. We had recently installed Tilde's parents in a new apartment in Rome with a balcony and terrace where her mother, now largely housebound, could enjoy the sunshine. For me there was a party to celebrate my twenty years of recording for His Master's Voice, complete with golden record. For Cecilia there was a ball on St. Valentine's Day, with our spacious garage turned into a ballroom of the 1920s. I painted frescoes on the walls, the place was rechristened "Au Chat Noir," the young people came in period dress, and Tilde and I and our old friend Albert White played doormen.

Professionally speaking, in addition to the usual variety of performances in Rome, I went as far afield as Tokyo to play Iago to Del Monaco's Otello. We were able to have a real family holiday in the summer at our country house in Santa Severa, with Tilde's parents and mine joining us, and several other members of the families coming too. Here, however, late in the summer, Tilde's mother slipped and injured herself and, although she characteristically made light of it, we persuaded her on our return to Rome to go to the hospital for an X-ray. It was then discovered that she had really broken her hip but, amazingly, the break had healed spontaneously.

Thankful to receive such reassuring news I went off without any special anxiety to fulfill engagements in Vienna and Zagreb. But quite suddenly, with Tilde beside her, she died on the morning of September 21. Our dear, good Mamma Giuseppina, who had scolded me all those years ago for walking her daughter through the streets of Rome without parental permission, and who had given me my first little book on stage make-up! She was so much a part of our lives, so very dear to all of us, and her passing left a sad gap in the close family circle.

But now our professional lives claimed us inexorably, and less than a month later Tilde and I had to go to Chicago for the usual fall season. It was on this occasion that we renewed contact with Sister Maria Michele of Rosary College, in circumstances which were later to have a profound influence on our life-pattern. Sister Maria, a splendid teacher and organizer, a woman of vision and an enthusiastic opera lover, invited me to give a concert at Rosary College. It was the second time this had happened and I decided to vary the program. In the first half, in formal evening attire, I sang the usual selection of arias and songs. In the second half I stripped off my jacket and tie and announced that I was inviting the audience to witness a rehearsal. Then, using obliging colleagues for Dr. Caius, Pistol, and Bardolph, and students for the scene-shifting, I rehearsed the first scene of *Falstaff*, guiding, correcting, encouraging, and explaining, exactly as though we were onstage.

For most of the audience this was their first experience of watching the early stages of a production, and they loved it. What was even more important from my point of view, however, was that Sister Maria Michele stored away an impression of the occasion in her memory and, years later, when she became principal of the Graduate School of Fine Arts established by Rosary College at the Villa Schifanoia in Florence, she decided to develop the germ of an idea which she had had in that autumn of 1959. She contacted me in Rome and asked if I would be willing to organize an Opera Workshop during the summer months at the Villa Schifanoia. I accepted immediately, and thus began the Opera Workshop to which advanced students now come each year from all over the world.

In those last weeks of 1959 I was more than usually busy, this time largely in Milan at the Scala, where we alternated *Otello* and *Tosca* well into the new year until the press observed that they were "squeezing Gobbi like a lemon." But the pips did not actually squeak and back in Rome I was immediately involved in rehearsals for *Don Giovanni,* in preparation for my first performance of this role in Rome. Maestro Gui was in charge and we worked together splendidly. I cannot say quite the same for the production of dear Margarete Wallman, whose stage rehearsals went on until two in the morning with a degree of on-the-spot changes that were difficult to bear. In the end all went well, though I think I played the Don rather more to my ideas than to hers.

March found us once more in London, which was almost our second European home by now. At Covent Garden a new production of *Macbeth* provided me with a memorable colleague in the person of Amy Shuard, a splendid Lady Macbeth. The performances were a great success and we were all enjoying ourselves when several of the cast were struck down by some kind of influenza. Under protest I agreed to be inoculated, and even now I am not sure whether I was allergic to something in the inoculation or whether I just became ill anyway. Suddenly in the middle of a performance I found myself with a hideously dry mouth, a sense of weakness and fatigue, and, worst of all, a large white spot of some sort of fungus on my tongue. A doctor was called and an announcement made to the effect that I was unwell but would finish the performance. This was the signal for the customary outburst of applause with which the sporting British audience tends to encourage any performer in difficulties.

Somehow I got through the evening but had to cancel the last two performances and returned to Italy really very sick. In fact, it was two months before I was fully recovered. There was no singing for me, apart from some recording, until the end of July, when I took part in the most gloriously staged *Otello* in my whole experience. It took place in the courtyard of the Ducal Palace in Venice, with the palace as our background. The Otello was Mario del Monaco, in my view the finest of my generation. A splendid stage figure, he always made Otello's entrance unforgettable, but to hear and see him delivering his great opening phrases from the top of the Scala dei Giganti was beyond description. As for me, I had the wonderful experience of singing the "Credo" leaning negligently against the magnificent bronzework which adorns the well. That was glamor, if you like!

There were five performances in all and as several of our American friends were in Venice at the time there was a great deal of pleasant social life as well. Indeed, it was a radiant time for Tilde and me, only slightly shadowed by the fact that a serious admirer had turned up in Cecilia's life—much too early in our opinion.

Do all parents worry about beautiful teen-aged daughters? I suppose they do—with or without reason. But, in the modern phrase, we tried to play it cool, knowing that excessive parental opposition can often have the opposite effect from the one intended.

During the autumn season in Chicago we had Franca and Boris (always Cecilia's devoted aunt and uncle) with us, as well as our good friend and valued colleague Giulietta Simionato. But when Franca and Boris left for Europe and it was time for Cecilia to return to school I still had further American engagements to fulfill, and Tilde and I decided that this was a time when our daughter should have at any rate one of her parents with her. So with a heavy heart I said good-by to both of my loved ones and returned alone to the apartment, feeling sadly bereft and asking myself: "Why did I let them go? Why didn't I go with them?"

To the disciplined professional there is unfortunately only one way to answer those questions: "Because it was necessary, and because that is part of your chosen way of life."

However, when I arrived in Los Angeles for my next assignment and found letters there from Tilde and Cecilia I wept like a fool and found it difficult to sleep that night. Throughout our married life Tilde and I had always been able to share our anxieties and reassure each other in any crisis. Now the Atlantic Ocean separated us, just as we were worrying about the one being most precious to both of us. It was therefore with indescribable relief that I rejoined them toward the end of the year.

In the early months of the new year (1961) I found myself traveling about a good deal on something other than professional engagements. I had been asked to help form a sort of union to look after singers' interests with agents, opera managements, and so on. Little headway was made, however, for ours is a competitive profession and it is difficult to get people to work in concert. Harmony may be our bread and butter, but it does not seem to color our relationships to any great extent.

Then, early in May, we held a memorable Gala Night at the Rome Opera in honor of Queen Elizabeth of England. We played *Falstaff* before a glittering house decked everywhere with flowers. The Queen was supposed to leave after the second act but enjoyed herself so much that she and Prince Philip stayed until the end; and I had the honor of quite a long conversation with them between the acts, discovering with pride and pleasure how accurately they recalled various occasions when I had sung at Covent Garden.

It was in the following February, while I was in Venice, that Cecilia's admirer, Piero Montagnaro, came to ask formally for permission to marry her. Tilde telephoned me and we decided at least to agree to their engagement. She was still in our view too young for marriage, but Tilde and I gave way with as good a grace as we could. Then on April 10 that year (1962) Tilde and I celebrated twenty-five years of our marriage. We did our best to make it the happy anniversary it should have been, including the new fiancé in the family party we held, but the realization that my mother had become seriously ill cast a deep shadow over the occasion.

During the ensuing months Tilde proved herself once more the best of daughters-in-law, giving unstinted love and care to my mother, even though this often meant attention at night after an exhausting day. I was mostly on my own at this time for short-term engagements, but in June, when I was at last to go to London to sing Iago, Tilde came too.

It was wonderful! All the disappointment of years ago was forgotten in one of the most heart-warming receptions I have ever had. The Queen Mother was present at the second performance, and David Webster—ever mindful of the fact that Tilde too had been bitterly disappointed when those earlier Iagos had been canceled—made it his business to see that Tilde was personally presented to her. The Queen Mother not only spoke most kindly about me but enchanted the blushing Tilde by saying, as one woman to another: "My, what a lovely coat you are wearing!" Tilde said she felt like a queen herself, and afterward rushed to embrace David Webster and thank him for providing her with her own great moment.

By the middle of July we realized that our young people were not willing to wait any longer for their wedding and we agreed that it should take place in Venice on August 11, because further performances of *Otello* were due to be held there then.

Once we had given our consent we determined that our daughter should have the most beautiful wedding day we could possibly devise; and for this we could hardly have chosen a more lovely setting than Venice. We practically took over the hotel, the Gritti Palace, and filled it with our guests. Then, as the ceremony was to take place on the island of Torcello across the lagoon, the whole wedding party embarked on the journey in a long procession of motorboats.

As we proceeded along the canal through the center of the city the Venetians lined the bridges and leaned over to shout their good wishes to the company and their blessings on the bride, who stood in her boat looking for all the world like a medieval princess.

It is generally conceded that it is the mother of the bride whose feelings are deepest and most mixed on such an occasion, and here is the entry in Tilde's diary: "The whole island was excited and took part. The marvellous cathedral, rather bare, was simply adorned with enormous plants of jasmine, and the ceremony was beautiful, simple and gay. Afterwards we all, including the whole *Otello* cast, went to the reception, the wedding-cake was cut and the sight of the two young people was very moving. Then we had to leave because, in spite of careful planning, it somehow turned out that there was a performance of *Otello* that evening. It was strange to leave the island without our girl, who stood on the balcony with her new husband, waving to us as the boats drew away!"

For me it was one of those occasions when the professional artist had the hardest struggle with the human being. To have left one's daughter —one's only child at that—and to have to rush to the theater to sing Iago, the villain totally without human feelings! But discipline is everything. We have a saying: "Die on the stage; you can cry afterward."

Tilde was with me backstage as usual and we were climbing together the great Scala dei Giganti when we thought we saw a familiar pair of feet descending: bare feet in sandals, worn by a girl in a cotton dress, no longer with an elaborate hair-do but with her hair down. It was our Cecilia, who with her young husband had come to be with us to show that, just as we had done everything we could for her great day, so she wanted to be with us for our performance. I was deeply moved. They stayed until the end and we had supper together afterward, united in a real family group.

The rest of the year was taken up with more or less the familiar program, but by the time we came home from Chicago and Los Angeles we knew that my mother was failing. She had terminal cancer, and she was in and out of the hospital until the end of the year. Then in the middle of January it was decided that she might come home for a spell, and Tilde and I hopefully drove to the hospital to fetch her. But, even as we were getting her ready for the short journey, she died in our arms.

We now had two bereaved old men to look after—not that Tilde's father, Papa Raffaello, ever caused us any difficulties. I am afraid it was Papa Giovanni who provided the firework displays during the next few ycars and like most firework displays, though they had a certain entertainment value, they were not exactly restful.

At the other end of the family age scale, however, the year 1963 brought us a beautiful blessing—our little granddaughter, Isabella.

15.

PROFESSIONALLY SPEAKING, the first half of 1963 provided some of the busiest months of my whole career. Apart from a variety of other commitments I made five visits to London, each time for a different opera at Covent Garden: *Falstaff* in January, *Tosca* in February, *Don Carlo* in April, *Don Giovanni* in May, and *Nozze di Figaro* in June.

It was my first Don Giovanni in London, and was under the musical direction of that splendid maestro Josef Krips. I had come a long way since those Salzburg performances a dozen or more years before and had given a great deal of thought to the complex character of the Don. (I still give thought to him, for he remains one of the great question marks of literature as well as music.) So much has been written about him and so much speculation made upon him that any explanation or comment of one's own must inevitably bear a very personal slant. Was he the archetype of love or a force of nature? Is he diabolical or the personification of exuberant sex itself?

For a man who has become a legend as the supremely gifted lover, a total of two thousand and sixty-four love affairs is not perhaps impossible. But Leporello's famous catalog is destined to stop there. No other name is ever going to be added to it. Every amorous attempt is doomed to failure. He is no longer a young man and it is with his decline that Mozart's opera begins. That being so, in my opinion one must keep in mind that his days of triumphant success are over. With the murder of the Commendatore he starts the avalanche which overwhelms and eventually destroys all that he has been but will never be again.

The first thing we see is his failure with Donna Anna—interrupted or rejected? Chased by the furious woman, he is exasperated but stimulated by the struggle, half enjoying, half sneering "Donna folle . . . sconsigliata . . . furia disperata . . ." If this is his first failure, why is he so exalted and fighting with such desperate vigor? Is he still sure of his own charm and power to succeed, or has the first doubt as to his own prowess already set in? The threat of impotence sharpens his awareness and the shadow of his guilt descends upon him, darkening his life.

It was not his intention to kill the Commendatore. The event overtook him rather than his directing events as he had been wont to do. The hand of the dying man, pointing at him and identifying him as the assassin, is the same hand which will be offered to him by the Statue in the last act. Here is the first stone which starts the avalanche. Something irreparable has happened to the core of Giovanni, though the outer "image" remains unchanged. Thus everyone still sees him as the legend which inwardly he has already ceased to be.

After the unsuccessful enterprise with Donna Anna he tries to dissipate his disappointment and insecurity with an attempt to seduce Zerlina. He is about to succeed when Elvira interrupts. Elvira, the only one of the women who has been physically close to him, bothers him with her presence, for she brings back memories of lost sensations. She is the living evidence of something he is not able to do any more, so he treats her shamefully, abusing her and finally thrusting her into the arms of his valet, while he tries his own luck with the maid.

The avalanche gathers power and momentum, and he is aware of it: "Mi par ch'oggi il demonio si diverta . . . vanno mal tutti quanti!" ("The devil's enjoying himself today . . . I've no success with any of them!") In a frenzy which covers his desperation he orders Leporello to prepare a big party, and in his aria "Fin ch'han dal vino" he imagines an orgy of love scenes in which abundant libations will enable him to add at least ten more names to that list of Leporello's.

Later, however, in the cemetery scene he confesses to Leporello that luck seems to have left him, since a girl friend of the servant rejected the master when she recognized him and fled screaming. Exasperated, increasingly aware of the unattainable, he laughs wildly, deliberately profaning the sacred ground on which he stands. Constitutionally arrogant, he remains defiantly unmoved even when the voice of the Commendatore addresses him from the stone Statue, and he boldly invites the Statue to dinner.

In the last act Giovanni stands before a richly laid table, alone with his useless challenge. He is rude to the musicians, sneering to Leporello, and insulting to Elvira when she arrives with a last appeal to him to repent. Then, as she flees from his fresh insults, the wind of a great storm brings thunder, lightning, and mist into the room and Giovanni's conscience materializes in the Statue. Courageously he faces it and grasps the icy hand which is offered to him. There is a brief struggle and then he is free: "Ah tempo piu'non v'e" ("Ah, there's no time left"). The vision disappears and Giovanni, torn with human desperation, his soul breaking down, feels himself being dragged down into the fire of hell where his myth will end.

Throughout the opera he is never a winner, the shadow of uncontrollable doubt being revealed in his voice and behavior. But he remains the towering figure in the work; all the rest are more or less "normal" people who, after the tragedy, will seek a normal life again. Only Elvira will never forget.

Leporello identifies himself with his master. His simple mind is full of admiration for him, discussing and criticizing but always ready to accept any kind of situation to please him. He is completely under his spell and will feel free only at the fall of his idol, when he will revert to his own modest personality.

Don Giovanni has a cold, often distant glance; his full mouth has a bitter curve; his face is pale, and he carries his head haughtily. His hands are nervous, his walk dashing and slightly feline, even when his soul is disturbed. With this idea of him in mind it is comparatively easy to complete the characterization musically. Mozart adheres perfectly to the idea born from the libretto of Da Ponte.

The supernatural happenings of the last scene become a logical development in Don Giovanni's mind. A large palette of vocal colors is at the complete disposal of this character, who is at first unaware of his own decline, which he disdainfully rejects. But the pain of growing self-knowledge worsens and he passes through violent reaction to a kind of madness—a madness which derives from the pride and traditional outlook of an absolute master in his own small world. His voice is in turn sharp and cutting or sweet and winning when he is attempting conquest. The "Serenade" is a test of pure bel canto, but when he is foiled even in this ironical courtship of Elvira's maid the coloring of the voice, the pronunciation of the words, the inflections, all underline the disappointment of the insecure hero.

Even his sword has lost its real power. It is used merely to trace the lettering on the funeral monument or to prick the quivering behind of Leporello. No longer is it a strong, effective weapon. Indeed, in the supper scene while he awaits the arrival of the Stone Guest, I would like to have him pacing up and down nervously twirling the sword in his hand

and slicing the candles in half—causing perhaps the fire which eventually consumes the scene. Vocal outbursts accompany the action, building up to his mad but heroic flare-up before the end.

One must pronounce the recitatives very clearly, calmly, and in a relaxed, thoughtful manner; one speaks because one is thinking and not because one already knows everything by heart. Quite often these recitatives are spoken in a childish way with the wrong cadence by people ignoring the Italian, the value of punctuation, and the rhythm suggested by the thinking and the action. It is not only what Giovanni says which is important but the meaning behind the words, reflecting his subconscious.

But then—after all this speculation about Don Giovanni—the thought comes unbidden that Mozart probably never dreamed on these lines at all. For one thing, he hardly had time to do so, composing as he did at such speed. He was certainly attracted by the libretto of Da Ponte, and this he eagerly enveloped in immortal music. Perhaps that is what really matters. Let Don Giovanni himself remain the enigma which everyone must interpret in his own way.

On the subject of those recitatives, I remember discussing the matter in great detail with Maestro Krips, who was used to the faster, slightly more inflexible rhythm favored by the Viennese school. My view was that, taken a fraction more slowly, they revealed much more of their inner meaning, particularly to those who had some (even slight) knowledge of Italian. We started our discussion in the opera house and then, as we became more deeply involved, I suggested that I should walk with him to his hotel, which was at the farther end of Piccadilly. We started off, talking and gesturing energetically and pausing sometimes to make a special point or even to sing a phrase.

When we arrived at his hotel we were still deeply immersed in our conversation, so we turned around and retraced our footsteps. How many times we walked up and down Piccadilly I really cannot say. But it must have been a remarkable sight—those two foreign gentlemen stepping first to one side and then the other to avoid the lunch-time crowds, totally oblivious of their surroundings as they talked volubly and gestured energetically and sang occasionally. One passer-by who recognized us, I suppose, happened to have a camera and (without our noticing anything) recorded the scene and later sent us each a copy of his photograph. We were both delighted, and my copy remains with me today as a cherished memento of stimulating days in London.

It was the following year (1964) which was to bring me, again in

London, the most exciting and moving offer ever made to me. The year opened with the drama and artistic satisfaction of Maria Callas' come-back, already described at some length earlier in the book. Then—it is always difficult to say when or why one operatic idea sparks off another —scarcely were the London *Toscas* completed than I was summoned urgently to New York for the return of Renata Tebaldi after nearly two years' absence from the operatic scene. She also was to sing Tosca and again I was called on to play Scarpia. I could not help thinking that the original of that splendid villain would surely have been surprised to know that he would ever be regarded as the man par excellence to reassure nervous sopranos. But so it was, and the success was considerable.

I was soon back in London for more television appearances and then, in April, we performed *Otello* at Covent Garden with James McCracken and that lovely Desdemona, Raina Kabaiwanska. I think it must have been then—or possibly in May, when I returned to sing the Count in *Nozze di Figaro*—that David Webster began to discuss future operatic possibilities with me. We had done this before and more than once I had suggested *Simone Boccanegra,* pointing out that most opera houses of note now included it in their repertoire and that Covent Garden surely could not be content to lag behind. So far I had not carried him with me but that day he said:

"I think, Tito, that perhaps it is time to consider your favorite *Simone Boccanegra* for Covent Garden—say, in the autumn of 1965. But"—I suppose I looked eager—"the conditions are going to be very stiff." I held my breath, and he went on: "They are that you should decide the cast, the conductor, the scenery, and the costumes. And that you should produce the opera and sing the title role."

Had I ever been given to fainting I would have fainted then. I had never before produced officially—only bits here and there, and always in the shadow of the main producer. It was the sort of offer one might dream about but never expect to happen.

"Think it over," Webster said. "You don't need to say yes to me now. Think it over—and say yes to me tomorrow morning."

I really had no need to think it over, of course, but I telephoned him the following morning and said: "If you have not changed your mind, I will not change mine. I accept this splendid offer with all my heart, but I shall need all your help."

He promised me all the support I could want. And then the day after the projected plans for the London *Simone* were leaked to the press I received a telegram from Chicago, saying that they had had the same idea.

Would I be prepared to produce *Simone Boccanegra* for them during the next season and sing the title role?

I naturally consulted David Webster before making any reply, particularly as the Chicago date would precede the London one, but he agreed immediately, remarking with typically whimsical humor: "That will give us five dress rehearsals." So it was decided that I should produce *Simone Boccanegra* and sing the title role in Chicago in October 1965 and do the same thing in London at Covent Garden in November, but with a different staging and a different cast.

It would be wrong to say that everything else seemed rather small beer in comparison with these heady offers, but I certainly viewed my other activities through a golden haze of greater things to come. One touching event in June, however, stands out in my memory. My hometown of Bassano del Grappa decided to honor me as a "famous citizen" and so, in company with the Gorlinskys, Tilde and I journeyed there. I was presented with a gold medal, the Mayor made a moving speech, there were various festivities, visits to factories, shops, and so on, all in company with old friends from the past. The whole town was in an affectionate turmoil, and it did my heart good to be welcomed so warmly.

In August Mario del Monaco and I were invited to take part in a performance of *Tosca* at Torre del Lago, the home of Puccini. Mario (as Del Monaco) was recovering from a very serious car accident but Mario (as Cavaradossi) was a splendid dashing hero who sang magnificently. Afterward, still in my Scarpia costume and followed by an enthusiastic crowd, I walked through the streets to Puccini's villa, where a horrible photograph was taken of me holding the maestro's guns. But nothing could detract from the strangely moving experience of standing in the room where Puccini had worked, surrounded by his personal things—not even the fact that the organizer omitted to pay the artists.

We spent some holiday weeks at Santa Severa as usual, and had so many visitors that Tilde declared she went around each night with a pillow and blanket looking for a corner to sleep in. None of us minded, however—least of all Tilde. At one time we used to call the house "Il Riposo," but after a while Bibi Bizzelli (who with his charming American wife, Alva, was a frequent visitor) wrote under the sign, "Ha! Ha!" and we all had to agree that however much fun we had there we could not claim that there was much "riposo" about those summer months.

By the middle of September Tilde and I had exchanged our "restful" summer break for work once more, starting in San Francisco. Here, with my *Simone* production ever in my mind, I visited the famous De Bellis Collection where I found some fascinating books on ancient Genoa, including a map of the port at the time of the real Simone Boccanegra.

I had, from the beginning, decided on Giancarlo Bartolini-Salimbeni for the scene designer. I admired his youthful vigor, the intrinsic beauty of his work, the absence of all gimmicks, and above all his wonderful "feel" for period. Later some critics were to complain that a few of the scenes were too stark. The fact was that they were totally authentic, which is why they lasted and can be—and are—used today. In the first year the murmur was: "Those walls are too bare." Later (perhaps after some further study of the period) this changed to "those beautiful bare walls."

Those beautiful bare walls were satisfying because they were *right,* as were the unexpectedly somber costumes of the period. Against just such a background and in just such clothing had the original revolt of Simone Boccanegra been played out. This kind of production will, in my experience, last an opera house for years and provide the basic background for any number of "new approaches" to a work. The production which sets *Tristan and Isolde* on a trans-Atlantic liner, *Falstaff* five hundred miles away from Windsor, or *Macbeth* in the middle of the nineteenth century may earn some headlines in the newspapers next morning but will be of little use to future budgeting in a seriously run opera house. Nor, I am prepared to insist, will the enjoyment of the audience be in any way enhanced.

Although both my productions were still a year in the future I was already absorbed in study and preparation. But in October, while we were still in the United States, by now in Chicago, Tilde and I received a frantic telephone call from Cecilia. Boris had become tragically ill and had to undergo a serious operation. It so happened that the very next evening I had to play Rodrigo in *Don Carlo* to Ghiaurov's King Philip, and inevitably I was haunted by the memory of the many times Boris and I had played those scenes together. Our anxiety was acute until, some while later, Cecilia was able to send us the news that the operation on Boris had been performed and all was well.

My American commitments still kept us away from Europe and it was almost Christmas before we were home again. In the new year David Webster joined us in Rome and after discussions—he agreed to everything I proposed!—he and I drove to Florence to see Maestro Gui and invite him to conduct the London performances of *Simone*. One of the finest and most cultured of musicians, Maestro Gui had known me and my work from the very beginning. Unfortunately, however, he was unable to accept the invitation and in the event it was none other than my old friend and colleague Maestro de Fabritiis who undertook the conducting. This was a far cry indeed from that terrible morning in December 1938 when he had telephoned to tell the wretched, unprepared young Tito Gobbi that he would be singing Lelio in *Le Donne Curiose* that night.

I returned to London with David Webster and, in addition to the long discussions on the *Simone* production, I enjoyed making a series of television programs based on a gallery of portraits from opera and produced by Patricia Foy. I remember particularly how intriguing it was to do both Falstaff and Ford, showing how the different coloring of the voice can enable the same artist to show the contrast between these two baritone roles even though they share the same scenes. Still more intriguing was the way in which, by clever photographic trickery, I was seen arm in arm with myself as both Falstaff and Ford and then, in a lengthening shot, as Tito Gobbi commenting on the two of them.

During the *Simone* discussions Sir David asked me whom I wanted for my understudy in the name part. I had been considering this with some care and so I was able to answer at once: "There's a very gifted fellow here, a man with a rather important nose. Good voice, good stage presence. The name is something like Shaw."

"John Shaw?" Sir David considered that. "N-o. I doubt if he is yet up to Simone Boccanegra."

"He is," I insisted. "All the possibilities are there. Let me coach him and have him in reserve. I don't intend to miss any of my performances, I assure you. But, in my view, if he studies well and develops as I hope, he should be given two performances anyway near the end of the run."

"Well, talk to him," said Sir David. So I sought out John Shaw and —my English does sometimes let me down rather badly—I said: "I've something I want to ask you. Will you be my undertaker in *Simone Boccanegra.*"

"Oh no, Tito—never!" he cried, laughing. "I wouldn't be your undertaker in any circumstances at all."

Well, we set that right, and he was delighted beyond measure at the prospect. I can say here and now that he worked splendidly and later became an excellent Simone Boccanegra. But there were still many performances and some personal crises between me and that first London production.

In February and March Maria Callas and I once more teamed up in

Paris for eight triumphant *Toscas*. Almost immediately after the first performance Cecilia once more had to telephone us with the frightening news this time that Tilde's father was dangerously ill. Papa Raffaello was eighty-six by now and, full of fears, Tilde left me and returned to Rome. It was a terribly anxious time, and I too went backward and forward from Paris whenever I could. But presently the dear old man rallied and by the middle of March I was able to leave for the United States for discussions with Maestro Donati and Salimbeni in Chicago, and then performances of *Tosca* with Maria in New York.

However, it was our year for family crises and tragedies. I almost immediately received the news that our much-loved Aunt Sisina had died suddenly. I felt quite desperate. I always seemed to be away from home when I was most needed, and at this juncture I could imagine how heavy the family demands would be upon Tilde. I managed two of my performances and then I went to Mr. Bing and explained my position, whereupon he kindly released me from the rest of my contract. Indeed, I should like to say here that, after that one difference concerning my first New York Scarpia, I always received the greatest consideration from him. It was a matter of real regret to me that I was unable to accept more of the Metropolitan offers made to me over the years, but the policy there entailed almost always a much longer stay than I was able or willing to make. On the whole I preferred engagements which took me to different places for two, three, or four weeks at a time. Longer engagements always seemed difficult to fit in.

I flew back to Rome where I was able to remain until April, when I went to London for four performances of the double-bill *Il Tabarro* and *Gianni Schicchi*. The Giorgetta in *Il Tabarro* was Marie Collier, with whom some years later I was to sing the last performances before her tragic death. The role of Giorgetta suited her wonderfully and she gave some memorable performances.

There followed several weeks of tremendous pressure: Hamburg and Mannheim for *Tosca*, back to London for three *Otellos*, Rome again for performances of *Falstaff*, Milan to inspect the scenery being built there for the Chicago *Simone*, followed by three *Toscas* in Rome, and then, still only half way through June, Tilde and I were in Athens. If the term "star" had ever been applicable to me I had become almost a shooting star at this period.

In Athens in the beautiful open-air theater of Herod Atticus we were to perform *Otello*, with Jon Vickers in the name part. The local gods were certainly not inclined to smile upon us at first, for it started to rain.

But the Princess Irene, who was in the audience, calmly remained seated and everyone followed suit. Consequently we began the performance and presently the weather cleared. In the first scene, by one of those strokes of genius beloved of producers but almost always dangerous to the performer, I was supposed to come leaping in down a flight of artistically broken steps. Naturally the light failed to come on at the crucial moment, so I missed my footing and came tumbling down the steps, arriving by a miracle, however, in time for my second cue.

After this I was expected to leap over a couple of barrels of doubtful solidity. They broke beneath my more than feather weight, and there I was with a leg in each barrel, scratched and with torn stockings, roaring the "Brindisi" with genuine venom breaking through my assumed gaiety.

Tilde, in the audience, was by now almost as shocked and scared as I was. As though all this were not enough a poor old man sitting near her suddenly dropped dead and had to be carried out. When she finally came backstage after the first act she was so enraged and nervous that she cried out to the producer: "What are you all doing? Do you want to kill my husband too?" So instead of giving vent to my own feelings I had to address myself to calming her.

And yet, in spite of everything, the rest of the evening went marvelously: a beautiful performance in a unique setting. At the banquet afterward I was saluted in a most charming speech, which ended: "Welcome home, Mr. Gobbi. For this, being the land of drama, is undoubtedly your natural home!" Who would not have been mollified by that?

Refreshed by our stay in Greece, cheered by five performances at Covent Garden with its ever-faithful and friendly audience, stimulated by an excellent recording of *Nabucco* in Vienna under Gardelli, I felt I was as ready as I was ever likely to be for my next great undertaking. On September 26 we flew from Rome to Chicago for the first staging of my life. I was welcomed with warmth and friendliness, but I was worried and anxious about this new venture.

"You must try to split yourself in two," Pino Donati told me. "You are both producer and singer. Look at yourself from the outside."

I did my best to follow this advice with the friendly co-operation of my conductor, Bruno Bartoletti, whose international career was then flourishing. I was fortunate to know him and his work almost from the outset, for he was a fine support to me during my first staging of *Simone,* and we were subsequently to work together on many occasions in great harmony and mutual understanding.

I was cheered by the fact that I had an excellent cast, including Arié,

Cioni, and Ligabue, and a splendid chorus, all of whom worked selflessly and well for me. At a stage party after the dress rehearsal the chorus presented me with a book and a beautifully designed parchment with all their signatures. I felt that everyone wished me well.

"October 11th," I wrote in my diary when the great night was over. *"My first production! The first performance I did myself.* Tilde says it was magnificent, but I won't say anything about the production myself. I only know that the atmosphere was tremendously exciting. My colleagues went out of their way to please me, and I have received the most moving demonstration of affection from every side—the audience, the stage, the direction, friends and unknown people sending mountains of wires from all parts of the world. Afterwards I gave a party in the Florentine Room at the Italian Village. The way the owners decorated the place was extraordinary: lights and candles and big stars hanging from the ceiling bearing the names of the artists, and fantastic trophies of flowers and fruit. What a night! I went to bed so deadly, beautifully tired!"

We gave three more performances, then Tilde and I returned to Rome to snatch a brief rest before going to London for the *Simone Boccanegra* there.

At Covent Garden the work was a good deal heavier. I had been promised absolute freedom, and I certainly had it. There was nothing of the "family party" atmosphere of Chicago, and sometimes I would almost have welcomed some interference in order to hear any opinion other than my own. In addition, I had virtually to train and direct two casts in order that the home team could later have their opportunity of playing the work.

Press, radio, and television people were around for a good deal of the time, which added to the stress. But I was aware of a feeling of great stimulation, as well as a sense of gratitude, because Sir David had believed in me sufficiently to entrust me with this task. I wish he were still alive for me to tell him now that *belief* in an artist is what so often lifts one to one's best achievement. But I expect he knew it, and that was one reason why he was such a fine opera director.

In the end all went well. The audience was enthusiastic, the critics well satisfied, and even the strictures on those "bare walls" were, as I have said, withdrawn at a later date. And so my great adventure was over, and we went home to Rome for Christmas in very good heart.

16.

FORTUNATE INDEED is the man or woman who is given the opportunity to plant in one decade the seeds which will flower in the next. That first excursion into production offered to me by Sir David Webster had the effect of almost immediately widening my artistic horizons, as similar invitations began to come in from other countries and other managements. The singer who is concerned solely with his or her own voice is a vulnerable creature, since no voice, however beautiful or well-schooled, can in the nature of things continue in full splendor indefinitely. For ten years more I was to remain a busy international singer, and some of my most treasured vocal experiences were to take place during that period, but now I became a busy producer too and my life was the richer because of it.

In a certain sense the year 1965 represents a line of demarcation, almost a watershed, in my career, and so I propose to pause here and take a bird's-eye view of the path I had so far followed, allowing myself the indulgence of recalling some of the fellow artists I encountered on the way. The fame of most of them is secure without any words of mine, but it is sometimes the personal glimpse which adds the touch of reality to a legend, a name on a gramophone record, or a photograph.

Look back then down the hill. Here comes the youthful Tito Gobbi on the lower slopes. And who is that genial, kindly looking gentleman pausing to give him an encouraging word? Can it possibly be Giuseppe de Luca of the golden tone? The tall, imposing man with the tremendous voice, booming out an unexpected expression of approval—could that be the legendary Titta Ruffo? That striking figure rising with a thoughtful air from his game of poker—is that really Riccardo Stracciari? It is, in each case, for I had the pleasure and honor of at least an acquaintance with all three.

To De Luca I owe two memorable lessons and some very kind interest and encouragement. He was in Rome when I first approached him to ask if he would hear and perhaps advise me. Immediately he invited me to his house, with Tilde accompanying me, and he heard me in *Don Carlo* and gave me some valuable advice on the phrasing and coloring of Rodrigo's music. He also gave me some hints on the presentation of the role, which I adapted somewhat to my own ideas, realizing that we were viewing the task from the standpoints of two different generations. Later he came to some of my performances and would usually come backstage afterward, often to express approval and sometimes to make further suggestions. Although acknowledged to be one of the greatest of all baritones, he did not stint his helpful advice and encouragement to a not very important young singer.

Titta Ruffo had already ceased singing when I entered the field, and was living in retirement. It must have been soon after the war, I think, when I came to Pisa to sing Rigoletto, and just before the performance someone came to me and said: "The maestro is in the house." Assuming that this referred to the conductor and thinking it was surely about time he was there anyway, I merely replied: "Oh yes." Then someone else came and said rather breathlessly: "The maestro is in the house!"

"Whereabouts in the house?" I asked.

"Why, in his box of course."

"In his *box?*" I repeated. "What is he doing in his box?"

Then it was finally explained to me that in Pisa "the maestro" meant only one person—Titta Ruffo.

I gulped slightly, tried not to think of the tremendous volume of sound for which Ruffo was famous, and resolved that, far from trying to emulate that, I must concentrate on giving my performance with all the subtlety and artistry at my command, making good use of the mezza voce, which can and should express so much in this heart-rending role. Within those terms I did my best, and was aware at the end that a tall figure had risen in one of the boxes and was applauding warmly. I bowed deeply in his direction and retired to my dressing room.

Hardly had I begun to remove my make-up when someone scuttled in with the announcement: "The maestro is coming." I got to my feet as he entered—about the most imposing figure I had ever seen. He stood just inside the doorway, dwarfing everything and everyone, and in deep, resonant tones he announced to the people accompanying him: "There are only two singers worthy to play Rigoletto in this house. One is Titta Ruffo and the other is Tito Gobbi." I think I made some suitably modest rejoinder, but in that moment the great Titta Ruffo made me feel at least six inches taller.

With Stracciari I was more closely acquainted than with either of the other famous baritones I have mentioned. I never heard him on the stage but sometimes in the studio, for among those who studied with him was my brother-in-law Boris. He was a handsome man—tall, strong, and with what is meant by "an air." He must have been tremendously impressive on stage and was famous for his magnificent costumes—as I have reason to know, since I came to possess some of them in rather intriguing circumstances.

Stracciari was an inveterate poker player, and heavy gambling played havoc with his fortunes. On one occasion when I met him he took out a beautiful gold watch and said: "I'm going to sell my watch—I need the money. Would you like to buy it, Tito?"

"Oh no," I protested. "If you need some money perhaps I can help you. You don't want to sell your watch."

He firmly refused my offer, however, and so I suggested: "Haven't you something else you'd rather sell?"

He thought for a moment and then said: "What about costumes? I have some very good ones, some of them never even worn."

I agreed this was something that would certainly interest me as we were near enough in size, and I went along to inspect the wonderful range of costumes made for him in better days by the famous Caramba. In the event I bought several costumes from him. These included the glorious Rodrigo costume which I wore many times in my career and which appears in several photographs, as well as the splendid armor and helmet for Charles V in *Ernani*. This I never actually wore onstage, and it hangs now on the wall of my studio, looking very impressive and known to my granddaughter, Isabella, as "the monster." I also bought his costume for Valentine in *Faust* and would willingly have included the beautiful costume he had for the elder Germont. But he said suddenly—and it moved me: "No, not that. I just might perhaps sing that again."

He was very well satisfied with the bargain we struck, and when I saw him some time later I said: "Hello, Riccardo. What is the time?"

Stracciari flashed his attractive smile at me and, drawing out the famous watch, replied: "It's all right, I've still got it."

Of the same vintage was Apollo Granforte, marvelously endowed both vocally and physically, a man of great simplicity and natural nobility. He told me once that he had had a very hard and unhappy childhood. In spite of this, or perhaps because of it, he was usually to be seen carrying a book of some deep philosophical character, which he would study perhaps for a year at a time, as though absorbing and meditating at length on something of the culture which had been denied him in his youth.

Of the older baritones with whom I myself sang I would have to say that my god was Stabile, to whose incomparable Falstaff I often sang Ford. His voice was not of supreme beauty but he used it with consummate skill and a sort of instinctive musicality, though he could not read music (like the tenor Masini, who once said that notes to him were just fly-dirts on the paper). The coloring and expression in Stabile's voice were marvelous and he presented some of the greatest character studies ever seen on the operatic stage.

In my own experience he was the greatest Falstaff; his Scarpia had a sort of deadly exquisiteness; he was a Malatesta in *Don Pasquale* to end all Malatestas and the finest Beckmesser I ever heard. To the Wagnerian purist this may sound heresy, but I stand by my statement: his Beckmesser was superior even to his Falstaff, and that is saying something indeed.

When Serafin finally asked me to take on the role of Falstaff for the first time I wrote to Stabile with the deepest respect, telling him of the offer which had been made to me, adding that having so often played Ford to his own great Falstaff I felt I had learned from him at least something about the role, and asking for his approval—in some sense his blessing—before, young as I was, accepting this great responsibility.

I received no reply and some time later I was told that he had taken what I had written amiss, and thought I was in some way making fun of him. When I told Serafin that I had apparently offended Stabile he said: "Nonsense! The world is wide and there are enough opera houses to accommodate two Falstaffs. I will tell Mariano that I myself chose you for the part."

So in the end I sang my Falstaff, but it continued to grieve me that I could, however inadvertently, have given Stabile the impression that I had less than complete admiration and respect for him.

In recalling some of the great artists with whom I came in contact it was perhaps natural for me to consider the baritones first. But lest I offend those rather easily offended gentlemen, the tenors, let me pass to them now with all speed. Of Gigli I have already written at some length.

To Pertile went the distinction of first showing me what a great tenor really means. One of the very finest of that period—Martinelli—I heard on the opera stage only once when I was quite young. But I knew him well in later life, and had the warmest regard for him (and he, I think, had affection for me).

What else could one feel for that handsome, generous, warm-hearted man who carried with him into old age something of the charm and gaiety and radiance usually associated with youth? But then he *was* ever young. He would come and sit in my dressing room at the Met or in Rome and talk about the performance knowledgeably but never ungenerously. He and my Maestro Crimi had known each other well. Indeed, when I recall Crimi (whom I never heard on the stage) it seems to me that he knew everyone, and he would often tell me stories of the great figures before my time.

One of these stories concerned Caruso and Titta Ruffo, both of whom he knew well. One evening Crimi found himself in the same box as Caruso during a performance in which Ruffo was singing, and on impulse he said: "Tell me, Enrico, what do you really think of him?"

"He's wonderful," replied Caruso without hesitation. "He frightens me."

Some time later, when Caruso was singing and Crimi ran into Titta Ruffo in the audience, he asked the same question: "Tell me, Titta, what do you really think of Enrico?"

"Oh, he's marvelous," Ruffo replied. Then he added slowly: "He frightens me."

Among the great tenors with whom I sang was the veteran Lauri-Volpi—still with us and still (at least up to a year or two ago) able to sing "Nessun dorma" with high notes of phenomenal power and mettle. A man of considerable culture, a writer of distinction, and a knowledgeable conversationalist, he was not among the subtlest of singers, but the sheer sound, particularly in the upper range, was electrifying. Tenors with lesser natural gifts, however, have been known to give more moving performances.

Though not ill-humored he was very much aware of his fame and liked special treatment to be meted out to him. Once when we were doing a performance of *Rigoletto* for the Italian radio he made it clear beforehand that he would like orchestra, cast, and chorus to be seated before he made his entrance for the first rehearsal. Then they should rise to their feet and he, in his turn, would say: "Thank you, thank you. Please sit down," on a note of charming protest.

This was accorded him; then he went and greeted his Gilda, the heavyweight but exquisitely voiced Lina Pagliughi. Next he paused before me (with whom he had sung several times before) and said graciously: "Tito Gobbi, if I am not wrong?"

"You are not wrong," I told him cheerfully, and then added doubtfully: "Lauri-Volpi?"

I must say he had the grace to laugh, but we sparred a little throughout the rehearsal and, when in the last scene the Duke crosses the back of the stage repeating the final phrases of "La donna è mobile," he let out a high note of really incredible power, hung onto it for seconds on end, and then turned to me and said challengingly, "How was that?" knowing that almost anyone else would have gone flat in similar circumstances and would have collapsed if they had tried to produce such a volume of tone.

"Not bad," I told him. "Not bad at all."

"Not bad?" he repeated crossly. "It was even *sharp*."

At this strange claim to improvement on the original, Pagliughi (who had an excellent sense of humor) was so overcome with laughter that she vowed she must "go and powder her nose." The phrase she used was more expressive, and she fled from the platform still laughing, to return a few minutes later to deliver Gilda's last farewell to life in that easy, beautifully colored voice and with infinite pathos.

The most subtle tenor singing of my experience came from Tito Schipa, with whom I often shared the stage and with whom I had a very happy relationship both professionally and personally. His was not a big "juicy" tenor, as can be judged from records, but the magic of his vocal projection was something unique. I remember once when he was singing in *Werther* at Caracalla, the great open-air theater, I asked myself how on earth he was going to make himself even faintly heard when he made his entry upstage on the almost conversationally uttered, "Ah tutto il core ho qui." Out of sheer curiosity I went to the very last row of the theater during the dress rehearsal and sat there waiting for his entry. When it came it was as though he were singing from the seat just in front of me. Of course Caracalla has fine acoustics (according to the wind) but I have known many a big voice which failed to reach the last row. With Schipa distance had no terrors. He, like Gigli, was a master of the art of projection.

I sang with him in *Traviata*, *L'Elisir d'Amore*, *L'Arlesiana*, and *Barbiere*. Once, late in his career, when we were singing *Barbiere* I had an enormous success after the "Largo al factotum." I thought the applause would never stop, for every time it showed signs of flagging some enthusiast or other would take it up from another part of the house. When the performance at last continued I found to my astonishment and dismay that I seemed to be in some sort of vocal trouble. There was some strange difficulty in getting my lower notes and I had to work very hard to produce the light, colorful tones required for the role.

In the interval I ran into Schipa and told him of my dilemma. "I can't imagine what happened," I said worriedly. "It's never happened to me before. I seemed to have to dig out my lower notes from some unusual depths."

"Oh." Schipa suddenly looked rather bashful. "I'm sorry, Tito. I should have told you, or someone should have told you. You see, nowadays I sometimes have a little trouble with those high notes in the scene that follows your 'Cavatina.' So they put down the pitch in the orchestra. That," he explained ingenuously, "is why you had such long applause. We see that it is kept up in the house so that the audience won't notice the alteration in key."

So much for my pride in my great reception!

Quite often when Schipa and I sang together in *Barbiere* our Rosina would be Toti dal Monte. Her beautifully clear, well-projected voice sometimes recorded with a fraction of an "edge" (due probably to the recording techniques of the period); but in reality it was a lovely voice, and she was a lovely stage artist. A cheerful little dumpling of a woman, she was a natural comedy actress. But—more unexpected, considering her build—she had a gift for pathos I have seldom seen equaled and never, in certain roles, surpassed. When she sang Lodoletta all Rome wept, and in the second act of *Butterfly* I never had a Butterfly who wrung my heart more completely with her childlike pathos and dignity.

In connection with this I have sometimes been commended for playing Sharpless in that scene almost entirely with my back to the audience, and I have more than once been asked how it is that I still manage to convey all that the consul is thinking. I am more than willing to put on record the fact that I *had* to learn to do it that way, for when Toti and I shared that scene I found her so moving that I never knew if I would be able to control my tears.

I am following no plan or list in recalling some of the artists I have known—merely following where my memory takes me. So without apology—and I trust without a break in the voice—I move from the exquisite high notes of Toti dal Monte to the deep commanding tones of Tancredi Pasero, the famous basso whose scene I cut short when I first leaped onto the stage of La Scala.

For years he didn't know the identity of the culprit. Then, one day when we had been colleagues for some years, we found ourselves together in Naples at the time of the bombardment. We came out of a restaurant and started to walk back to our lodgings; and on impulse I said: "Tell me, Tancredi, wasn't there some incident—some mishap—when you sang in the first performance of Pizzetti's *Orseolo?*"

He frowned thoughtfully but replied: "N-no. I don't remember anything of the kind."

"Some young fellow interrupted you at the point when—"

"Oh, oh, oh!" he cried. "Don't even remind me of it! I know what you mean. That young idiot! If I knew who he was, I'd kick him from here to the other side of the town. There I'd been singing for twenty minutes and had just gotten to the cadenza when this donkey came galloping onto the stage and spoiled the whole effect."

"And you never found out who it was?" I asked sympathetically.

"No. I only wish I had. If—"

"That was me," I told him; and started to run. Laughing, he gave chase for I don't know how far, but I managed to keep ahead of him and his remembered wrath.

We were good friends and colleagues and shared some amusing experiences. He was a bit of a ladies' man and once invoked my assistance in impressing the lady of his choice.

"Tito," he said, "I know you do some rather clever sketches and paintings. Do me a favor. Make a nice little sketch for me and I'll sign it and send it to someone I'd like to please."

So I did a fetching little sketch of the Bay of Naples on which we were gazing and he signed it and sent it off to his inamorata of the moment. I never heard any more about it, but I hope that someone somewhere still likes her Tito Gobbi sketch signed "Tancredi Pasero."

To attempt anything like a comprehensive list of the fine artists with whom I sang would be futile, and I am already aware of glaring omissions which trouble me. Any choice is naturally dictated to a large extent by the theaters in which I sang, the number of times I partnered certain artists, and so on. High on the list of those who have an irrefutable claim on all counts, however, would come my great partner in so many operas, Maria Caniglia, family friend (with her husband Maestro Donati) for so many years.

I have mentioned her unforgettable Minnie in *La Fanciulla del West*. She was also a fine Aïda, a thrilling Tosca, an outstanding Maddalena in *Andrea Chenier* (well captured on the full recording with Gigli); indeed that unusually rich, beautifully colored voice was a joy in any role she sang. In addition she was a delightful colleague, generous and loyal, with a strong sense of humor and resourceful in an emergency. She once combined the two last qualities in a performance of *Simone Boccanegra* when suddenly the words escaped her. She never faltered but continued in some sort of Esperanto of her own, and only when she came off the stage did she gasp: "Dio! Whatever was I talking about?"

At much the same period came Rosetta Pampanini with her clear, exquisitely lyrical soprano and Pederzini, one of the best mezzos of my whole experience. Hers was not perhaps one of the greatest vocal organs, but she used it splendidly and had a beautiful vocal intensity onstage which made her performances riveting. When she sang the role of the mother in *L'Arlesiana* and began "Esser Madre è un inferno" a sort of shiver would run through the house and the whole audience would go tense. She was also a superb Fedora—so much so that Giordano transposed the role for her—and for as long as she was on the operatic scene hardly anyone else even attempted the role.

Then there was the beautifully stylish and intelligent Magda Olivero, with whom I often sang in what might be called her first career. For, unlike any other artist I can recall, she enjoyed a successful career, retired for ten years, and then came back to attain even higher honors than in her earlier days.

Later, in the same period as Callas, there was Renata Tebaldi, with her very individual, exquisitely creamy tone, her great musicality, and her touching characterization in many of the lyric roles. Among other parts she sang a matchless Desdemona. This was also the time of the adorable Victoria de Los Angeles, with whom I shared many performances and recordings. The voice—still to be heard in recitals and on countless gramophone records—has a beautiful quality all its own: appealing, intensely feminine, and with a capacity for bringing a lump into the listener's throat unrivaled in my experience.

Like Dal Monte she was an unbearably touching Butterfly, and I am still ashamed to remember how Pippo di Stefano and I, in an inexcusable mood of teasing, actually made her cry during the lovely recording of the work which we did together. I tell the story with shame but also as a serious warning of how easily a singer's confidence can be shaken. It was during the recording of "Un bel di vedremo," and after two "takes"

Pippo and I were thinking hard of lunch. When a third "take" was decided upon we planted ourselves behind the conductor, exchanged grave and worried looks, pretended to be astonished, shook our heads, and so on. At which poor Victoria stopped, burst into tears, and sobbed: "What is wrong? Why do you look like that?"

Full of remorse we rushed onstage, embraced her, told her she was wonderful and begged to be forgiven. Forgiven we were, but we never played the fool like that again.

Naturally a special place must be found on any list of mine for Ferrucio Tagliavini and Italo Tajo, the other two of "The Three T's" and "The Flying Musketeers of La Scala." We shared our youth and many of our professional years together, and I think I can say that our voices and our personalities integrated particularly well onstage. Ferrucio's voice was a true lyric tenor—full without being absolutely "robusto," with a marvelous color, a natural flexibility, and most admirably schooled. It can be heard on many records in almost its full beauty, for it is a voice which recorded well.

Italo Tajo, one of the real singing actors of my time, was, like myself, absorbed in the quest for a new degree of naturalness on the operatic stage. Still active in the field of opera, he is a master of make-up and justly famed for the subtlety of his characterization. His impersonation of Don Quichotte remains for me one of the finest pieces of stagecraft and dramatic projection.

Also with me for the greater part of my career was Giulietta Simionato, for she was at La Scala when I myself was too insignificant to aspire to even the humblest rung of the ladder. Indeed, she and I still recall with amusement one occasion when I offered to escort her home though neither of us could afford a taxi. We walked the whole way—and a long way at that—and just as I said good night to her it began to snow with such ferocity that, somewhat unrealistically, she offered to call a taxi for me. I airily assured her that I *liked* walking in the snow, and off I went. Within two minutes I was half blinded and completely lost in a blizzard. The few people I encountered were strangers in the district (they always are) and the few directions I received only served to confuse me further. I don't remember how long it took me to reach home, but it seemed like hours. Strangely enough, however, I escaped without a trace of a cold— a fact which so impressed Gino del Signore, one of my colleagues, that he declared he was going to follow my habit of dispensing with a thick scarf and refusing to coddle myself. I agreed that it would be wonderful if he could free himself from his bundled-up regime and go untrammeled for the rest of his career. The poor fellow, as a result, caught the worst cold of his life, and for nearly a month I remorsefully visited him with fruit and other small offerings to assuage my feelings of guilt.

As my career burgeoned, so did Giulietta's. In my view she went too long unrecognized, for any management worth its salt should have picked her out from the ranks of the small-parters at an early stage. In the end she made her way to well-deserved stardom, among other things creating a portrait of Jane Seymour which stood up on equal terms to Callas' famous Anna Bolena, for she was an outstanding actress as well as singer.

Another mezzo of great distinction and wonderful professionalism is Fedora Barbieri. Hers is a vocal organ of great richness, with formidable chest notes. Her stage work is excellent—particularly in comedy—and her musicality superb. She was the finest Quickly of my experience, and when I was asked to sing in and direct *Falstaff* in Paris for the first time at the Opéra and then a full-length color television performance of the work, I agreed to an all-French cast for everyone but Quickly. For those wonderful comedy exchanges with Sir John I *had* to have Fedora Barbieri.

Finally I want to pay tribute to the *comprimarios,* who play such a vital part in any company and who provide perhaps the most useful lesson of all to the aspiring young singer. We are not all cut out to be Dukes, Manricos, or Otellos, nor Aïdas, Violettas, or Toscas. But some of the best careers—and incidentally some of the most financially rewarding—are carved out by the clever, versatile, small-voiced singers who fill the secondary roles.

It is well to remember that a fine *comprimario* is always in demand. His fee may not be among the highest, but he will probably sing five times a week while the "star" may sing twice in ten days. Also he will probably still be pursuing his career even after the best of his vocal powers are spent. Nor must it be supposed that his contribution to the artistic whole is negligible. On the contrary, men like De Paolis, Zagonara, Mariano Caruso, and De Palma, with their versatility, musicality, and practiced sense of rhythm, could sometimes "make" a scene, just as a clumsy performer in the same part could ruin it.

Mariano Caruso is a good example of someone who assessed his own potential with great intelligence and realism. I remember so well his coming to me after a performance of *Rigoletto.* It was what is called a "popular-priced" performance in which he had been given an opportunity to sing the Duke, and he had made a very good job of it.

"Tito," he said to me, "I respect your judgment and think you will give me an honest reply. After this success, do you think I should go on and try my luck in some leading tenor roles?"

With absolute frankness I replied: "Since you ask me, Mariano, I must say in all friendly candor that in my view you would be rather far down the list of the leading tenors. As a *comprimario* you could be the king."

"Thank you," he said. "That is my opinion too. I'll stay a *comprimario*." Which he did, for the rest of his fine and distinguished career.

I am deliberately not pursuing my reminiscences beyond this point. It is unnecessary—indeed, it would be presumptuous of me—to tell listeners what to think about those artists who are still pursuing an active career and can therefore be heard, seen, and judged according to individual taste. With many of them I have sung; with still others I have been the producer in performances in which they have appeared. But it is not my province to play the music critic at this point. The modest intention of this chapter is, as I said at the beginning, to attempt to give a touch of reality to some of those with whom I worked. Interpretative art is in its very nature transitory. A record, however good and however intelligently played (which is the exception rather than the rule), can give little idea of a personality. Perhaps my words may add a little here or there. I hope so.

Inevitably when one looks back one is tempted to draw deep conclusions and offer advice, but this practice should be indulged in with caution. One thing which strikes me quite forcibly, however, is that, although I counted a few of my real friends among other singers, they were singularly few. And I ask myself why.

Certainly I enjoyed pleasant relationships with most of my colleagues, and there are few whom I recall with any real bitterness. But real friends? That is another matter. To me a friend is someone who accepts me with all my faults, virtues, and peculiarities—for life, as I accept him: someone, if you like, who is close to me in spirit as well as in fact, and to whom time and distance make no difference.

As I try to express my exact meaning, I at once call to mind Nanni Ghibelli, whom I met on my first day at school when I was six. He it was who shared those food parcels pressed upon me by my nurse, Maria, when she feared that her poor little Tito might be underfed. His was the house where I stayed the very first time I spent a night away from home, at nine years of age. In the course of our lives we have met and parted many times, for we married and followed different professions. Now,

Three social studies, featuring good food and good fellowship: with Maestro Serafin at a birthday party; with Carol Fox in Chicago; with my Ghost and my Assistant Ghost (Ida and Louise Cook) at a party given by the Verdi Society of Liverpool, of which I was president for some years.

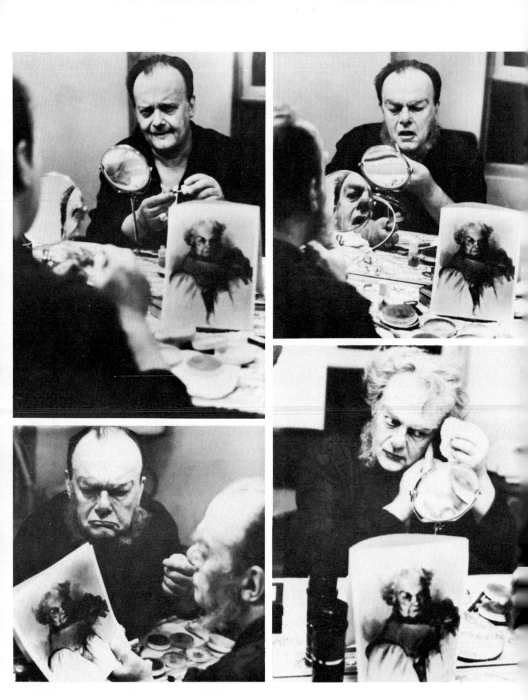

Four studies showing the makeup for the title role in Verdi's Falstaff.

Opposite, Falstaff in three contrasting moods: top, authoritative as he delivers the Honor Monologue in Act I; below, chilled and disillusioned after his ducking in the river; in the guise of the ghostly Herne the Hunter, he goes to his second assignation with Alice.

Two "royal" moments backstage: the Italian ex-king Umberto congratulates me on being a head of state in the person of Simone Boccanegra; below, Del Monaco and I are presented to the Queen Mother after a performance of Otello at Covent Garden.

My own brief appearance as "royalty"–King Moomba for a day in Melbourne, Australia.

Tilde between my parents on the occasion of their Golden Wedding.

My father, Papa Giovanni, and Tilde's father, Papa Raffaello.

My girls! My daughter Cecilia as a little girl with her lion cub, Figaro.

Cecilia today.

Grandpa and granddaughter Isabella.

Three teaching "shots" at the Opera Workshop in the Villa Schifanoia.

when we are no longer young, we have arranged to live quite near each other. I cannot recall our having had any difference in our lives; but even if we were to do so now it would not alter the ease and depth of our relationship. We are friends.

To ask so much of a colleague in a competitive profession is probably unrealistic. And yet—and yet! Need the spirit of competition operate quite so harshly, when artists working together desperately need warmth and sympathy? If I were starting out again or speaking to those setting out I would stress the fact that *of course* it is natural and right to strive to reach the top, but the person whose best efforts one should try to surpass is oneself. It is difficult not to resent and fear the fellow you regard as a dangerous rival. It is impossible to resent and fear oneself.

17.

FOLLOWING THE Chicago *Simone* Carol Fox asked me to produce *Otello* in Chicago in the autumn of 1966, a proposal to which I willingly agreed. But before this production came along a strange and harrowing experience involving another *Otello* occurred. During the previous year Pippo di Stefano had telephoned me one day to tell me that he had an opportunity to sing Otello in California. Would I be his Iago and also direct the performance? Either I am a masochist or an idiot because on the spur of the moment I thought perhaps Pippo, with that heavenly lyric voice, could be made to sing Otello in some individual sort of way. I warned him that he would have to work hard and prepare himself with the utmost thoroughness. He assured me that he would, that he had a year in which to prepare, and so on and so on. With some misgiving I agreed.

It was not until the early months of 1966 that I began to feel the shadow of the impending performance cast a chill over my optimistic heart. I was in New York at the time singing in *Falstaff,* and as Mr. Bing had allowed me to make some changes in the standing production I was enjoying myself. Equally Tilde and I were enjoying our social life for it is a truism that Americans are the most hospitable people on earth. There would be dinner one evening with our friend John Coveney of EMI Records and Francis Robinson from the Metropolitan, with his marvelous fund of anecdotes. Next day we might have lunch with our bosom friends, Dario and Dorle Soria, or perhaps Lauder Greenway, a prince of hosts, or we might dine with our old friend Gregorio Sciltian, the artist, exhibiting in New York for the first time. It was on this visit also that we first met Nathan Milstein, the great violinist, and found him as fine a raconteur as musician. No New York visit would be complete to us without at least a glimpse of Mary Peltz, the incomparable archivist of the Metropolitan, or Max de Schauensee on one of his frequent visits from Philadelphia. Max, one of the most perceptive and literary of music critics, has a gift of "total recall" which is second to none, and as he has heard almost every singer since Caruso his conversation is riveting. It flatters and pleases me enormously that he remembers hearing me as Silvio at the Castello Sforzesco in Milan in 1937, and is kind enough to say that he noted: "The young Silvio has a good voice and should make quite a career for himself."

With all these distractions to charm me it is not to be wondered at that I pushed the thought of the Californian *Otello* into the background of my mind. But inexorable time always has the last word, and presently the rather quixotic experiment was not only rapidly approaching but was actually upon me. Tilde and I flew to Los Angeles, where we were collected and driven to Pasadena. Hospitality abounded, but in the midst of this paradise a sort of nightmare began. To begin with, no one (including the conductor) appeared to know much about the work, and for some days the Otello himself did not turn up. For nearly a week we did not even see the place where the performance was eventually to take place. Instead we drove around night and day rehearsing (with Otello usually missing) in school halls and private houses. At the first chorus rehearsal it turned out that there was no chorus master, that the chorus, though willing, had no idea what the work was all about, and that the prompter for some reason did not want to prompt. Perhaps he didn't know what it was all about either.

After various get-togethers which could hardly be described as rehearsals since on no single occasion did everyone manage to attend at the same time, it became clear to me that Pippo had very shaky ideas indeed about Otello. He ignored Act III (which requires the most meticulous rehearsing of all) and had already almost reduced his Desdemona, Marcella Pobbe, to hysterics. Under protest I canceled the proposed first night on March 28, postponing it until the 31st. On the 29th we at last all got together for a sort of dress rehearsal. Everyone was in costume except for my wretched self. I was too busy rushing about repairing this and that ever to get into my Iago costume.

I had presented the conductor with a recording of the work in the hope that he might correct some of his more eccentric tempi, and the chorus struggled manfully to do their best. We had a simple sort of dance for them which worked quite effectively during the "fuochi di gioia," the "fuochi" being made by me with my own hands rather on the plan described by Marco Polo in his book. The chorus touchingly presented me with a small silver cup inscribed "The World's Greatest Teacher," and for the first time Pippo sang his role in its entirety (or rather, the little he knew of it).

On March 31 the show, incredibly, went on. I began to think perhaps I was a stage director of genius after all. Pippo was both frightened and frightening; and after the second act his wife called me urgently to say he was not prepared to continue. In costume and sweating like an ox I rushed down the stairs to his dressing room, let him explain he had "no voice, no strength left, etc.," and then told him grimly: "You are going to die on this stage tonight to the very end, or I'll kick you all the way there myself."

He went on, but as he did not know the third act it was up to me to improvise madly and somehow make the pieces fit together. The last act was strangely good, with some of that beautiful lyric singing he could do so well.

Afterward there was an enormous party, but Pippo and family did not turn up. I thought perhaps it was belated shame over the massacre of a performance, but not at all. They had been robbed—he of five thousand dollars and she of a gold powder case set with sapphires. I did not see him again, nor did I hear from him—not even a word of thanks.

The next day I glanced at the calendar just before we left and felt there was grim significance in the fact that it was April 1. But I did not know the half of it yet. We drove to Los Angeles to catch the plane, but when we had been flying for two hours we had to turn back because something was wrong with the aircraft. We waited and waited, tired and irritated beyond belief, and were then informed that there would not be another flight until the following day. There was no taxi to take us to the hotel, just lines and lines of people queuing up for any kind of transport. Finally we reached the hotel and tried to snatch a little sleep.

The next day we had a horrible flight to New York and then another one to Rome. But there, joy of joys, were Cecilia and Piero, who had come to meet us with the car. Thankfully we sank back into it, whereupon it promptly broke down in the middle of the road and we had to push it for a mile. By the time we reached home we were wrecks. After a few days' rest I went to Maestro Ricci to ask him to put my Iago right, for I feared I might have lost him altogether in the melee.

Later in the month we went to Paris, where I had been invited to take part in performances of *Otello* and *Don Carlo*. The *Otellos* were to be something quite special, according to Monsieur Auric, the director of the

Opéra. They had recovered the original scenery made for Verdi and I was to wear the costume of Maurel, who created the role of Iago. In theory these things sound fine, but it was not my year. I arrived to find that the scenery and costumes did indeed date from 1894 and threatened to disintegrate at the lightest touch. The producer who had last used them had died thirty years before and they had never been replaced. As for the famous costume of Maurel, it fell to pieces as I shook the moths out of it.

I hastily telephoned Tilde to bring my own costume. We did the best we could with four brief rehearsals, and the success of the first performance was remarkable (in the circumstances almost miraculous). The press was enthusiastic, but I was extremely unhappy since it was not at all my way of working.

The one bright spot at this point was the first of what we were later to know as "The Cooks' Parties." Among our warmest and most devoted admirers—introduced to us by our dear friend, the incomparable Dame Eva Turner—were Louise and Ida Cook, lifelong opera fans and confirmed star-gazers. Apart from their enthusiasm they have an exceptional talent for gathering around them a group of fellow enthusiasts who will come together for a London party from as far afield as Liverpool, Leeds, Birmingham, and Northumberland, and will also be prepared at the drop of a hat to journey abroad for any operatic occasion which attracts them.

There they were, our Cooks' Party, in Paris, and they had arranged with their enchanting friend Ginette Spanier and her husband Dr. Seidmann that the party should take place in the Seidmanns' large apartment. Not until we arrived did we discover that extra glamor was to be added to the occasion by the presence of Marlene Dietrich, who made a superb entrance as the last arrival. Within minutes I found myself engaged in an intriguing conversation with her on the uses of advertisement. She asked me if I smoked, in spite of being a singer, and if I always smoked the same brand of cigarette. I said I did and told her the brand, at which, with that dark intensity of tone which sends a *frisson* down one's spine, she said:

"My dear, you could make *millions!* You only need to be photographed smoking one of those cigarettes and saying, 'I always smoke So-and-so.'"

At that I laughed and suddenly confessed that when I have to offer Tosca a glass of Spanish wine in Act II, I am frequently tempted to change the wording "è vin di Spagna" to "è Coca-Cola," the drink which I use for the occasion. She thought this a marvelous idea and begged me to use it, but I have never yet found the courage to do so.

We were getting on splendidly by now, when she said plaintively that she would like to come and hear me sing but did not know how to get a ticket. (Imagine Marlene Dietrich asking in vain for any ticket she wanted!) I removed my glasses, gave her my best Act II Scarpia glance, and said: "Give me your telephone number." All in all it was quite a party, and made up for the moths in poor Maurel's costume.

To compensate for the mishaps over the *Otello* production Monsieur Auric promised wonders for the *Don Carlo* and I hoped for the best. But when I arrived in Paris once more for the first rehearsals none of the cast were there except myself and Renato Cioni, who was singing Carlo for the first time, and no one seemed to be sure when anyone else was coming.

I became nervous and anxious. *Otello* without much preparation is bad enough, but *Don Carlo,* with its great crowd scenes and amount of ensemble singing, requires even more rehearsal and attention. There was no scenery on view, and one can hardly work from sketches. For me the proper presentation of opera means slow, patient preparatory work and a lot of rehearsing. Presently, in despair, I went to Maestro Dervaux (who had still not decided which cuts were proposed in this difficult work, with its varied versions) and told him that I could not go on like this. Whereupon, with something less than old-world courtesy, he told me that if I did not like the situation I knew where the door was.

So I went to Monsieur Auric, with whom I had always been on pleasant terms, and explained my embarrassment and my feeling that I could not participate in a production of which I saw nothing and nobody. I leaned over backward to take some of the blame, saying that I understood the conditions might be difficult at the Opéra at this time and that perhaps I had been spoiled by the standards elsewhere. I added that I had no wish to be difficult—which could be judged from my acceptance of the *Otello* crises—but would he please release me from my contract?

He seemed to understand my point of view completely and a statement was prepared for the press in which I said in all sincerity: "It is with deep regret that I renounce participation in the performance of *Don Carlo,* solely for artistic reasons. The very few rehearsals make it impossible for me to integrate in the production or give of my best. In view of the inadequate preparations available for this opera, which requires such particular care in this respect, I have asked the administration of the Opéra to release me from my contract."

Having apparently agreed to this Monsieur Auric then proceeded to loose upon me a veritable press campaign in terms which earned a place in my press-cutting collection not surpassed for violence and rudeness to this day. "Tito Gobbi is a deserter or he is afraid, and shows disquieting signs of senility," and so on. I was fifty-two at that time and at the peak of my career. He was seventeen years older and, although a good musician, not conspicuous for his temperate habits. In the circumstances, to challenge me on the grounds of senility was not perhaps the wisest course. I had no choice but to sue him.

The international press—most of whom were on my side—took the case to heart. I had never been involved in a scandal before and found myself hailed as a sort of hero—the one who had at last challenged the pitiful conditions obtaining at the Opéra. So-called friends were zealous in pushing me into the fight, and I felt a bit like Don Quixote tilting against the windmills. My good Sander—always on the side of the artist —buckled on his armor and prepared to charge. It was quite something.

My replacement as Posa was the excellent Louis Quilico, and the Paris *Presse* said that nobody missed Gobbi. Paris *Jour,* on the other hand, declared that there were cries of "Gobbi, Gobbi!" when he first appeared. I was not there, having gone home by then, leaving them all to fight it out. Everyone of prominence I had ever known was approached for their comments, and to this day I am surprised at some who declined to comment (what did I say about few colleagues being real friends?). But I record with gratitude that Cioni immediately wrote to me to say that he was at my disposal if he could help me in any way.

At this point a gentleman called Bacquier (of whom in my perhaps deplorable ignorance I had never heard and whom to the best of my belief I had never met) rushed into print with the statement that I was too old to sing Posa anyway, and that I had threatened the Chicago Lyric Opera that I would never sing there again if they dared to engage *him.* It seemed that I was a much more influential fellow than I had ever supposed.

The case went on for two years and in the end I won it. By then Monsieur Auric had retired from the Opéra, and I had little interest in the affair any more—even in the quite heavy damages which were eventually awarded me.

At the height of the great brouhaha in the summer of 1966 I went home, as I have said, and sought the soothing company of my wife and my dog. Here Tilde reminds me reproachfully that I have never yet mentioned Onyx, a valued member of our family, the best-mannered poodle ever created, a seasoned traveler yet always ready to welcome us home *senza rancor* whenever we had to leave him behind. All three of us spent two relaxing weeks at Abano, with excursions to Bassano to visit our beloved Baby Zanchetta, who still plays the perfect hostess in the villa where we gathered as children and where her father, the barone, once called me from the tennis court and told me I had a voice which might possibly be worth cultivating.

The mischances of this extraordinary year, however, had by no means yet exhausted themselves. After a flying visit to Milan to inspect the lovely sets being built for the Chicago *Otello* and a pause in Rome to spend a few days with our good friends George Marek from RCA New York and his wife Muriel, we set out for Montreal for performances of *Otello* in company with the Del Monacos, Renata Tebaldi, and Marcella Pobbe (a sad mix-up here since it transpired that *two* distinguished Desdemonas had been engaged, although Shakespeare and Verdi surely envisaged only one).

It soon became clear that the financial background of this undertaking was very dubious and I was glad that the ever-watchful Sander had insisted on my fees being deposited in the bank beforehand. His forethought was fully justified when, although we had the artistic satisfaction of seeing our performance described in the press as "The Singing of the Gods," it turned out that this was to be the limit of our reward, for there was no money available to pay "the gods." The situation was serious indeed for the company, and no sooner had I arrived back in Rome than I received a cable asking if I would be willing to have my deposited fees used to help with the company's traveling costs. With Sander calling me a fool, I agreed.

I never saw my money again but at least the company all got home. Tilde and I were warmly welcomed by Onyx and we retreated to Santa Severa, if not to lick our wounds, at least to enjoy what we felt was a well-earned rest in company with such old friends as Betty Eliot, Albert White, and Stella Chitty, who, in a quiet and tactful way, always seems to have the answer to any problem backstage at Covent Garden. Fate, however, was not to be satisfied with merely professional crises. We were almost immediately summoned back to Rome by the news that my father had fallen and broken his hip.

We settled him in a suite in the Orthopedic Center, with his housekeeper, and I discovered (if I had not known it before) that the principal exponent of drama in the Gobbi family was not Tito but Giovanni. Given such a splendid opportunity to hold the stage, my father put on a magnificent performance as the distinguished invalid. He lived in the Orthopedic Center like an emperor, ringing the bell every five seconds, delighting everyone with his charm when not driving them mad with his demands. The poor doctor in charge kept on explaining to me that it was customary for a patient to go home once the plaster was on and not to be brought back until the plaster had to be removed. But not my father! There he stayed for three months, at enormous expense, playing the star role and loving every minute of it.

The rest of the year was taken up with more run-of-the-mill experiences, although during the production of *Otello* in Chicago I suffered from both tooth trouble and tenor trouble, and it would be difficult for me to say which was the more agonizing. Sustained by the friendly company of Terry McEwen, Vice-president of Decca-London Records—one of the most *simpatico* and helpful people in the record world—and our good friend Norman Ross, I managed to surmount all difficulties, and then in December I went to London to fulfill a role which was entirely new to me.

With far more nervous trepidation than I ever experienced over a singing engagement I made my debut as a lecturer, speaking for the British Italian Society at Chelsea Town Hall. The head of the society was Sir Ashley Clarke, for years the distinguished and popular British ambassador to Rome, and he and Lady Clarke were both old friends of ours. Lord Drogheda, Chairman of the Covent Garden Board, introduced me and the place was full of friends—among them Margaret and Leonard Boden, Dame Eva Turner, Betty Eliot, the Cooks, and Harold Rosenthal, who edits the unique magazine *Opera* (without which few of us would know what is happening in the international opera world) and has gathered around him such a remarkable team of musical writers. To two of them I should like to pay a personal tribute at this point: Arthur Jacobs, who produces that splendid reference book *The British Music Yearbook* and was kind enough to nominate me for Musician of the Year in 1975, and Alan Blyth, who wrote the wonderful article about me for inclusion in the yearbook on that occasion.

My lecture was on *Simone Boccanegra,* and although I drew a certain amount of moral support from the presence of so many friends I also felt doubly responsible because they had come. I remember it as a beautiful but unnerving occasion, but what I remember still more clearly is the incredible display of British calm, good manners, and humanity displayed by Frances Clarke at the dinner party which she and Sir Ashley later gave for us. I still wince to remember the agonizing crash when a waiter, carrying a pile of superb Wedgwood plates, stumbled and broke the lot. Frances did not even blink; she was concerned solely for the waiter, lest he might have hurt himself.

The following year provided fewer crises but included a great deal of traveling for me, the highlights of which I shall describe in a later chapter. I was immensely busy in my double role of singer and producer, but I loved every moment. Then, at the beginning of 1968, an event occurred which must stand as a melancholy milestone in my life. On February 4 Maestro Serafin died in Rome.

I owed so much to him throughout my career that even then I felt suddenly lost without him. His guidance had always been so secure, an invaluable gift to a young singer. With him the Rome Opera House reached its maximum splendor, and he built a whole generation of singers, repetiteurs, conductors, dancers, producers, technicians. His performances were like an arch, beautifully shaped in a curve from the first to the last bar, and we all took part, body and soul, with the same devotion and enthusiasm as he himself showed.

We had no right to be wrong, but if we did err his prompt baton would put everything back in order, and I still love to remember him during some especially difficult passage, smiling from his rostrum. He was always ready to sacrifice his personal ambition to help one of us for the sake of the performance. But woe to anyone who was wrong through carelessness! Black looks and a few sharp words would strike like a whiplash to prima donna or supporting singer alike: all in the family, naturally, never a public scandal.

He used to call me "my son" and he inculcated in me the feeling that any obstacle must be overcome for the sake of the performance. It was a strict sense of duty, a sense almost of life and death. It gave one such a firm foundation—an awareness of every possible emergency and the certainty that one could somehow make it. He demanded the same standards throughout all the years I knew him. I remember once in Chicago Renata Tebaldi had asked especially for me to be in her Michonnet in *Adriana Lecouvreur*. I had not sung the role for several years, though I always loved it and thought I remembered it well. But I had not remembered those awkward little bars and cues as well as I supposed and during the rehearsal I made several mistakes. I was aware of this but was in a happy, perhaps careless mood. No comment was made at the time, but we all went out together afterward and at the door I stood aside to let Maestro Serafin pass. He turned to me and merely said: "Gobbi, just call a repetiteur and go over the role, will you?" And I blushed until my face was hot.

My diary entry at the time of Serafin's passing speaks, I think, for many others besides myself: "We all met in the church of Santa Maria degli Angeli to give the last salute to the maestro, whose body was going back to the small, tree-shaded village near Venice where he was born ninety years ago. I feel strangely lonely, as though he were taking away with him the glorious days which he had created."

18.

ONE OF THE HARDEST things for an international artist to become accustomed to is the continual traveling. Since one person's joy may be another's purgatory it is well to discover as early as possible one's limitations in this respect. I myself love fast cars, detest trains, am a happy air traveler but grudge the time lost traveling by sea. Nevertheless, traveling the world was never to me just a question of rushing from one engagement to another. I was always eager to gather some real impression of the countries I visited, and when such opportunities came my way I seized them willingly.

Such an occasion occurred in April of 1967 when I was in Cairo for some performances of *Tosca*. Tilde had been prevented by family commitments from accompanying me, and I was sight-seeing on my own one day when I paused at the entrance to an ancient mosque to examine a curious, highly polished stone which was set in the wall at the side of the entrance. As I did so an Egyptian approached me and said courteously: "You seem to be interested in that stone, sir. Do you know what its purpose was?"

It so happened that I had read something about it a few days previously and I replied that I believed it to have been set there originally as a sort of mirror in which the ladies of the time could see themselves before entering the mosque and so check that they were suitably attired. We fell into conversation and entered the mosque together. I told him that I was singing at the opera house, and after he had explained to me the special points of interest of the place, with such a wealth of fascinating information that I was entranced, I found out that he was a professor of fine arts, employed by the government to look after historical monuments. He spoke both English and French fluently, and we got on so well that in the end he also became my guide when I visited the Pyramids and the Sphinx. By then I was so fascinated by the extent of his knowledge and the charm with which he imparted it that I went to the opera house and managed to be released from my last performance. With some days now at my disposal I went to my professor once more and begged him to accompany me to Aswan and Luxor, persuading him to let me pay his plane fare and expenses. No price would have been too high to pay for his knowledge and guidance, and I remember his companionship to this day with the greatest pleasure.

Early in the following year Tilde and I joined forces with Sander and Edith Gorlinsky for a winter holiday in Israel. It was almost twenty years since I had sung there and I looked forward immensely to seeing the changes which I knew I would find.

We started in unpromising circumstances, meeting at Rome Airport in the most frightful storm, which accompanied us all the way to Tel Aviv and forced us to make three hair-raising attempts to land. We made it in the end, however, and after a night's rest continued to Eilat where our hotel proved to be something short of the tour operator's description "luxurious." But the situation was marvelous. Although our room was so small that I had to jump over Tilde's bed to get to the bathroom and when I picked up my razor from one end of the shelf, the other end leaped up unexpectedly, we were inexpressibly happy.

It was wonderful to be able to swim in January, the water unbelievably clear and the beautiful glass-bottomed boats revealing a wealth of corals and sea flora and so many kinds of beautiful fish. In the afternoon we would go sight-seeing by jeep and at night we visited the little night clubs and cabarets, where the show invariably consisted of some celebration of the Six Days' War—and rightly so. It was incredibly moving and stimulating to see this handful of courageous people against so many enemies.

There was a certain amount of bombing, especially at night when we played our own special kind of poker and gambled with the shells we had collected on the beach. From time to time a big blast would startle everyone, but we refused to move, Edith declaring that as she had been brought up in England it was against her principles to let anything disturb her.

Though we were strictly incognito we received after a few days an invitation from the government of Israel to tour the country. A car (with driver) was provided for us and in this we set out for Jerusalem. All of a sudden in the middle of the desert a violent storm broke out, and the radio announced that there was snow in Jerusalem. I laughed incredulously at first, but as we journeyed on we began to see people on the road with a sprinkling of snow on them, and as we approached the city we found the going so slippery that the car was reluctant to climb the steep road and the driver became very nervous.

I proposed that I should take the wheel, at which the usually imperturbable Sander unexpectedly yelled: *"Leave him alone!"* But the driver was more than happy to accept my offer and we changed places. Then Edith—still the calm Britisher—gazed thoughtfully at a shoe shop we were passing and said: "I wonder if they have any Wellington boots."

Knowing her for a compulsive shopper and finding the idea of Wellington boots in Jerusalem deliciously incongruous we all shouted with laughter and told her that *of course* they wouldn't have any such thing. But it takes more than that to deflect Edith when her mind is on shopping. She insisted on stopping the car, went into the shop, and emerged again triumphantly carrying two pairs of Wellingtons, one for herself and one for Tilde. Now they were able to walk around in the snow looking smug and superior while Sander and I trudged about in our shoes.

After we left the shop we finally arrived at the King David Hotel, the snow being incredibly deep. We tumbled out in search of porters, still naïvely unaware of the seriousness of the crisis, and found the hotel hall already crammed with people stranded by the weather. I approached the desk and brazenly asked for two suites. The receptionist looked at me as though I were mad and pointed to all the people who were sitting on their luggage for lack of chairs. But I pressed my request and the poor clerk resignedly said he would see what he could do.

I returned to my party and said to Sander: "Go and whisper the magic name."

"What magic name?" inquired Sander in his most deflating manner.

"What magic name?" I repeated arrogantly. "Mine of course."

"Oh, my dear fellow!" Sander looked pityingly at me. "Who do you suppose would know you in this mess?"

"Go and *ask,*" I urged him, and the poor man, being used to capricious artists, went and did so.

Hardly had he pronounced the words, "You know, the gentleman over there is Tito Gobbi," than the manageress let out a gratifying scream: "Which one? *You, sir?"*

Sander hastily disclaimed any idea of his being the eccentric singer, and the manageress immediately promised to do whatever was possible if we would have dinner in the meantime. Sander was so dumbfounded that his cigar almost fell out of his mouth.

After dinner we were taken up to a beautiful suite, where the previous occupants were making haste to pack their things and go, declaring all the time: "It is perfectly all right, Mr. Gobbi, we are only too happy. We can catch a cold, but not you!" Before such kindness I lost all my arrogance and was thoroughly ashamed, but they would hear no apologies. The suite was ours, and it overlooked the most breathtaking view. There before us lay the old city of Jerusalem under snow, with the moon shining on it: unbelievable in its beauty.

Our friend the manageress even brought us a few red carnations, and the next morning the Italian flag was flying from the balcony of the hotel. By then the storm had blown itself out and the stranded passengers had all left. We virtually had Jerusalem to ourselves. We wandered at our leisure, visiting all the holy places, walking the Via Dolorosa with a little donkey—perhaps as Jesus did. We saw the house of Pilate, the Mosque, the country roundabout, and the heartbreaking but discreet museums. On every side we met with the kindest hospitality: we visited shops and factories, and watched precious stones being cut and polished, and at every turn I marveled afresh at the progress made since I had been there in the earliest days of this remarkable state.

Within weeks of that Israeli holiday I went much further afield—to Australia, where I was to sing Scarpia in Adelaide with the Australian Marie Collier as Tosca, Donald Smith (also Australian) as Cavaradossi, and my friend Maestro Cillario as conductor. The performances were successful and the hospitality staggering. When I had a chance to drive out into the country I was overwhelmed by the beauty of the scenery and the invigorating quality of the atmosphere. It made me feel younger, full of life, and immensely refreshed.

I was tempted to expand my journey home and to visit places which I had always longed to visit but had regarded as too far off the beaten track for a busy singer. So I postponed the date of my return and took off instead for Singapore, deciding to include Djakarta, Bali, and Cambodia in my travels.

The airline was called Garuda, which means "god of the wind," well named since the wind is capricious and so was the airline. But I didn't mind. It merely added to the feeling of being suddenly free from my usual routine. On my way to and from places I several times ran into a delightful group of Americans whose average age was about seventy. I noticed one particularly attractive old lady who was carrying a string bag containing a casket, and I was told that as her husband had died at the beginning of the trip she had had him cremated and brought him along. After all, the poor man had looked forward greatly to the trip, for which he had paid in advance. He occupied his seat on the plane and his chair in restaurants (or rather the casket did). Sometimes a kind companion would borrow "Charlie" and give the widow a break by taking him to a museum or temple. I could not decide whether to take this seriously or to laugh, but apparently it was quite a solemn matter, so I controlled my amusement and merely record it here as one of the most curious "traveler's tales" which ever came my way.

When I try to describe the beauty and mystery of the temples of Angkor-Wat I am lost for words, and I can hardly bear to think of that lovely country now torn with strife. I usually had for my guide a small boy with a round face, starry eyes, and broad smile. He took me in a wheeled cart driven by a small motor, and in this I sat wearing a curious cotton hat, presented to me by my Australian friends, from which hung corks to keep away the insects.

My little guide would take me to the edge of the forest and I would walk alone for miles through the great silent woods—silent, that is, except for the sounds of birds and sometimes strange animals. It was in these huge mysterious forests that one would come upon temples of indescribable beauty and size. Sometimes nature had encroached to an alarming degree upon these marvelous buildings, sometimes it had been kept at bay and one could see—or guess at—the whole of the original plan. The almost fearful solitude, the indefinable atmosphere, and the awareness of a great culture now vanished from the earth combined to give an overwhelming impression which was spiritual as well as physical.

On one of these expeditions of mine I had a curious experience. I had been exploring one of the half-ruined temples when, misjudging the height of a stone archway, I hit the top of my head a tremendous blow, gashing it badly and knocking myself unconscious. When I came to, there were a couple of small boys standing beside me chattering softly, and they indicated that they wished me to accompany them to another part of the ruins.

I contrived to stand up and follow them to an open space where water had gathered in a stone depression. Here they made me sit down and with a piece of white cloth they gently washed my injured head and managed to make me understand that I must sit there bare-headed in the sun. This seemed to me rather drastic, for the sun was terrifically strong. However, they were so insistent that I did as I was told. Almost immediately, to my astonishment, I felt the edges of the gash drawing together. The blood ceased to flow and the faintness passed. Within a very short time I was able to go on my way again, though I have the mark to this day. I only wish I knew what eventually happened to my two small guardian angels in the troubled years ahead.

Another time I heard a lot of mynah birds singing and calling. Ever since I had seen a tame mynah in Harrods in London I had wanted to own one, and I eagerly asked my guide where I could acquire one.

"One, sir?" He looked surprised. "But there they are—many of them."

"No, no," I explained. "I want to buy one."

"Buy one, sir?" Again he repeated my words in a surprised tone. "But they are free, sir. You can buy one only from God."

I felt very ashamed of myself; I, who had supposed myself to be a civilized European, to be taught such a lesson!

That was not my only trip to the other side of the world, for in the following March I accepted an invitation to sing Falstaff in Melbourne. Then, to my mingled gratification and embarrassment I found myself nominated "King for a Day" or King Moomba, as the strange title goes.

This "day" is devoted to all forms of sport, shows, and competitions of every variety. The honor of being King Moomba usually goes to an Australian. Thus the choice of a visiting Italian was not uniformly popular and quite a controversy broke out. I was astonished to receive a number of threatening letters, and local Italians wrote begging me to refuse the honor, assuring me I would be in some danger. The story got into the Italian press and poor Tilde read: "Tito Gobbi receives death threats."

I was not especially eager to be King Moomba, but the governor of South Australia supported the choice and I was irritated by the absurd opposition and intrigued by the spice of danger. So I went ahead with the project, and there I was, King Moomba for the day, driving through the streets in an open white Alfa-Romeo, visiting the various "events" for four sweltering hours. The sun was blazing and I myself was perspiring under the weight of a heavy crown and a "royal" cloak of red velvet lined with fake ermine. Police were ahead, behind, and on either side of me, and armed police were stationed at strategic windows. I saw my colleagues from the opera from time to time, looking pale in spite of the sun, and Maestro Cillario's frightened face as he rushed up and down with a camera, checking the safety of the route. I, however, was as happy as a lark, being kissed by beautiful girls in scanty bikinis. Finally I arrived in front of the official building where the governor received me, rather relieved to find I was alive, and at last I could take off my royal robes and have a welcome drink. All very amusing for one day, but I came to the conclusion that opera singing is lighter work than being royalty.

The rest of that very full year, 1969, saw me in London, New York, Chicago, Rome, Copenhagen, Florence, Berlin, Monte Carlo, and Edinburgh. Berlin was particularly moving for, when I went there in September to sing Scarpia, under Maazel, it was the first time I had sung there since 1942. I doubt if many of the audience remembered those earlier performances, but the welcome and scenes of enthusiasm at the stage door after the opera were stupefying. I was assaulted by supporters and nearly torn to pieces. Indeed, when I examined my coat afterward I found that all the buttons had been removed in the fray—whether as souvenirs or merely because they could not resist what might be called the pressure of events I do not know. So much for the "stolid" Germans.

In Edinburgh, as might be expected, enthusiasm was kept within more decorous bounds, but it was still very heart-warming. It was Tilde's and my first visit to the Edinburgh Festival, and I was looking forward tremendously to producing *Gianni Schicchi* and singing the title role, a great favorite of mine ever since I first sang it in Rome in 1951. Undoubtedly one of the most brilliant one-act masterpieces ever conceived, the work is difficult to produce with its large cast in which even the most minor character is of unique importance, but infinitely rewarding when properly handled. There is a temptation to overdo the comedy (a temptation to which almost all inexperienced producers succumb), and then it degenerates into farce. Nothing was further from Puccini's intention.

I had a good and responsive cast, and the festival atmosphere which dominates Edinburgh at this time seemed wonderfully in keeping with *Schicchi*. Tilde and I enjoyed ourselves both inside and outside the theater, meeting such treasured friends as Lord Harewood, that knowledgeable and enthusiastic supporter of worthwhile opera wherever it is to be found, Walter Legge and his lovely wife Elisabeth Schwarzkopf, Harold Rosenthal, Patricia Foy, and many others. Among our professional friends we were especially glad to see Magda Olivero and Maestro Giulini, who was conducting concerts there.

I had worked with Giulini on several occasions and was among his most sincere admirers. I was therefore pleased and curious when he asked me to meet him one morning as there was something he wanted to discuss with me. I turned up promptly and was all attention when he said with that serious charm of his: "I would like to tell you how much I have admired your work and how highly I think of you as a man and an artist." I hastened to reply that this was also how I regarded him. Then he went on: "I feel therefore that the time has come when you and I should drop the formal type of address to each other and use the more intimate 'tu.' "

Only Giulini could have made such a courteous occasion out of what is usually a most casual change in relationships. With anyone else I might have been amused. With him I felt touched and honored, and we sealed the bargain over a soft drink. But the extraordinary sequel is that from that day to this we have never met for any length of time. We speak to each other sometimes on the telephone—always using the "tu," we visit the same cities, theaters, and festivals, but never at precisely the same time. I leave as he arrives, or he leaves as I arrive. The vagaries of an artist's life could not be better illustrated. But I still hope one day we shall meet again and possibly even work together, and that we shall then be able to address each other as "tu" in all seriousness.

Most of us who have some talent for which we have won praise are perverse enough to entertain a secret wish to be noticed for some other quality. I own to pleasure and pride in being a professional singer, but in my heart of hearts I long to be told that my work as an amateur painter has also a certain merit. During the Edinburgh Festival, to my undying gratification, I was asked to contribute a picture to an exhibition of paintings organized by the *Scotsman.* I sent in a canvas of "Waterloo Bridge, London" which I had painted from the window of our suite at the Savoy when Tilde and I had been staying there, and with great pride I inspected the "hanging" of my picture on the huge open staircase where the exhibition took place. Toward the end of the festival some of the pictures were auctioned for charity and Tilde and I went along, smiling for the photographers but secretly wondering how we would hide our mortification if no one made a bid for my offering. My heart was beating when the bidding started, but to my astonished delight my picture was bought for over £200 by the owner of a restaurant, who afterward hung it in a place of honor. That sealed my devotion to Edinburgh. I had not only sung in that lovely city but sold a picture there as well.

To complete that splendid year, Tilde and I paid no less than three visits to the enchanting fairy-tale principality of Monte Carlo. In May I went to record *Fedora* with Olivero and Del Monaco; and from the window of our suite at the Hermitage we had a glorious view of the harbor and a grandstand view of the Grand Prix.

In July we returned for a concert in which I was to sing under the baton of Sir John Barbirolli—a delightful man as well as a wonderful musician, who loved to hold conversations with me in Venetian dialect. The concert took place at the palace in the presence of Prince Rainier and Princess Grace, and the program included the delicious little "Quand'ero paggio" from *Falstaff*. At the end of this Barbirolli turned to the royal hosts, who were sitting in the front row, and said: "This air is so lovely and so short, and Tito sings it so well, that we are going to do it again." And we did.

Afterward, at the grand reception, I was much amused when Prince Rainier greeted me with "Here is my enemy!" in reference to the fact that it was Simone Boccanegra who exiled the Grimaldi family from Genoa, and we were immediately lost in a historical discussion.

Our third visit provided a fittingly glamorous finale to the year when Tilde and I joined the Gorlinskys for a brief holiday there and met Rudolf Nureyev. Party followed party, on land and on Sam Spiegel's yacht in the harbor, the last one ending around six o'clock in the morning. Tired but enthralled, Tilde and Edith voted that evening the highlight of the year, for Rudi had danced with them in turn. Well, Sander and I had to concede that they had a point there, for what woman would not rate middle-aged baritones and impresarios at two a penny when given the opportunity to dance with Rudi Nureyev?

19.

IF I WERE to divide my career into decades and describe each section in a few words I suppose it would be roughly correct to say that the 1940s covered my years of training, trying out my operatic wings, and arriving at relative maturity; the 1950s saw my establishment as an international artist and brought me the consequent rewards of work and experience; the 1960s, while multiplying those rewards both artistically and materially, provided me with fresh fields to conquer in the world of operatic production. I am a fortunate man—and I know it.

In addition, during those years I did a large amount of recording, and here a very special approach is called for. Bereft of the stage and everything which helps to build up the scene in which you create your character, you face not a living audience but a battery of recording equipment —and an unnerving moment of truth. For the voice alone is going to have to express every emotion, every nuance of tragedy, comedy, or pathos. No telling gesture or subtle facial expression is going to be of any help now. You will have to concentrate solely on sound and convey everything you wish to convey by that medium.

It pleases me to remember that Walter Legge of EMI Records once coined a phrase to describe my recording work when he called me "the Acting Voice." In fact I came to enjoy recording, particularly when the circumstances verged on the informal, such as the time when I was recording with Gerald Moore and we found ourselves in such harmony that we went on and on until one of the engineers said good-humoredly: "That's all right; we've got more than we need now!" (The "overspill" was used years later for my "Venice in Peril" disc.)

Now that this story enters the 1970s there is naturally a certain shift of emphasis. People tend to think that the end of a singing career is a sad business, but this need not be true, unless one has been foolish enough to view vocal successes as the be-all and end-all of existence. The 1970s, in the nature of things, saw a gradual reduction of my singing life but a steady increase in my production work. Above all, it brought me to the third—and in some senses the most exciting and satisfying—aspect of my career: the master classes and my Opera Workshop.

In the first years of this decade I was tremendously busy, singing and producing and often doing both in the same performance, a double activity which requires a really enormous amount of energy. It also requires a meticulous attention to detail and at the same time a capacity to view the enterprise as an artistic whole, as well as a willingness to listen to experienced advice while holding firmly to one's own convictions. In other words, as an experienced singing-actor I knew perhaps more about singers' problems than most operatic producers; but, as a producer who was to some extent feeling his way, I had at first quite a lot to discover.

This was when I was glad that I had long ago learned the value of listening as well as talking. If a lighting expert was anxious to explain everything to me from A to Z, I was only too willing to listen. Perhaps half of what he told me I had already absorbed during my years of stage experience, but it was not important that I should brush up my ego by telling him this; on the contrary, if I were ready to be the attentive beginner I was usually given all kinds of information that later proved invaluable.

Combining the two lines of approach—those of performer and producer—was fascinating to me, and although the work was intensive I was happy to find myself already in 1970 producing as well as singing my usual roles in *Tosca* in Zurich (with my old friend Maestro Nello Santi conducting), *Gianni Schicchi* in Chicago, and *Falstaff* in Lisbon and in Paris, where I also had to reproduce the work for color television.

I asked myself whether the success which attended these enterprises owed something to the blessing of an unexpected patron saint. For while I was singing and producing *Falstaff* in Lisbon I was summoned between the acts to appear before the President of the Republic in his box. Having generously referred to my "services" over the years to the Lisbon Opera, he presented me with a beautiful decoration and informed me that I was now invested with the Order of Officer of Saint Iago. I thought I had known most things about Iago, but never that he had managed to become a saint. That smart fellow must surely have pulled some strings and done some of his familiar intriguing over there. Anyway, I now wear his decoration with pride on state occasions and hope he looks after me.

This year also saw the end of an era, for Sir David Webster retired from Covent Garden. It would be difficult to overestimate the debt all concerned with that great opera house owed to him. I myself have been witness to the skill, vision, and good judgment with which he built up the company, always alert to see—and sometimes to create—opportunities for British artists to step into bigger and better roles, but always making his decisions on the basis of genuine merit and not hesitating to integrate into his company outstanding artists from all over the world when this was required.

He knew how to handle artists to a degree rare in my experience; he knew how to encourage and to assess and develop potential and how to be firm when firmness was required. But my most valued memory of him as a friend is of the times when he would come to my dressing room between the acts after a particularly enthusiastic reception and say, with that charming British understatement which is so much more flattering than fulsome praise: "It seems they rather like you, my boy."

To him, as I have described, I owed my first opportunity to produce, and to him we all owe much for the smoothness with which he relinquished the reins of office and withdrew from management, leaving the admirable John Tooley to succeed him, virtually without hitch or upset. This takes some doing in any opera house, and in my view reflects great credit on both men.

Another experience which I had during that year—memorable for quite different reasons—was my first visit to Russia, not to sing or produce but to take part in "judging" contestants in the Tchaikovsky Competition for singers. We were all classed as international judges and prepared to exercise our powers of assessment to the best of our ability. In the event we might just as well have stayed at home. We listened attentively to each contestant; our opinions were respectfully sought and then totally ignored. It became clear that the verdicts had been reached before we arrived and the spate of meaningless words poured upon us could not disguise the fact. It would have been insulting if it had not been farcical.

On the same level was our "independent sight-seeing." We were shown what we were supposed to see, and every polite obstacle was put in the way of our seeing, hearing, or experiencing anything else. One morning, determined to defeat this absurd system, I got up very early, dressed silently, and prepared to sally forth on my own. As I stepped out into the corridor of my hotel my charming guide/jailer emerged from further down the corridor and smilingly greeted me with: "I somehow thought you might like to do some early sight-seeing this morning and I am ready and happy to guide you."

Among the more personal events of the early 1970s our little Isabella lost her distinction of having two great-grandfathers when Tilde's father died in November 1970 and my father in May of the following year. They had both lived to a great age and neither event could be described as unexpected, though each was nonetheless a sorrowful occasion.

Of the many professional engagements in 1971 one of my most poignant memories was of my visit to South Africa to sing Scarpia to Marie Collier's Tosca. Marie had done some remarkably good work at Covent Garden, as I knew personally from her Giorgetta in *Il Tabarro* and certainly from some of her Toscas. But she could sometimes be wild and undisciplined and needed a firm hand. When I arrived in Johannesburg I found an agitated Mr. Reinecke, the head of the company, declaring that Marie was not at all good, that she was wild in her ideas about Tosca, and that, in effect, he proposed to engage someone else in her place.

"Oh no," I said. "Let me talk to her. We are old colleagues." Indeed, Marie often called me "Zio Tito" (Uncle Tito) and I felt she probably had some confidence in me.

At first she behaved like a rebellious child and shook her head when I said mildly: "Marie, have you ever thought where Tosca came from? No? Well, she came from the Veneto, and we people who come from that region tend to have very strong feelings which we have to keep in check. In addition—" (and please note this, all you violent first-act Toscas!) "she was the prima donna of Rome, which is to say, in those days, the prima donna of the world. There was only one woman whose conduct would be more closely observed, and that was the Queen. So she conducted herself with dignity and style and 'class'—and that is how you must play her."

Whereupon she began to cry and suddenly came and put her head against me and said: "I don't really know anything about it, and I'm very frightened. Help me, Zio Tito—please help me."

Oh, dear God! and the public think we have only vocal problems.

I said to her: "This, for instance, is a very good gesture of yours. Now we'll talk about it." So we had a long talk about Tosca, and she was attentive and intelligent and docile, and in the end she gave a lovely performance. I shall always be glad of that chance to have given a little professional help and a little human encouragement, for those were her last performances before her tragic death some months later.

While we were in Africa Tilde and I met many friends from the earlier tours; and we were also happy to find there Maestro Fasano and his beautiful Virtuosi, who take the music of Vivaldi all over the world. Later Sander joined us and at the kind invitation of the government of South Africa we spent six marvelous days in the Kruger Park game reserve.

We were provided with two cars, lived in a big comfortable bungalow, and drove out each day in search of wild animals. For the first three days we saw only giraffes and thousands of springbok and wildebeests, but when we were back in our bungalow we would hear among the sounds of the night the roar of a lion.

Then one day we saw him—a big one, a real king of beasts, followed by his lioness and cubs. We got quite close in our cars, but the animals never gave us so much as a glance—absolutely superior and indifferent to mere humans. On another occasion we actually saw the birth of an elephant. The female elephants made a circle around the mother, thrusting out the male elephant, doubtless judging him superfluous on this occasion. He, in fury, pulled up the surrounding trees with his trunk—whether to demonstrate his anxiety as the expectant father or his rage at being excluded, I don't know. As the circle of female elephants moved slowly around the mother in a sort of dance there finally appeared among them the baby elephant. Immediately they started to clean him, spreading sand on his wet body, and in a short time he was on his feet walking in procession with all the other elephants, including the previously discarded father.

The end of the year found us in Chicago once more, where again I was to sing Scarpia—this time in ideal circumstances, under the conductorship of Maestro Sanzogno—and also to produce the work.

Janis Martin was the Tosca, Bergonzi the Cavaradossi, and (a delightful surprise for me) Italo Tajo was Sacristan. I studied the production very carefully with the stage designer, Pier Luigi Pizzi, and was delighted to find him totally in agreement with my view of Scarpia—that he was a refined man with an appreciation of art and beautiful things.

We covered the walls in the second act with paintings by Vanvitelli; my dinner table and desk had fine glass, silver, and precious objets d'art. This Scarpia was really something—no wonder he imagined he could "collect" everything, even the prima donna of Rome. My personal assistant was David Sell, hard-working and utterly reliable as I was to find again and again in the future.

It was the custom then to give a special performance for students and, realizing that they knew rather little about the work, I gave them a talk beforehand. Their response to the drama of that second act which never fails was both gratifying and startling. When Janis Martin stabbed me they rose as one and cheered my assassin to the echo. Down with the Bad Man in no uncertain terms.

It was certainly the baron's year. I sang Scarpia again in New York in November, with Placido Domingo as a thrilling Cavaradossi, whose spectacular "Vittoria" brought down the house, and Grace Bumbry as the most distant Tosca I have ever partnered. As far as she was concerned I simply was not there in the second act. She was playing all by herself and was literally so far away that when I had to say, "Sedete qui" ("Sit here"), she was so distant that I sang, "Sedete lì" ("Sit there").

However, as always in New York, there was the joy of seeing old friends. The apartment was full of flowers, food, and fruit from Terry McEwen, John Coveney, and Lydia Popper and her husband—all of whom tended to spoil us in this way. Erika Davidson, the busy photographer from *Opera News* (and a great friend of Isabella's), was always in and out—usually accompanied by a dog or two. George Jellinek came to interview me for radio, putting me in such a good (and loquacious) mood that I rated him one of the best of interviewers. There was a most interesting meeting with the distinguished critic Irving Kolodin and dinner with Alice Tully, who is not only a wonderful patron of the arts but an enchanting hostess with whom we always feel we have a very special rapport.

Back in Chicago I did something very unusual for me. *I went to the opera,* and, of all things, I chose *Rheingold.* Maestro Ferdinand Leitner, a great favorite of ours, was conducting and that was what tempted me. I will not say that I didn't envy Tilde and Carol Fox when they slipped out of the box for a surreptitious cigarette, but I did demonstrate my superior operatic stamina by remaining in my seat.

In marked contrast I myself produced *Barbiere,* with Bartoletti conducting brilliantly and Marilyn Horne making a great job of Rosina once I had, with difficulty, persuaded her to cut at least 50 per cent of the unnecessary embellishments which at that time she favored.

From Chicago Tilde and I flew to London, to finish the year at an occasion of sadness and pride. At St. James's Palace a memorial concert was held for Sir John Barbirolli in the presence of Her Majesty the Queen Mother. I sang exactly the same program I had sung with Sir John himself that evening in Monte Carlo, and when I came to "Quand'ero paggio" I turned to the audience as he had done and asked the permission of Her Majesty to repeat the little aria, just as Sir John had wished. Permission was granted, and I saw that Lady Barbirolli was deeply touched—and who will say that the spirit of Sir John was not among us at that moment?

Quite early in the following year we were back again in London, first for me to hold master classes at the London Opera Center, then to speak briefly but with feeling at the memorial service for Marie Collier in St. Paul's Church, Covent Garden, and finally to produce *Simone Boccanegra* (but not to sing in it). One must tear these things from one's heart eventually if one is to face realities. As with my beloved Rigoletto earlier, I had to tell myself that the sheer vocal and physical energy required to do full justice to the role was mine no longer. And so for the first time I took my bow at Covent Garden as producer only.

But, in that delightful English expression, as one door closes another opens. During the previous summer I had already held the first, rather tentative Opera Workshop in Florence and, like a prospector looking for gold, I was on the alert for any unusual talent. I already had high hopes for a Greek baritone called Louis Manikas, who had turned up in Florence the previous summer, and now, here in London, Tilde and I were asked to audition a young American-Israeli soprano by the name of Mani Mekler. I hope she will not mind my saying so now, but she was a trifle undisciplined both vocally and in appearance. That was a year when all the girls wore ridiculously long dresses and their hair in waterfalls on either side of their faces, which made it hard to take them seriously. But between those waterfalls was an intelligent and attractive face, and somewhere in that girl and that voice was something which Tilde and I knew had to be brought out.

What to do about her? Her family, though devoted, were in Los Angeles. At that point our friends the Cooks stepped in and undertook to send her to the workshop that summer, so that we could see what signs of real development she might show under supervision. Her family agreed, and her mother flew over from Los Angeles to see for herself (very properly) that her daughter was not doing anything quite mad. It was a challenge and a gamble for us all, but it was one of the things which convinced me that, even if I myself were saying good-by to some of my favorite roles, a new door was opening through which might come some truly talented youngsters whom I could help with my own experience. It was an exciting discovery.

Meanwhile I had been invited by the Welsh National Opera to sing Falstaff in Cardiff and Bristol under the conductorship of James Lockhart, with whom I had and still have a particularly happy musical association. The production, originally by Geraint Evans, was an excellent one. There was of course a Cooks' Party: Hello, Jim! Hello, Ena!—Ted, Una, Charles, Kathleen, Reuben, May and Olive, Joan, Joe and Anne—so many of them, known to us on countless occasions by name or by personality—friends of the family, one might almost say—our big operatic family. Albert White was there from Washington, the Bodens of course; Pauline Clarke turned up and made a charming picture of me as Falstaff in the Basket. I even learned to sing the Welsh national anthem in Welsh, and was commended for my pronunciation.

Change and variety are indispensable features of an international artist's life, and within days I found myself a whole world away in outlook and surroundings. I was in Bucharest to sing in *Tosca,* brought there by circumstances that were both curious and touching. For some years I had been receiving letters from an admirer in Rumania, and finally he had hinted broadly that he would so much like to come to Rome and meet me in person but that "as he was not an important person there were difficulties."

I got the message and promptly wrote a cordial letter as though we were lifelong friends, saying how much I wanted him to come to Rome. There was a long silence, and then one day our doorbell rang. There, standing outside, was my Rumanian friend—Constantin Bonig—carrying a bag containing two bottles of Rumanian wine and a piece of embroidery for Tilde. On the strength of my letter he had at last gotten permission to travel abroad for a month—but without a penny and nothing but what he stood up in.

We put him in a pensione, I gave him some lessons—since he turned out to have a pleasant light baritone voice—and everyone in the family took turns to entertain him. He begged me to come to Bucharest to sing, explaining that it would confer some sort of authority on him if I did so. Though it took two or three years to arrange I finally went to Bucharest for an enjoyable and successful *Tosca.* My friend accompanied me everywhere, basking in whatever glory emanated from me, and I was eventually able to leave him my Rumanian money (worth much more inside Rumania than outside). As a result of all this he presently got permission to work abroad, and now he sings in small opera houses in Switzerland and Germany.

If this experience might have given me exaggerated ideas of my importance, I was soon put in my place by my own country. Maestro Fasano proposed Boris Christoff and me as academicians of the Accademia di Santa Cecilia in Rome. There was a long period of consultation, and then we were both turned down. Was it because he had proposed us, or were we both unworthy?

In marked contrast the Royal Academy of Music in London wrote to me to say that they had made me an Honorary Member—without fuss. Next time I was in London the Certificate of Honorary Membership was presented to me at a party where warmth, friendliness, and sincerity were the outstanding features.

The following year, 1973, opened with the sound of trumpets. In honor of Great Britain's entry into the Common Market a great gala was held at Covent Garden on January 3 in the presence of the Queen and Prince Philip. Representatives from the European Community were invited to perform, and I was asked to represent Italy. Tilde and I flew over, leaving Rome in sunshine but arriving in such dense fog that the plane had to be diverted to Manchester.

Dismayed at the delay, I showed what amounted to my invitation to dinner with the Queen and explained the urgency of the position; whereupon our luggage was extracted in record time, a customs officer drove us from the airport to another waiting car—engine already running—and off we were wafted into a world of mist at such speed that we felt like the hero and heroine in the last reel of an old-fashioned film. We arrived in London at midnight but next morning were ready for the rehearsal and the subsequent performance.

Again I was to sing "Quand'ero paggio" (a favorite for royal occasions, it seems), only this time it was introduced by no less than Sir Laurence Olivier speaking the Shakespearean lines which lead up to it in that beautiful voice of his. It was like being announced by an archangel and I walked in on clouds. Later, at the royal reception at Lancaster House, Tilde and I were presented to the Queen by the Prime Minister, Mr. Edward Heath, with such an impeccable pronunciation of our name that I was constrained to call him "Maestro" later and tell him that only someone with a musical ear would have done it so well.

For much of the evening Tilde and I were in the company of the Oliviers, and when he and I were laughingly examining each other's decorations he suddenly exclaimed: "You haven't got a star to your

Grand' Ufficiale of the Italian Republic. Here, have mine! You deserve it and it looks better on you." It was something to be decorated by Laurence Olivier—more exciting than when I received the star later from my own government. It was also like meeting old friends. There was so much for us to talk about, discuss, compare, that we could hardly tear ourselves away from each other when the time came.

I have sometimes found that before—not with other singers, but with great men of the theater. It was the same with Vittorio Gassman, I remember. We met in his dressing room in London as strangers, exchanged a few pleasant words and then suddenly on parting embraced each other as friends.

By this time Tilde and I had achieved a long-desired ambition. We had at last discovered and bought an attractive small estate on the outskirts of Rome. Large enough to accommodate guests but small enough to retain a homely air of intimacy, it was something between a manor house and a farm—what in Italy we call a *casale*. There was a good deal to be done to it, but we were prepared to take time. For the moment I was still pursuing an active career, with engagements in several parts of the world. But to me, a countryman at heart, there was an irresistible attraction in the prospect of eventually growing my own fruit and vegetables, raising my own hens, whistling in answer to the birds in my own trees—even mockingly copying the croaking of the little frogs on the edge of my own land.

Meanwhile, with that prospect still in the not-too-distant future, I was due to sing Falstaff in London in June and July of 1974. During and after the earlier performances I was aware as always of the wonderfully warm rapport between my audience and me. It is something special at Covent Garden, and I do not mean only the great, heart-warming ovations, but a sort of beautiful relationship which seems to make each of them personally known to me. We would often talk pleasantly and at leisure in Floral Street outside the stage door. Rain, snow, or cold wind—nothing deterred them. They would wait until the last minute just to wave their hands or tap against the window of Betty Eliot's car. They have been so *good* to me throughout the years. And then—I don't know how the report could have originated—a rumor apparently began to circulate that the performance on July 9 would be my last at Covent Garden.

I found my dressing room full of flowers and gifts, and when at the end of the performance I took my solo calls a great rain of flowers fell on me from the upper boxes and circle and "slips." I was overwhelmed by emotion and my throat went tight at the cries of, "Tito, Tito, don't go! Come back!" I bowed again and again to the most loving, wonderful audience any artist ever had.

Afterward visitors poured into my dressing room, some with tears in their eyes, and outside the longest line imaginable filled Floral Street. I thought: "If this is indeed my last performance at Covent Garden, what a beautiful, incredible finale."

Later the report was contradicted. I took many more solo bows in opera houses in other parts of the world. But if I were asked to name the half-dozen times in my life when I have been most deeply moved by the public I should have to put high on the list that extraordinary night when my dear faithful London audience thought they were bidding me good-by.

20.

THE STRETCH of country lying between Florence and the even older hill-town of Fiesole is one of the loveliest in all Italy, and it is here, in the Medici villa of Schifanoia, surrounded by gardens of breath-taking splendor, that I have held my Opera Workshop for six weeks each summer since June 1971.

The last owner of the villa was Myron Taylor, American ambassador to the Vatican, and he presented it to the Holy See, along with its furniture, pictures, and art treasures, to be used as a Graduate School of Fine Arts of Rosary College, Illinois—a Catholic school run by Dominican Sisters. Sister Maria Michele, whom we first met in Chicago in the 1960s, was the one who had the magnificent idea of an opera workshop to be held during the long summer break, and it was her vision and drive which put the enterprise on its feet and incidentally presented me with one of the most thrilling challenges of my career.

When she left to rejoin the community the new principal, Sister Jean Richter, picked up all the threads of the workshop organization, in what was to her an unfamiliar world, with a skill and devotion which earned our eternal gratitude and admiration. Nor would any reference to the workshop be complete without our affectionate acknowledgment of the unending kindness and co-operation we receive from the sisters at the villa—not to mention Maria Lintas, with Natale and Albertina, without whose superb domestic management nothing could function as smoothly as it does.

The choice of students, who come from all over the world, is made during the early months of the year. Then from the middle of June for six intensive weeks the villa and its gardens resound daily to music and song, laughter and discussion, the trilling of coloraturas, the booming of basses, the competition of birdsong in the garden and the crisp commands of operatic coaches. From four in the afternoon until eight in the evening—with one brief interval for iced tea on the terrace—the students gather together in the great salon for my sessions of coaching in the singing, acting, and presentation of a role.

To say that I teach them is not an expression I favor—at least not if one uses the term "teach" in the strictest sense, implying that one has all the answers—a sort of recipe for "how it is done." Of course one can guide, encourage, and inspire, giving specific instructions on the mechanics of the job, how to approach individual study, how to discipline oneself for the long hard pull ahead. But even more important than this is to *bring out* what is already inherent somewhere within the heart and soul—and body—of the student, and to show him or her how to present this at its best.

After all, what *is* a voice? Air passing through vocal chords, that is all. Naturally the voice differs according to the structure of those chords and the throat and body containing them, but the whole art of becoming a worthwhile performer depends on an immense complexity of qualities. So when I am selecting the twenty or so students I can handle during the weeks of the workshop, what do I look for?

First of all there must *be* a voice. A pianist without a piano cannot play, a singer without a vocal organ of some distinction and promise had better choose another profession. Yet once this has been established, paradoxical though it may seem, the voice alone is not of paramount importance. Other gifts are going to be required to make it important. I look for musicality, presence, personality, capacity to work, a natural (though maybe latent) sense of drama, projection, rhythm—and a highly developed capacity for observation.

A good presence can be a great advantage, but again without the rest it is not much help: marvelous to be a fine, upstanding fellow if you are posing for a monument, but if that is all you can do you will be overlooked on a stage while someone smaller but with an arresting personality will dominate the scene. Capacity for work is vital. Many young people imagine that a stage life is a thrilling, but not too arduous job. They do not realize that they will have to learn the meaning—even the implication—of every word they sing, and to learn how to walk, to stand, to control their limbs and body; they will have to study carefully how different people comport themselves in different periods, countries, age-groups, classes. Then will come the refinement of learning how to convey a thought or a mood by facial expression or the way one turns the head or listens to another artist. Thrilling it may be, but not easy. Nor is it learned in a week, a month, or a year.

They come, with their fresh young voices and their eager faces. Usually I can tell how their voices should sound when properly developed. Often—though by no means invariably—I can tell if they have been taught by a man or a woman (or perhaps they have changed teachers midstream), what the teacher's nationality was, whether the teacher was young or old. This may sound a bold claim to make, but it is really the fruit of long experience and close observation. For the truth is that although I have enjoyed my life greatly, as an artist I worked very seriously and with great concentration.

As I have admitted, I am intensely curious, and I tend to ask myself *why* someone does this or that, or what it is that weakens an otherwise strong face: is it the chin, the nose, a nervous lack of repose? Why does some essentially pretty woman fail to attract, while someone else of quite moderate looks has everyone around her? Quite early in life I learned to know what I was looking for, like the time when I realized that a man asleep opposite me in a train had the kind of nose I needed to make my Scarpia intimidating. I began to sketch him immediately, and he was not very pleased when he woke up, saw what I was doing, and demanded an explanation. (Not an intelligent or a co-operative man obviously, but he had the right nose; and its counterpart has appeared on many stages since, whether he would have liked it or not.)

This attitude to my work and art (to life too, I suppose) has provided me with a store of observed and considered experience, which is vital to anyone taking the responsibility of passing on to others some degree of "teaching." In addition, no student has ever been merely a student to me, or to Tilde either, for she plays a great part in what I might call the human management of the young people who come to the villa. They are all people to us, with their own individual interests and importance.

We now know very quickly who is teachable and who is not. I don't care if they come from the humblest background hardly knowing how to handle a knife and fork at the dinner table. (Indeed, we had one gifted youngster who plunged her fork into her meat and went to work around it with her knife like a sculptor on a block of stone.) It doesn't matter. With tact and friendliness and affection one can alter all that. What cannot be altered is arrogance and an assumption of "knowing it all." If they are really young—well under thirty, say—one can sometimes brush them up and set their values right. After thirty this is very difficult, though we try.

Almost from the outset … e began to develop a sort of camaraderie which embraced everyon … udents, coaches, accompanists, the man who dealt with the record … and Tilde and me. This being so it was not long before we found ou … es involved in far more than merely vocal problems. Perhaps a sm … young fellow who appeared to be holding his own well would bre … own in sudden tears. I would know it was not his singing that was … bling him, and so I would say: "All right— leave it for the mome … ome and have supper with us tonight and we'll talk things over."

Then, over a glass … ine and a dish of pasta, out would come the problem. We would … ss it sympathetically (also bracingly if there was too much self-p … an indulgence favored by most of us in our youth) and endeavor … ffer practical and friendly advice.

Sometimes we wo … find that one student would know best how to help another. Somet … we would discover that we had more or less to stand *in loco parent* … there were real distress. And more than once we have come across n … ng depths of feeling, courage, and a sort of naïve wisdom in member … our workshop family.

Situated on the … step of the great art treasure house of Florence, we take every opport … y to encourage our students to be aware of other aspects of art. Per … s relating my remarks to something in their musical studies, I will ask … hey have seen such-and-such a picture, building, or statue—right th … n Florence, almost waiting for them to feed their eyes and minds … n it. Sometimes they will already have begun their own artistic voy … of discovery; but if not, I say: "Why don't you ask Maestro Podic … u can go with him when he is next going into town? He will show y … nd tell you about things you have never dreamed of."

For Baldo P … who has coached at the villa for several summers and still, though n … sident conductor in Düsseldorf, returns to us each year, is a mar … at culture and knowledge with a delightful way of opening up fi … izons to youthful minds. All this contributes greatly to the development of artistic awareness so essential to a complete person and performer.

Past students often return to us year after year, to work on roles they are now singing in opera houses throughout the world. One of the most popular is Björn Asker from Stockholm, who, although a successful artist himself these days, seems to have a very special understanding of and rapport with the young singers. These "Schifanoia veterans," as we call them, are a great help and inspiration to those starting out on the lower rungs of the ladder—rather like big brothers and sisters who remember all about their early steps and are now living examples of what can be done by hard work, intelligence, and a determination to make the grade.

From time to time one or other of my colleagues will drop in to see me and listen with interest to all that is happening at the workshop. This is also an inspiration to the young singers and affords an exciting glimpse of famous figures from the world they themselves hope to enter. (A little stardust is a pleasant thing, particularly when one is young.) Or it may be Dr. Peter Mennin, president of the famous Juilliard School of Music in New York, or John Tooley from Covent Garden, or some other authority from the world of music who finds real interest in observing the beginnings of an operatic artist.

Six weeks is a short time in which to effect sensational developments; but I am constantly moved and excited to find how much can be accomplished if on one side there is experience, on the other a passionate desire to learn, and on both sides an almost affectionate involvement with the work at hand. Above all, the links forged at Schifanoia tend to remain unbroken when the six weeks come to an end. It is very usual for some of the young singers to follow us to the *casale* or to turn up some months— or even a year or two—later to ask for special coaching and help.

Louis Manikas (our Greek baritone from the very first year in Schifanoia) will come from his engagements throughout Europe to Schifanoia and to the *casale*, particularly if I am going to produce some performance for which he is studying. Mani Mekler (hair beautifully done now and with an air which arrests attention) comes to the *casale* almost as a "house daughter," perhaps from Stockholm or Düsseldorf or the Wexford Festival. Paulette Berman, usually with Maestro Fagen, her husband, whom she first met at Schifanoia, is another ever-welcome visitor. They used to come to us from Holland but in the future they will be coming from Kassel, where he has been appointed a conductor. Now they bring their baby daughter too. (We believe in starting them early, and at least she can enjoy lying there listening to the songbirds—both those in the trees of the *casale* and those who are working hard in the studio.)

Among the latter may well be Janice Cairns from England, putting the finishing touches to her Desdemona for the performances in Greece which I shall be producing and in which Manikas will be singing Iago. Wolfgang Lenz and his wife, Doris, may quite likely be there too, having come over from Darmstadt to give an extra polish to his Don Giovanni. Lovely Marta Márquez is coming too, working hard at her Konstanze before going to Germany. There is no end to the meetings, the reunions,

the involvement with each other's fortunes—or to the pleas for advice:
"What would you suggest, Maestro?" "Is it too early for me to try so-
and-so?" (It usually is.) "I am to audition for This or That or The
Other, Maestro. Please would you advise me—help me—coach me."
"I'm having difficulty with my high notes—my low notes—a particular
passage. I don't seem to have confidence."

How could they be to me just students whom I teach? They are all
people, artists at different stages on the difficult, thrilling road I myself
have traveled. I was also once a scared and doubtful young singer, trying
to find the way. I also was gifted by God with the responsibility of a
voice. But in addition I was blessed beyond measure by the fact that I
fell into the right hands for training, disciplining, development, and artistic understanding.

In my most earnest view, to be given so much is in a sense a trust—
something which must be handed on; for to serve any great art is a wonderful and enriching experience, however humble a servant one may be.
What the great maestros of my youth gave to me was a treasure beyond
price, and I cannot believe that this was intended solely for my own
profit and enjoyment. There is a debt I owe to those who helped me,
which is to pass on as much of their wisdom and training as I can to
those who are coming after me. If I failed to do so, I should also be
failing Serafin, my good Maestro Crimi, my father-in-law, the Watchdog
of my youth at the Rome Opera, and so many others.

These thoughts occupy my mind sometimes in the few leisure hours I
have at the *casale*—the haven to which I return whenever I can; for
none of the often tempting offers I receive could induce me to make my
home elsewhere. Here I *am* at home—an Italian in my beloved Italy.
But operatic production takes me to many of the cities of Europe still, to
the Metropolitan in New York and often to Chicago. It was in Chicago
that I first met Luciano Pavarotti when I was producing *Tosca* there.
We formed an instant rapport and I adapted his powerful physique not
to a romantic type of Cavaradossi but to a big, boyish, extrovert fellow
who was yet sufficiently clear-sighted to know that Tosca's plan for their
escape would never succeed, and while she poured out her hopes for
their future he already knew that there *was* no future.

At home at the *casale*, when there are no young singers singing, plung-
ing in and out of the swimming pool or helping to cook in the kitchen, I
naturally take time to enjoy old friends. Nanni Ghibelli and his wife
often come. So does Dr. Leoni, for more than thirty years the compas-
sionate doctor of the Rome Opera House who knows more than almost

anyone else about that house. Another friend we love to welcome is Ettore della Giovanna and his wife, Eva. He is an outstanding journalist, and it was he who suddenly said one day, as we idled away the afternoon under the trees, that he wanted to interview me on my personal attitude toward operatic production. I replied that I was not in the mood to be interviewed, but he said: "Just talk about it. Reflect aloud, if you like."

So I found myself explaining that when I approach the production of any opera my first feeling is one of responsibility toward the composer and the librettist. I do not aim at headlines proclaiming "Tito Gobbi's controversial production." I have no ambition to read in any newspaper: "A piquant experience awaited us at the opera last night, for when the curtain rose on Tito Gobbi's production of *Otello* we found ourselves in the world of Watteau (or Breughel, or God knows who)." My simple intention is that the audience should find themselves on such an occasion in the world of Verdi and Shakespeare.

Naturally fresh angles must be sought in presenting a work which has been performed many times before, but these must be within the frame of the period and the composer's intention. The truth is that most great opera composers were great men of the theater too. They do not require to have their masterpieces rehashed for them in one eccentric form or other.

The eminent music critic Desmond Shawe-Taylor has often expressed his disagreement with what he calls "cultural schizophrenia," and I find myself in such complete agreement with him that there is one article of his (published some time ago in the *Sunday Times*) I keep permanently on my writing desk. It deals at length with crazy directions and in my view sends a welcome breath of common sense across the operatic scene.

Often I have found that the simplest idea will serve to heighten the drama, the comedy, the sheer charm of a scene, and I found myself telling Ettore how once in the first act of *Tosca* I had the desperate Angelotti dart into hiding in a confessional box, and every time the Sacristan idly flicked his duster around that box you could almost feel the audience sharing Angelotti's agonized anxiety. In a totally different mood, I found opportunities for charming new touches in *Barbiere* by setting the scene in a country house on the outskirts of the town. Again, the opening scene of *Gianni Schicchi* was made much more effective (and more immediately understandable) by the simple expedient of first showing all the relations, against a drop-scene, converging greedily on the house where Buoso Donati lay dead. Similarly, the last magical scene of *Falstaff* was beautifully enhanced by having the people of Windsor seen beforehand passing across the stage in their lovely masks and carnival costumes on the way to the forest.

But what I want most of all in any production of mine is to have my singers become real characters who convey their feelings to the audience. *This* is what emphasizes the drama or heightens the comedy, and this I believe to be the true work of the producer or stage director. For it should be remembered that he is not a creator; he is simply the interpreter of someone else's creation.

In brief, then, I put the claims of the work and its creators first. As an experienced singing actor I next consider the difficulties of the performers and do my utmost to smooth their paths so that they shall give of their very best. Finally, I always remember that we are serving the public, who have paid for their tickets and have every right to enjoy themselves.

Ettore said that was fine. Then he took his leave—but returned a few minutes later to say that he could not start his car and would I see what sort of production job I could do on that? To his surprise—and mine too —I discovered what was wrong and he finally departed with so many flattering words (most of them about the car, I am bound to say) that I decided he was a prince of newspapermen.

The title of "King of Newspapermen" I reserve, in all seriousness and admiration, for Indro Montanelli, the bravest and finest man in the newspaper world of Italy. It is a great thing to recognize the truth; it is an even greater one to tell the truth; but greatest of all is to refuse to yield to any threat from those who seek to suppress the truth. I am very proud to know him and to mention his name in a book which is largely about me.

As that book comes to an end a few sobering reflections inevitably spring to mind. To be made the subject of a biography is in a certain sense to be put on trial. To write an autobiography is to put oneself on trial, but with the advantage of presenting the case in person and presenting it in a favorable light. Have I favored myself too far? Certainly there are things I have left out, for indeed I have lived my life to the full. But though it is said that confession is good for the soul it can also be profoundly boring to a captive audience. For the man who insists on discoursing at length on his follies is just as vain as the one who talks endlessly of his virtues.

Here then is the case of Tito Gobbi, presented with some favoritism but also with some twinges of conscience for the things which have been omitted. This being so, too kind a verdict would be embarrassing, too harsh a verdict rather wounding. Might I ask humbly for something in between? Such as: "Certainly no saint, but not really a bad fellow either. At least it can be said of him that he was faithful to his art and to his friends."

So the curtain goes down—but there is always the overture tomorrow. I do not say good-by to you, my friends who have meant so much to me on both sides of that curtain. Who knows? We might meet and talk again tomorrow. Instead I say

ARRIVEDERCI.

My Dear Ghost,

Having used all my irresistible charm and diplomacy to persuade you to help me with this story of mine, I have had my moments of remorse for the immensity of the task I asked you to undertake. In retrospect I see you at the *casale* almost buried under the mountains of material I heaped upon you, fighting daily but relentlessly my overwhelming desire to include everything about my green sixty-five years.

You listen patiently to an anecdote I have told you a dozen times before and then, smiling but ruthless, you cut out all my nonsense. I am truly sorry, and even tear my thinning hair and sprinkle a few ashes; yet we are both, I know, so happy about this joint work of ours that we shall feel bereft when it is over.

There in the serene atmosphere of the *casale,* enlivened by the song of the birds and the croaking of the frogs, with the delicious scent of flowers around, is my ghost—with an assistant ghost in the person of Louise; vigilant and alert, settling a doubtful passage, supplying the right word, making a point with sudden, unexpectedly sharp wit. In short, acting the reader.

Dear Ida, you have lent your beautifully expressive pen to my life and reflections. I wish that I myself could borrow that pen now, for only so could I find the right wording to express my affectionate gratitude.

Tito.

DISCOGRAPHY

John Steane

A "Chronological List of Recordings" on 78 rpm and on 33⅓ rpm is followed by a note on unpublished and "private" recordings. Then comes a "Listing By Composers" (with specification of roles, orchestras, etc.), divided into operatic and non-operatic. Abbreviations of orchestras' names (the use of the orchestra's associated chorus being understood, when appropriate) are as follows:

CG	Orchestra of the Royal Opera House, Covent Garden	PCO	Paris Conservatoire Orchestra
LSM	Orchestra of La Scala, Milan	PO	Philharmonia Orchestra
LSO	London Symphony Orchestra	POO	Paris Opera Orchestra
MCO	Monte Carlo Opera Orchestra	RO	Rome Opera Orchestra
MMF	Orchestra of the Maggio Musicale Fiorentino	VPO	Vienna Philharmonic Orchestra
NPO	National Philharmonic Orchestra	VSO	Vienna State Opera Orchestra

All records are 33⅓ rpm except where marked 78 or 45 below. A disc of reissues of 33⅓ rpm which did not appear in the United States or Great Britain and bears an Italian number (QBLP 5056) is also included, but

Italian reissues on 45 rpm are excluded. Proprietary labels are indicated as follows:

ALP	HMV	LPM	RCA Victor
ALPS	MV	QBLP	Voce del Padrone
ANG	Angel (USA)		(Italy)
ASD	HMV	RCA	RCA Victor (USA)
COL	Columbia (USA)	RLS	HMV
D	Decca	SAN	HMV–Angel
DA (78)	HMV	SAX	Columbia
DB (78)	HMV	SERA	Seraphim (USA)
DGG	Deutsche Grammo-	SET	Decca
	phon	SLS	HMV
HLM	HMV	33CX	Columbia
LDS	RCA Victor	7ER (45)	HMV
LM	Victor (USA)	7R (45)	HMV
LO	Cetra Live	76563	CBS
LON	London (USA)		

I: CHRONOLOGICAL LIST OF RECORDINGS

These early 78-rpm recordings have been reissued (in Great Britain only) in two separate albums: "Operatic Arias and Songs" (HLM 7018); and "The Art of Tito Gobbi" (RLS 738)—the latter not to be confused with an earlier album also called "The Art of Tito Gobbi" (ALP 2057/8) which has been issued in the United States on the Seraphim label (SERA 6021). In addition, certain of these songs have been collected on an old RCA Victor 10-inch album entitled "Around the World in Music—Italy—Vol. 1" (LPM 3090). This album may be found in the Rodgers and Hammerstein Archives of Recorded Sound of the New York Public Library at Lincoln Center in New York City, along with other privately made recordings of Gobbi performances (*see* Section D).

A. On 78 rpm HMV recordings

	78 rpm		45 rpm	33⅓ rpm (reissue nos.)

July 1942   Italy   Orchestra/
Umberto Berrettoni

Cilèa: *L'Arlesiana*—Come due tizzi accesi	DB	5400		RLS 738
Leoncavallo: *Zazà*—Buona Zazà del mio buon tempo	DA	5429		RLS 738
Leoncavallo: *Zazà*—Zazà, piccola zingara	DA	5429		RLS 738
Mozart: *Don Giovanni*—Deh vieni alla finestra	DA	5430		HLM 7018
Verdi: *Don Carlo*—Convien . . . Per me giunto	DB	5447		HLM 7018
Puccini: *La Fanciulla del West*—Minnie, dalla mia casa	DA	5430		RLS 738
Verdi: *Don Carlo*—O Carlo ascolta . . . Io morrò	DB	5447		RLS 738

	78 rpm	45 rpm	33⅓ rpm
			(reissue nos.)

July 1943   Orchestra/Dino Olivieri

| Gastaldon: Musica proibita (Film – "Musica Proibita") | OBA 5167[1] | | RCA[2] |
| Ruccione: Famma sunna cu'tte (Film – "Musica Proibita") | OBA 5166 | | RCA[3] |

February 2, 1948   England Orchestra/Alberto Erede

Verdi: *Otello* – Era la notte	DB 6626	7R 107	RLS 738
Rossini: *Il Barbiere di Siviglia* – Largo al factotum	DB 6626	7R 107	HLM 7018
Leoncavallo: *Pagliacci* – Si può (Prologue)	DB 6822	7R 165	HLM 7018

February 17, 1948   England Orchestra/Alberto Erede[4]

Valente: Torna	DB 6876	7ER 5091	RLS 738
Tosti: 'a vucchella	DA 1887		RLS 738
Denza: Occhi di fata	DA 1887	7ER 5091	RLS 738
Falvo: Dicitencello vuje	DB 6876	7ER 5091	RLS 738

March 14, 1950   England Philharmonia Orchestra/ James Robertson[5]

Verdi: *La Forza del Destino* – Urna fatale	DB 21071	7R 171	RLS 738
Verdi: *Otello* – Vanne . . . Credo in un Dio crudel	DB 21071	7R 171	RLS 738
Mozart: *Le Nozze di Figaro* – Non più andrai	DA 1946		HLM 7018

[1] La Voce del Padrone AV Red Label European Issue.
[2] RCA Victor Purple Label 25-7158-A (53-4017-A) American Issue.
[3] RCA Victor 25-7158-B (53-4017-B).
[4] Labels do not credit Erede with OEA 12727 & 12728.
[5] Labels do not credit Philharmonia Orchestra with OEA 14464 & 14465.

	78 rpm	45 rpm	33⅓ rpm (reissue nos.)

	78 rpm	45 rpm		33⅓ rpm (reissue nos.)
Mozart: *Le Nozze di Figaro* – Aprite un po'	DA 1946			RLS 738

March 29, 1950   England
Orchestra/Philip Green

Rota: Take the sun (Film – "The Glass Mountain")	DA 1940	7P	240	RLS 738
Pigarelli: Song of the mountains (Film – "The Glass Mountain") (*with accordion & guitar*)	DA 1940	7P	240	RLS 738
Sadero: Gondoliera Veneziana	(*unpublished*)			RLS 738
Sadero: Amuri, amuri				RLS 738

September 24, 1950   England
Philharmonia Orchestra/Walter Susskind

Verdi: *La Traviata* – Di Provenza il mar	DB 21227	7R	154	HLM 7018
Verdi: *Rigoletto* – Pari siamo!	DB 21227	7R	154	HLM 7018

September 30, 1950   England
London Symphony Orchestra/ Warwick Braithwaite

Verdi: *Macbeth* – Pietà, rispetto	(*unpublished*)		RLS 738
Verdi: *Un Ballo in Maschera* – Alzati, là tuo figlio . . . Eri tu	DB 21606		RLS 738

1951   Italy

Rossini: *Guglielmo Tell* (excerpts)[6]			LPM 3090

[6] 10 inch version Royale VLP 6072.
12 inch version Royale 1212.

	78 rpm	45 rpm	33⅓ rpm (reissue nos.)

October 2, 1952   England
London Symphony Orchestra/
Armando la rosa Parodi

Cottrau arr Gibilaro: Santa Lucia	DA 2022		RLS 738
di Capua: O sole mio	DA 2026		RLS 738
Tosti: Marechiare	DA 2022	7ER 5091	RLS 738
Bellini arr Meglio: Fenesta che lucive	DA 2026		RLS 738

October 18, 1953   Italy
Orchestra/Dino Olivieri

Olivieri: Nenia d'amore Film – "Canzoni a due voci")	DA 11352		RLS 738

June 1953   Italy   Nicola Monti/
Rome Opera Orchestra/
Gabriele Santini[7]

Donizetti: *L'Elisir d'Amore* – La donna è un animale . . . Venti scudi	DB 21612		RLS 738

B. On 33⅓ rpm

No discography of any artist can hope to be complete. Recordings are constantly being added to and deleted from the catalog by the various companies. In particular it should be noted that many of the old Angel recordings, long out of print, have been reissued on the lower-priced Seraphim label. Listed below are the U.S. catalog numbers and the corre-

[7] Dubbing made 31 December 1953 from complete recording (ALP 1067/8).

sponding U.K. catalog numbers. A blank in the USA column indicates the record was never issued in this country. Bold type indicates recordings in print in the United States as of press time for this book. The dates listed are those of original issue. (For reissues, e.g. highlights albums, *see* Part II.)

		USA	*UK*
Oct 1953	Donizetti, *L'Elisir d'Amore*	LM 6024	ALP 1067/8
Dec 1953	Puccini, *Tosca*	**ANG 3508**	33CX 1094/5
Mar 1954	Donizetti, *Lucia di Lammermoor*	**SERA 6032**	33CX 1131/2
Mar 1955	Puccini, *Madama Butterfly*	**SERA 6090**	ALP 1215/7
Sep 1955	Leoncavallo, *Pagliacci*	ANG 3528[8]	33CX 1211/2
Nov 1955	Verdi, *Don Carlo*	**SERA 6004**	ALP 1289/1292
Jan 1956	Verdi, *Aïda*	**ANG 3525**	33CX 1318/1320
Feb 1956	Verdi, *Rigoletto*	**ANG 3537**	33CX 1324/6
May 1956	Puccini, *Il Tabarro*	LM 2057[9]	ALP 1355
Sep 1956	Verdi, *La Traviata*	**ANG 3545**	33CX 1370/1
Mar 1957	Verdi, *Falstaff*	**ANG 3552**	33CX 1410/2
Oct 1957	Verdi, *Un Ballo in Maschera*	**SERA 6087**	33CX 1472/4
Jan 1958	"Tito Gobbi at La Scala":[10]	ANG 35563	33CX 1501
Feb 1958	Rossini, *Il Barbiere di Siviglia*	**ANG 3559**	33CX 1507/9
Dec 1958	Verdi, *Simone Boccanegra*	ANG 3617	ALPS 1634/5
Dec 1959	Puccini, *Gianni Schicchi*	ANG 35473[9]	ALP 1726
Sep 1961	Leoncavallo, *Pagliacci*	**ANG 3618**	33CX 1752/3
Nov 1961	Verdi, *Otello*	**RCA-AGL3-1969**	LDS 6155

[8] ANG 3528 was a combined *Cav* and *Pag* album with Callas and Di Stefano (but not Gobbi) appearing in *Cavalleria*. The *Pagliacci* was issued separately as ANG 3527.

[9] A combined *Il Trittico* (with Gobbi appearing in *Tabarro* and *Gianni Schicchi* but not in *Suor Angelica*) has been issued as ANG 3849.

[10] Excerpts from previously recorded complete versions of *Pagliacci, Un Ballo in Maschera, Rigoletto, La Traviata, Tosca*.

			USA	UK
Dec	1962	Puccini, *La Bohème*	DGG 138764/5	SLPM 138764/5
Dec	1964	"The Art of Tito Gobbi":[11]	SERA 6021	ALP 2057/8
Jul	1965	Puccini, *Tosca*	ANG 3655	SAN 149/150
May	1966	Verdi, *Nabucco*	LON 1382	SET 298/230
Oct	1967	Mascagni, *Cavalleria Rusticana*	LON 1266	SET 343/4
Oct	1968	Verdi, *Otello:* "Fuoco di gioia . . . Inaffia l'ugola" (in Royal Opera House Anniversary Album)		SET 392/3
Mar	1970	Giordano, *Fedora*	LON 1283	SET 435/6
Feb	1973	"Operatic arias and songs"[12]		HLM 7018
May	1977	Puccini, *Gianni Schicchi*	COL 34534	76563
Jul	1977	Leoni, *L'Oracolo*	LON 12107	D 34D 2
May	1979	"The Art of Tito Gobbi"[13]		RLS 738

[11] Operatic arias, classical songs, romantic songs, popular songs. Rossini, *Guglielmo Tell:* "Resta Immobile"/Dionizetti, *L'Elisir d'Amore:* "Come Paride"/Verdi, *Simone Boccanegra:* "Plebe! Patrizi!"/Cilèa, *Adriana Lecouvreur:* "Ecco il monologo"/Giordano, *Fedora:* "La donna russa"/Verdi, *Falstaff:* "Quand'ero paggio"; *Otello:* "Vanne . . . Credo in un Dio crudel"/Cavalli, *Serse:* "Beato chi può"/Vivaldi: "Piango, gemo"/Carissimi: "Vittoria, mio cor"/Durante: "Vergin, tutto amore preghiera"/Giordani: "Caro mio ben"/Paisiello, *La Molinara:* "Nel cor più non mi sento"/Pergolesi (*attrib.*) "Tre giorni son che Nina"/A. Scarlatti, *Pompeo:* "O cessate di piagarmi"/Monteverdi, *Orfeo:* "Rosa del ciel"/Bellini: "Fenesta che lucive"/Cottrau: "Santa Lucia"/Lama: "Silenzio, cantatore"/Pigarelli: "La montanara"/Tagliaferri: "Piscatore 'e Pusilecco"/D'Anzi: "Madonnina," "Mattinata fiorentina"/Sadero: "Gondoliera veneziana," "Amuri, amuri"/Tosti: "Malia," "Donna, vorrei morir," " 'a vucchella," "Ideale"/Gastaldon: "Musica proibita"/ Respighi: "Nebbie"/Wolf-Ferrari: "Se gli alberi," "Serenata commiato."
[12] (Issued in aid of Venice in Peril fund); excerpts from previously recorded complete versions of *Pagliacci, Rigoletto, Don Carlo, Simone Boccanegra, Otello, Falstaff, Don Giovanni, Le Nozze di Figaro, La Traviata, Il Barbiere di Siviglia, Gianni Schicchi;* and, previously unpublished: Cilèa, *Adriana Lecouvreur:* "Ecco il monologo"/Brogi: "Visione veneziana"/Mascagni: "Serenata"/Denza: "Occhi di fata"/ Mayr: "Biondina in gondoletta."
[13] The early recordings, 1942–1953; unpublished recordings of 1955 and Italian songs (*see* sections I-A and C).

C. Unpublished recordings

The following recital record was made in Rome in October 1955 for EMI (matrix nos. 2XBA 30, 2XBA 31) with Orchestra conducted by Oliviero de Fabritiis:

Verdi, *Otello:* "Credo in un Dio crudel" Cilèa, *Adriana Lecouvreur:* "Ecco il monologo"/Wolf-Ferrari, *I Gioielli della Madonna:* "Serenata" Puccini, *La Fanciulla del West:* "Minnie, dalla mia casa"/Giordano, *Fedora:* "La donna russa"; *Andrea Chenier:* "Nemico della patria"/Rossini, *Guglielmo Tell:* "La valanga che volge," "Resta immobile"/Berlioz, *La Damnation de Faust:* "Chanson de la puce"/Verdi, *Macbeth:* "Pietà, rispetto"; *Falstaff:* "Quand'ero paggio"; *Nabucco:* "Ah, prigioniero sono io."

D. Private recordings

The comments made above about the necessary incompleteness of any discography are even more true when it comes to the question of "private" or pirate recordings. There seems little point in listing private recordings that may have been available years ago but have long since disappeared. Accordingly, we have set forth below the recordings which are generally available in New York at press time for this book:

Bruno Walter Society

> Mozart, *Don Giovanni.* Gobbi, Schwarzkopf, Greindl, Welitsch, Dermota, Kunz, Poell. Salzburg Festival, 1950. Vienna Philharmonic, Wilhelm Furtwängler conducting. RR 407.

Cetra Live

Rossini, *Il Barbiere di Siviglia.* Callas, Gobbi, Alva, Rossi-Lemeni, Luise. La Scala Orchestra, Carlo Giulini conducting. LO 34.

Historical Recording Enterprises

Puccini, *La Fanciulla del West.* Corelli, Gobbi, Frazzoni, Zaccaria. La Scala. Antonino Votto conducting. April 4, 1956. HRE 278-3.

Puccini, *Tosca.* Callas, Gobbi, Corelli. Metropolitan Opera Orchestra and Chorus, Fausto Cleva conducting. March 25, 1965. HRE 306-2. 275-2.

Puccini, *Tosca.* Callas, Gobbi, Tucker. Metropolitan Opera Orchestra and Chorus, Fausto Cleva conducting, March 25, 1965. HRE 306-2.

Verdi, *Falstaff.* Gobbi, Tebaldi, Simionato, MacNeil, Moffo, Canali. Tullio Serafin conducting. 1958. HRE 282-2.

Voce

Puccini, *Tosca.* Callas, Gobbi, Cioni. Royal Opera House. Georges Prêtre conducting. July 5, 1965. VOCE 13. [Callas' final performance.]

Verdi, *Otello.* Gobbi, Di Stefano, Pobbe. Allen Jensen conducting. March 31, 1966. VOCE 14.

In addition, the Rodgers and Hammerstein Archives of Recorded Sound, located at the New York Public Library at Lincoln Center, New York City, possesses a number of rare tapes of Gobbi performances, including the following:

Puccini, *Tosca.* Callas, Gobbi, Cioni. Royal Opera House at Covent Garden. Carlo Felice Cillario conducting. January 24, 1964.

Puccini, *Tosca.* Callas, Corelli, Gobbi. Metropolitan Opera Orchestra and Chorus, Fausto Cleva conducting. March 19, 1965.

Verdi, *Falstaff.* Schwarzkopf, Moffo, Simionato, Gobbi, Panerai. Salzburg Festival. Vienna Philharmonic Orchestra, Herbert von Karajan conducting.

Verdi, *Otello.* Zeani, McCracken, Gobbi. Rome, 1963.

Verdi, *Rigoletto* (selections). Pagliughi, Lauri-Volpi, Gobbi. June 27, 1947.

II. LISTING BY COMPOSERS

Items are listed by composer, alphabetically, with the year of issue and the American catalog number. A bold print listing indicates an item in print at press time for this book. In situations where the recording was never issued in the United States, the British catalog number is listed in brackets. Further details can be found by reference to Part I. The order followed in the list below is: composer (alphabetically), work (alphabetically), and chronological order of issue where the same work or extract has been recorded more than once. Complete recordings of operas take precedence over excerpts, and extracts from such complete recordings are listed immediately under the entry for that recording itself.

Where a complete opera is recorded, but not otherwise, Gobbi's role is indicated. Conductor's name follows an oblique stroke after specification of the orchestra.

A. Operatic — Complete Works and Extracts

Berlioz
La Damnation de Faust, "Chanson de la   [RLS   738]
    puce" (RO/De Fabritiis) 1955

Cavalli
Serse "Beato chi può," 1964   **SERA   6021**

Cilèa
Adriana Lecouvreur "Ecco il monologo"   [HLM   7018]
    (RO/De Fabritiis), 1973 (r 1955)
—— "Ecco il monologo" (PO/Erede)   **SERA   6021**
    1964
Arlesiana, L' "Come due tizzi accesi"   [RLS   738]
    (r 1942)

Donizetti
Elisir d'Amore, L' (as Belcore, with Ca-   LM   6024
    rosio, Monti, Luise, RO/Santini)
    1953

—— "La donna è un animale . . . Venti   [RLS   738]
scudi" (*from preceding*) 1953

—— "Come Paride" (PO/Erede) 1964   SERA 6021
Lucia di Lammermoor (as Enrico, with   SERA 6032
Callas, Di Stefano, Arié, MMF/
Serafin) 1954

—— "Il pallor funesto," "Chi mi frena"   [33CX 1385]
(*from preceding*) 1957

Giordano

Fedora (as De Sirieux, with Olivero, Del   LON 1283
Monaco, MCO/Gardelli) 1970

—— "La donna russa" (O/de Fabritiis)   [RLS   738]
1955

—— "La donna russa" (PO/Erede)   SERA 6021
1964

Andrea Chenier (O/de Fabritiis) 1955   [RLS   738]

Leoncavallo

Pagliacci (as Tonio and Prologue, with   ANG 3528
Callas, Di Stefano, Monti, Panerai,
LSM/Serafin) 1955

—— Prologue (*from preceding*) 1957   ANG 35345
—— Prologue (*from preceding*) 1958   [33CX 1501]
—— (as Tonio and Prologue, with   ANG 3618
Amara, Corelli, LSM/Matacic)
1961

—— Prologue (orch/Erede) 1948   [HLM 7018]
Zazà "Buona Zazà," "Zazà, piccola zin-   [RLS   738]
gara." 1942

Leoni

L'Oracolo (as Cim-Fen, with Suth-   LON 12107
erland, Tourangeau, Davies, NPO/
Bonynge) 1977

Mascagni

Cavalleria Rusticana (as Alfio, with   LON 1266
Suliotis, Del Monaco, RO/Varviso)
1967

Monteverdi

Orfeo "Rosa del ciel" (PO/Erede) 1964   SERA 6021

Mozart

Don Giovanni (as Don Giovanni, with

Welitsch, Schwarzkopf, Seefried,
Dermota, Kunz, VPO/Furtwäng-
ler) 1950

—— "Deh, vieni alla finestra" (*r* 1942)   [HLM   7018]

Nozze di Figaro, Le "Non più andrai,"   [HLM   7018] [RLS   738]
"Aprite un po' " (PO/Robertson)
1950

Paisiello

Molinara, La "Nel cor più non mi sento"   SERA   6021
(PO/Erede) 1964

Puccini

Bohème, La (as Marcello, with Scotto,   DGG   138764/5
Poggi, MMO/Votto) 1962

—— Excerpts (*from preceding*) 1963   [DGG   19275]

Fanciulla del West, La "Minnie, dalla   [RLS   738]
mia casa" (*r* 1942)

—— 1955   [RLS   738]

Gianni Schicchi (as Schicchi, with De   ANG   35473
Los Angeles, Del Monte, RO/San-
tini) 1959

—— "Ah! Vittoria!," "Ditemi, voi   [HLM   7018]
signori" (*from preceding*) 1973

—— (as Schicchi, with Cotrubas, Do-   COL   34534
mingo, LSO/Maazel) 1977

Madama Butterfly (as Sharpless, with   SERA   6090
De Los Angeles, Di Stefano, RO/
Gavazzeni) 1955

—— "Dovunque al mondo" (*from pre-*   [7ER   5073]
ceding) 1957

—— "Ebbene, che fareste" (*from pre-*   [7ER   5068]
ceding) 1957

Tabarro, Il (as Michele, with Mas,   LM   2057
Prandelli, RO/Bellezza) 1956

Tosca (as Scarpia, with Callas, Di Ste-   ANG   3508
fano, LSM/Sabata) 1953

—— "Tre sbirri," "Già mi dicon venal,"   [33CX   1893]
"Sei troppo bella" (*from preceding*)
1964

—— "Tre sbirri," "Tosca è un buon   ANG   35563
falco" (*from preceding*) 1958

—— (as Scarpia, with Callas, Bergonzi,   ANG   3655
PCO/Pretre) 1965

—— "Tre sbirri" (*from preceding*) 1967   ANG   36326

—— (as Scarpia, with Callas, Cioni, CG/Cillario) (*r* 1964)

Rossini

Barbiere di Siviglia, Il (as Figaro, with   ANG   3559
Callas, Alva, Zaccaria, PO/Galliera) 1958

—— "Largo al factotum," "All' idea,"   ANG   35936
"Dunque io son," "Freddo ed immobile," "Buona Sera," "Ah! qual colpo," "Dì si felice" (*from preceding*) 1962

—— "Largo al factotum" (orch/Erede)   [HLM   7018]
1948

—— (as Figaro with Callas, Alva, Rossi-Lemeni, Luise, LSM/Giulini) (*r* 1956)

Guglielmo Tell, La valanga che volge   [RLS   738]
(RO/De Fabritiis) 1955

—— "Resta immobile" (O/De Fabritiis)   [RLS   738]
1955

—— "Resta immobile" (PO/Erede)   SERA   6021
1964

Scarlatti, Alessandro

Pompeo "O cessate di piagarmi" (with   SERA   6021
Roy Jesson *hpchd,* Derek Simpson *vcl* and Freddie Phillips *gtr*) 1964

Verdi

Aïda (as Amonasro, with Callas, Barbieri, Tucker, LSM/Serafin) 1956   ANG   3525

—— "Ciel, mio padre" (*from preceding*) 1965   ANG   35938

Ballo in Maschera, Un (as Renato, with   SERA   6087
Callas, Barbieri, Di Stefano, LSM/Votto) 1957

—— "Alla vita," "Eri tu" (*from preceding*) 1958   ANG   35563

—— "Eri tu" (LSO/Braithwaite) 1953   [RLS   738]

Don Carlo (as Rodrigo, with Stella,   SERA   6004

Niccolai, Filippeschi, Christoff, RO/
Santini) 1955

—— "Per me giunto," "Io morrò," "Dio,   [ALP 1700]
che nell' alma" (*from preceding*)
1959

—— "Per me giunto," "Io morrò" 1942   [HLM 7018]

Falstaff (as Falstaff, with Schwarzkopf,   ANG 3552
Moffo, Merriman, Barbieri, Alva,
Panerai, PO/Karajan) 1957

—— "Reverenza," "C'è a Windsor,"   [33CX 1939]
"Qua una sedia," "Ehi! Taver-
niere!," "Pizzica" (*from preceding*)
1965

—— "L'onore! Ladri!" (*from preced-*   [HLM 7018]
ing) 1973

—— "Quand'ero paggio" (PO/Erede)   SERA 6021
1964

Forza del Destino, La "Urna fatale"   [RLS 738]
(PO/Erede) 1950

Macbeth, "Perfidi . . . Pietà, rispetto   [RLS 738]
amore" (1950) (1955)

Nabucco (as Nabucco, with Suliotis,   LON 1382
Prevedi, Cava, VSO/Gardelli)
1966

—— "S'appressan gl'instani," "Donna   LON 26059
chi sei," "Dio di Giuda," "Oh, chi
vegg'io" (*from preceding*) 1968

Otello (as Iago, with Rysanek, Vickers,   RCA AGL 3-1969
RO/Serafin) 1961

—— "Era la notte" (orch/Erede) 1948   [RLS 738]

—— "Fuoco di gioia . . . Inaffia l'ugola"   [SET 392/3]
(with Lanigan, Dobson, CG/Solti)

—— "Vanne . . . Credo in un Dio   [RLS 738]
crudel" (PO/Robertson) 1950

—— "Vanne . . . Credo in un Dio   [RLS 738]
crudel" (RO/De Fabritiis) 1955

—— "Vanne . . . Credo in un Dio   SERA 6021
crudel" (PO/Erede) 1964

Rigoletto (as Rigoletto, with Callas, Di   ANG 3537
Stefano, LSM/Serafin) 1956

—— "Pari siamo," "Povero Rigoletto,"   ANG 35518
"Tutte le feste," "Bella figlia del-
l'amore" (*from preceding*) 1958

—— "Pari siamo," "Cortigiani, vil razza" (*from preceding*) 1958 — ANG 35563

—— "Pari siamo" (PO/Susskind) 1950 — [HLM 7018]

Simone Boccanegra (as Boccanegra, with De Los Angeles, Campora, Christoff, RO/Santini) 1958 — ANG 3617

—— "Del mar sul lido," "Dinne alcun," "Messeri, il re," "Plebe! Patrizi!," "Parla, il tuo cor," "Gran Dio, li benedici" (*from preceding*) 1965 — [ALP 2067]

—— "Plebe! Patrizi!" (PO/Erede) 1964 — SERA 6021

Traviata, La (as Germont, with Callas, Di Stefano, LSM/Serafin) 1956 — ANG 3545

—— "Di Provenza" (*from preceding*) 1958 — ANG 35563

—— "Di Provenza" (PO/Susskind) 1950 — [RLS 738]

Wolf-Ferrari

I Gioielli della Madonna (1955) — [RLS 738]

B. Non-Operatic

Bellini

"Fenesta che lucive" (LSO/Parodi) 1953 — [RLS 738]

—— "Fenesta che lucive" (orch/Bizzelli) 1964 — SERA 6021

Brogi

"Visione veneziana" (Gerald Moore *pno*) 1973 — [HLM 7018]

Carissimi

"Vittoria, mio cor" (Roy Jesson *hpchd*, Derek Simpson *vcl*, Freddie Phillips *gtr*) 1964 — SERA 6021

Cottrau

"Santa Lucia" (LSO/Parodi) 1952 — [RLS 738]

—— "Santa Lucia" (orch/Bizzelli) 1964 — SERA 6021

D'Anzi

"Madonnina," "Mattinata fiorentina" (orch/Bizzelli) 1964 — SERA 6021

Denza
"Occhi di fata" 1948   [RLS 738]
—— "Occhi di fata" (Gerald Moore   [HLM 7018]
pno) 1973

Durante
"Vergin, tutto amor preghiera" (Roy   SERA 6021
Jesson *hpchd,* Derek Simpson *vcl,*
Freddie Phillips *gtr*) 1964

Falvo
"Dicitincello vuje" (orch/Erede) 1949   [RLS 738]

Gastaldon
"Musica proibita" (Gerald Moore *pno*)   SERA 6021
1964

Giordani
"Caro mio ben" (Roy Jesson *hpchd,*   SERA 6021
Derek Simpson *vcl,* Freddie Phillips
gtr) 1964

Lama
"Silenzio cantatore" (orch/Bizzelli) 1964   SERA 6021

Mascagni
"Serenata" (Gerald Moore *pno*) 1973   [HLM 7018] [RLS 738]

Mayr
"Biondina in gondoletta" (Gerald Moore   [HLM 7018]
pno) 1973

Olivieri
"Nenia d'amore," (*r* 1953)   [RLS 738]

Pigarelli
"La montanara" (orch/Bizzelli) 1964   SERA 6021

Respighi
"Nebbie" (Gerald Moore *pno*) 1964   SERA 6021

Rota
"Take the sun," "Song of the mountain"   [RLS 738]
1950

Sadero
"Gondoliera veneziana," "Amuri, amuri"   SERA 6021
(orch/Bizzelli) 1964

Tagliaferri

"Piscatore 'e Pusilleco" (orch/Bizzelli) 1964	SERA 6021

Tosti

"'a vucchella," "Malia," "Ideale," "Donna, vorrei morir" (Gerald Moore *pno*) 1964	SERA 6021
——"'a vucchella" 1948	[RLS 738]
—— "Marechiare" (LSO/Parodi) 1952	[RLS 738]

Pergolesi (*attrib*)

"Tre giorni son che Nina" (Roy Jesson *hpchd*, Derek Simpson *vcl*, Freddie Phillips *gtr*) 1964	SERA 6021

Valente

"Torna" (orch/Erede) 1948	[RLS 738]

Vivaldi

"Piango, gemo" (Roy Jesson *hpchd*, Derek Simpson *vcl*, Freddie Phillips *gtr*) 1964	SERA 6021

Wolf-Ferrari

"Se gli alberi," "Serenata commiato" (Gerald Moore *pno*) 1964	SERA 6021

ACKNOWLEDGMENTS

The Tito Gobbi discography by John Steane first appeared in the *British Music Yearbook* of 1975 (editor: Arthur Jacobs), published by the Bowker Publishing Company Ltd. The section on "78 rpm HMV recordings" was prepared by Bryan Crimp. The entire discography has been revised and updated for the American edition of this book by Stanley A. Bowker, to whom special thanks are due.

Index